Accessible Gardening

Tips & Techniques for Seniors & the Disabled

Joann Woy

STACKPOLE BOOKS

Copyright © 1997 by Stackpole Books

Published by
STACKPOLE BOOKS
5067 Ritter Road
Mechanicsburg, PA 17055

Printed in the United States of America

10 9 8 7 6 5 4 3 2 1

FIRST EDITION

Cover design by Wendy Reynolds
Cover photograph courtesy of Gardener's Supply Co.
Line drawings by Steve Hoeft

Library of Congress Cataloging-in-Publication Data

Woy, Joann.
    Accessible gardening : tips & techniques for seniors
& the disabled / Joann Woy.—1st ed.
        p.   cm.
    Includes bibliographical references and index.
    ISBN 0-8117-2652-5
    1. Gardening for the aged.   2. Gardening for the
physically handicapped.   I. Title.
SB457.4.A34W68   1997
635´.087—dc20   96-30332
                                                          CIP

In loving memory of my father,
Walter F. Micik,
who taught me to love gardens.

To own a bit a ground, to scratch it with a hoe, to plant seeds, and watch the renewal of life—this is the commonest delight of the race, the most satisfactory thing a man can do.

—Charles Dudley Warner (1870)

• CONTENTS •

ACKNOWLEDGMENTS xiii

INTRODUCTION ix

CHAPTER ONE   Planning and Layout of the
Accessible Garden 1

CHAPTER TWO   Garden Construction 15

CHAPTER THREE   Raised Beds, Containers, and Trellises . . 29

CHAPTER FOUR   Soil Testing and Preparation 46

CHAPTER FIVE   Easy Composting 58

CHAPTER SIX   Water for the Accessible Garden 71

CHAPTER SEVEN   Tools for Accessibility 84

CHAPTER EIGHT   Lawn Care 108

CHAPTER NINE   Accessible Landscapes 131

CHAPTER TEN   Accessories for Accessibility 161

CHAPTER ELEVEN   Horticultural Therapy for
Professionals 176

APPENDIX A   Accessible Public Gardens 190

APPENDIX B   Sources of Tools, Supplies,
and Information 198

APPENDIX C   USDA Hardiness Zones 209

BIBLIOGRAPHY 210

INDEX 213

• ACKNOWLEDGMENTS •

I would like to thank the following individuals and organizations for their help and encouragement in preparing this book: Gene Rothart and the Chicago Botanic Garden's Horticultural Therapy Services; the American Horticultural Therapy Association (AHTA); the Arthritis Foundation; Abeldata Database, the Department of Education, and Macro International, Inc.; the National Federation of the Blind; the Easter Seals Society; the National Council on Disability; the National Multiple Sclerosis Society; the National Association for Visually Handicapped; the American Horticultural Society; Queen's Botanical Garden; Steve Hoeft; Jess H. Dehnz, Jr.; Duane Clupper; Roger Pearson; Mary Kight; Melanie Trelaine; and all of the others who offered their time, encouragement, and expertise to make this book possible.

Special thanks to Winnie Wagaman for her help and encouragement, and to my husband, Rodger, for his patience.

• INTRODUCTION •

Who loves a garden still his Eden keeps,
Perennial pleasures plants, and wholesome
harvests reaps.
                              —Bronson Alcott (1868)

To a gardener, few things in life are as rewarding as growing green
things. There is something ineffable about the joy of bringing up a
tomato from seed to seedling, watching it grow, blossom, and set fruit,
and finally bringing that fruit to the dinner table. What can compare to
the anticipation of waiting for that first rose to bloom or that first pea to
sprout? Will it? Won't it? Is it too hot? Too cold? Too wet? Too dry?
Can any TV drama come close to the fierce battle waged daily against
the bean beetle, the slug, the cutworm, the wily raccoon? Let the crash
of a stock market wait; put on pause the rise and fall of nations. Will
there be enough rain for a good crop of sweet corn this year? Nongar-
deners can have no concept; true gardeners need no explanation.

During the average lifetime, one in every five Americans will be
faced with either temporary or permanent disability. And unfortunately,
very often the ability to continue gardening as accustomed is either
diminished or lost because of illness, accident, or advancing age. Too
often, for the estimated 43 million Americans who are living with
either permanent or temporary disabilities, gardening as an active and
participatory part of life is abandoned as being too difficult, and a vital
and enriching part of life is allowed to slip away. This is tragic, especially when one considers the many assistive and adaptive tools and
techniques developed specifically for special-needs gardeners. This book
presents ideas, tools, and sources of equipment and information that
may serve to keep many more people gardening, even in the face of
physical disability.

Numbers in parentheses follow many items mentioned in the text.
These numbers refer you to the suppliers Appendix.

The accessible garden nourishes both soul and body. The psychological benefits of gardening are undeniable: In the garden, the world and the entire cycle of life are captured in miniature, and here, as nowhere else, we are given some control, some mastery over fate. In the growth, fruition, seed time, and death of plants, and in the interactions of animals and plants in the garden, we begin to comprehend our own place in the greater scheme of things. To the garden we bring our frustrations, our pain, our sense of the unfairness of it all, and we see that we are not alone; that our sufferings are not a cruel and unique punishment visited on us alone, but merely the burden of living, borne by all life. With understanding comes peace of mind, and with peace of mind comes healing.

Gardening's physical benefits are also undeniable. Gardening activities provide unequaled fresh-air exercise, taken at whatever pace is comfortable for the gardener. From the gentle pace of flower gathering to the strenuous aerobic workout provided by spading up the earth, gardening is a balanced exercise program of bending, stretching, breathing, moving, and flexing. Better circulation, better respiratory health, lower blood pressure, and reduced stress are all beneficial side effects of a daily "workout" in the garden.

Besides exercise, the gardener who grows his or her own produce enjoys the benefits of fresher, more nutritious vegetables and fruits, safe from the contamination of agricultural chemicals and unsafe handling practices. A clean, well-balanced, nutrient-dense diet high in fruits and vegetables contributes to better overall health and may even help to slow chronic or progressive ailments.

Using the garden as a therapeutic aid is nothing new. As far back as ancient Egypt, physicians and philosophers recognized the soothing and healing benefits of gardening. In the modern era, horticultural therapy is moving rapidly to the forefront of rehabilitative programs, providing hands-on work rehabilitation that can lead to increased physical strength and mobility, mental and emotional improvements, and increased self-esteem and self-confidence. The last chapter of the book is devoted to the professional caregiver or therapist who wishes to incorporate a therapeutic garden into the rehabilitation program of his or her institution.

I hope that the information and ideas presented in *Accessible Gardening* will encourage you to maintain a garden, be it a windowbox of flowers or an acre of vegetables.

CHAPTER ONE

Planning and Layout of the Accessible Garden

Proper planning is important in any gardening venture, but with special-use gardens, it becomes essential that careful thought be given to the layout and design of the garden.

Begin by assessing your needs and limitations. Do you have problems with eye-hand coordination, endurance, balance, visual acuity? Do you experience spells of dizziness or disorientation? Is getting around the garden a problem, or does working with your hands present the biggest obstacle? Will others garden with you? Do they have special needs or preferences? Will special allowances have to be made for children, pets, or guide dogs in the garden? Will you need access and maneuvering room for wheelchairs or walkers? Make an honest assessment of your abilities and consider whether your condition will improve or deteriorate with time. There is little point in designing a garden that is accessible now, only to have it become obsolete in a few years' time.

No style or type of garden is out of reach—not even a formal rose garden or an intricately graveled Japanese stone garden—but as with so many things in life, you may have to be a little more creative, a little more ingenious, and a little more adaptive to achieve the results you want.

Take your time when assessing an existing garden or landscape and planning changes. A full year is not too long to spend on this important first step. By observing the full cycle of seasons and the changes they bring to your landscape, you can more accurately determine what features of your garden you would like to keep and what you would like to change.

ASSESSING YOUR LANDSCAPE

Probably the biggest change you will want to make is one of scale. Because it may now take you more time or effort to perform your regular gardening chores, reduce those areas of the garden or landscape that require irksome amounts of time and labor, and concentrate on those areas where your efforts give you the most pleasure and satisfaction. If, for example, you find that trying to maintain an acre of lush, weedless lawn demands too much time, consider ways to reduce the amount of lawn that surrounds your house.

Explore all the alternatives. Huge expanses of high-maintenance lawns can be broken down into smaller, more manageable sections by the use of attractively paved areas, low-maintenance plantings and ground covers, and durable, eye-pleasing mulches. Lawn-care routines can be made easier with the use of new "high-accessibility" products and the adaptive techniques described in chapter 8. If you find it difficult to clip the hedges, replace them either with attractive fences or walls, or with varieties of plants that are smaller, slower-growing, and more self-contained (see chapter 9). Steep, hilly sites that are difficult to mow or even navigate can be transformed with the use of stairways, ramps, or terraces.

Fallen leaves each autumn can require intensive labor, especially if those leaves litter a manicured lawn. The obvious solution—removal of the offending trees—is usually not the best, in terms of aesthetics, property values, or environmental concerns. Consider, instead, removing the lawn. Trees surrounded by a wide bed of heavily mulched under-

---

From Rob Wade, South Orange, New Jersey:

" I am a left hemi, as a result of a stroke five years ago, so I have some mobility. My best advice is that less is more. From an 8-by-10-foot plot, I have gotten three or four bushels of tomatoes and a bushel of cucumbers. I put in rows of lettuce and radishes along the long edge of the garden just by leaning out of my chair.

"I can drag myself through the mud to plant the four tomato plants I limit myself to. It's kind of fun getting all dirty . . . but it's also more practical to invite my Mom up from Baltimore and then get *her* to plant my tomatoes!"

TABLE 1-1:
Yields for a Family of Two, with Intensive Spacing

This list gives the amount of vegetables two adults need to grow for fresh eating. If you want to can, freeze, or otherwise store your homegrown produce, double the amounts listed in the Grow column.

Vegetable	Grow	Plant	Interspace
Beets	4 pounds	8 feet	2–6 inches
Broccoli	8	14	15–18
Cabbage	10	5	12–15
Carrots	7	10	2–3
Cauliflower	12	10	15–18
Corn	12	33	18–22
Cucumbers	15	10	18–36
Green beans	20	30	4–9
Lettuce	10	15	6–9
Okra	5	9	2–18
Onions	25	25	4–6
Peas	8	40	2–6
Peppers	7	12	12–18
Potatoes	25	12	10–12
Radishes	5	5	2–3
Spinach	7	15	4–6
Squash	7	4	18–24
Sweet potatoes	8	10	10–12
Tomatoes	20	17	18–24
Turnips	4	4	4–6

story plantings, such as laurels, rhododendrons, or azaleas, can transform a suburban lot into a lovely corner of woodland, and their fallen leaves disappear effortlessly and naturally into the carpet of mulch.

If you want the color and fragrance of summertime flowers, but the yearly chore of setting out flowering annuals has become too much for you, consider a low-maintenance perennial bed of hardy daylilies, mums, irises, sedums, peonies, or other tough, easy-care plants. Or replace the beds altogether with planters or windowboxes.

If you enjoy growing your own produce but the annual job of canning, preserving, or freezing the excess has become more of a burden than a joy, consider scaling back. A vegetable garden that is only 150 square feet can supply two people with plenty of fresh produce, especially if you take advantage of new space-saving varieties of traditional favorites like pole beans, melons, cucumbers, and tomatoes.

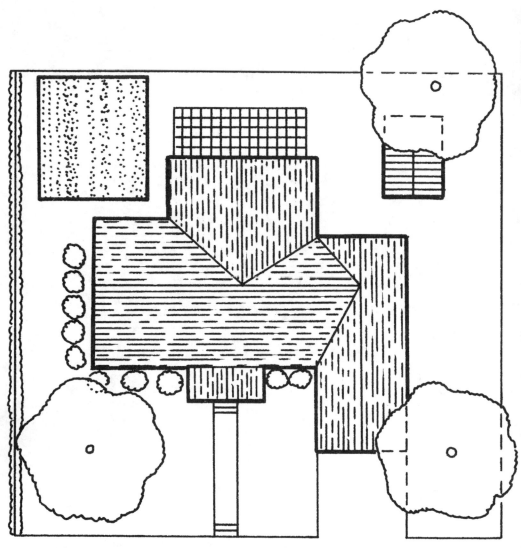

The typical high-maintenance suburban lot landscape is highly inaccessible to wheelchair or walker gardeners. Often there is no direct access from the driveway to the house, and barriers of steps lead up from the public sidewalk to the entry path and from the entry path to the front door. Big trees shed tons of leaves on the large lawn every autumn, and their roots are hard to mow over. Formally trimmed foundation shrubs and a boundary hedge need constant attention. In the backyard, access to the garden and the distant tool shed is over the lawn, presenting difficulties in wet, muddy weather.

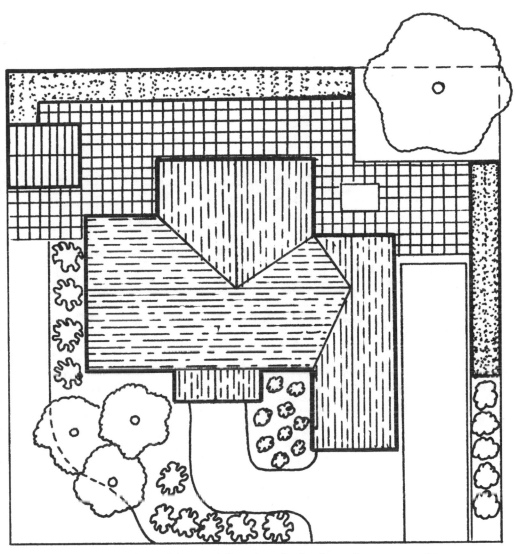

The same lot, redesigned for accessibility. A gently sloped, paved area connects driveway and front door and allows unimpeded access to the backyard. Small ornamental trees in an understory planting bed have replaced the original large specimens, eliminating the leaf-raking and mowing problems. The formal hedge has been removed and foundation shrubs allowed to grow in a more natural, and thus easier-to-care-for shape. In the back-yard, the tool shed has been moved and the paved patio extended. An underplanting of no-mow ground cover surrounds the remaining large tree, and a small water feature breaks up the monotony of the paved terrace. The vegetable garden has been transformed into two long, narrow raised beds along the north and east boundary lines and it actually measures several square feet bigger than before.

The ability to adapt and to change obstacles into assets is the key to success in gardening and landscaping, as it is in life. Rather than continuing an ongoing battle to grow grass in dense shade, plant shade-loving ferns, astilbes, and impatiens. Transform a low-lying or damp portion of the yard into a marsh or water garden, and create low-maintenance alpine terraces in a steep or rocky area, or simply plant it with wildflowers or ground cover.

Evaluate everything in your existing landscape and consider changes that will make your life easier.

• Is your existing garden near enough to the house to be easily and quickly accessible, or would it be better moved?

• Is it close enough to a driveway so that bringing plants and materials to the garden is easy?

• Are tools and supplies close to your garden site, or could your storage shed be relocated to a more convenient location?

• Does your garden have a source of water nearby, or will a special line have to be run? Few things are more difficult than transporting full buckets and watering cans or more frustrating than unwinding miles of hose.

• Is there a close source of electricity available to power hand tools, lights, and heating cables?

• Do exposed areas require fences or screening to provide privacy or shelter from wind, noise, or unattractive views?

Keep in mind, too, that wide, paved walkways or ramps for wheelchair and walker use may require considerable room. Plan their placement—and the size and shape of adjoining landscaped or garden areas—very carefully.

IMPORTANT CONSIDERATIONS

When laying out a new garden or planning changes to an existing garden or landscape, consider accessibility, safety, and maneuverability.

Avoid narrow pathways. A standard wheelchair or walker is 24 to 27 inches wide; add 1½ inches on either side for finger clearance, plus an inch or two for maneuvering, and you have a total minimum passage width of 29 to 32 inches. If possible, garden paths should be no less than 4 feet wide to allow room for a single wheelchair or walker, or for two people to walk side by side for support or companionship. Pathways that may experience two-way wheelchair or scooter traffic must be a minimum of 7 feet wide. Walkways ending in cul-de-sacs need a wheelchair turnaround space of at least 6 by 6 feet. Edge guides placed

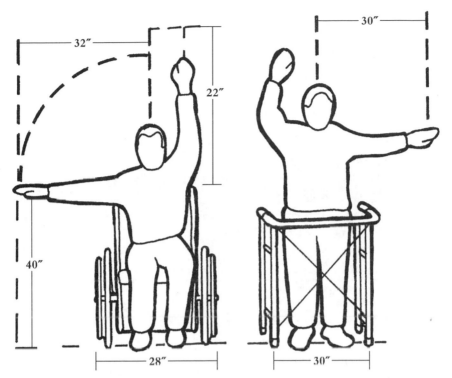

Wheelchair and walker gardeners must consider their maximum comfortable working reach when designing raised beds, gateways, paths, and the placement of hanging baskets and pots. The measurements given are for typical adults and should be used as a general guideline only. Take your own measurements and customize your accessible garden for your greatest comfort. What is an easy reach now may become more difficult over time, so plan for the future as well. Forward reach from a wheelchair, without bending, is about 30 inches, and for a walker user, a little more.

along pathways can be useful to visually impaired gardeners and will keep wheelchair wheels off planting areas.

Slopes and varied levels in the garden can add great visual interest, but they can present problems for those with impaired mobility or vision. If steps are not out of the question, keep them fairly wide and shallow, with an easy gradient. Risers should be no higher than 4 inches. Things that provide audible signals, such as wind chimes or a splashing water fountain, may be placed near the top and bottom of stairs or ramps as cues for visually impaired or easily disoriented gardeners.

Ramps with a gradient of 1:20 (a rise of 1 foot for every 20 feet of length) are negotiable by most wheelchairs, but a shallower 1:25 gradient

TABLE 1-2:
Wheelchair Dimensions

Typical Adult Wheelchair

Length	42 inches
Width	26
Seat height	19.5
Armrest height	29
Wheel height	26
Push-handle height (rear)	36
Fixed turn radius, wheel to wheel	18
Fixed turn radius, front to back	31.5
Average turn space	60 x 60
Minimum passing space for two wheelchairs	60

Adult reach from wheelchair

Unilateral vertical reach (straight overhead)	60
Horizontal working reach (one arm out from chair)	30
Bilateral horizontal reach (both arms outstretched	64
Diagonal reach to wall	48

(1 foot for every 25 feet) is better. If a steeper slope is necessary, allow an additional level approach of at least 5 1/2 feet at both the top and bottom of the ramp. More is better; up to 10 feet of runway is not excessive.

Stairways and ramps should always be equipped with sturdy handrails, placed at a comfortable height. To aid those with poor vision, paint or outline handrails and the edges of steps, paths, and ramps with bright white or yellow paint.

When designing pathways, keep in mind that straight lines and gentle curves are easiest to navigate and that angles, narrow places, and tight curves can present real difficulties for wheelchair, scooter, or walker gardeners. Gardeners who are easily disoriented may find straight paths preferable to curves.

Planting beds with paths on all sides should be no more than 4 feet wide, and beds with a path on only one side should not exceed 2 feet in width. Wider than this, it will be virtually impossible to reach the center of the bed from a standing or seated position. Bed height must be determined by the individual gardener's range of reach. A gardener in a wheelchair is limited to a maximum side reach of about 30 inches and a maximum frontal reach of about 48 inches. The lowest easy reach from a seated position is about 9 inches to the sides and 12 inches to the front, so raised beds should be no lower than 9 or 10 inches above ground level—and even this will be a stretch.

Gates should be at least 4 feet wide and have an unobstructed clearance of 24 to 36 inches beyond the latch side so that they can swing fully open to accommodate the passage of garden carts and wheelbarrows, as well as wheelchairs.

From Joseph Trappa, Idaho Falls, Idaho:

"Nothing is really impossible in a vegetable garden for blind people. Not at all! If the gardener is an elderly blind or partially sighted person who doesn't use Braille, a numbering system can work equally as well for labeling rows.

"For example, you have ten rows with strings between the sticks to mark your rows. The gardener can number those sticks with a very large number on a piece of paper, and then write behind it what is growing in that row.

"You don't really have to know Braille. Just be willing to devote some time to planning the garden on paper. You can lay out your garden on a large piece of cardboard or drawing board, say 2 by 3 feet, and glue strings or whatever you want in a pattern just like your garden, and write in very large print or in Braille what is where."

MEASURING AND MAPPING THE EXISTING SITE

Begin by making a rough sketch of your yard, drawing in any prominent features such as existing garden beds, walls, walks, trees, and plantings.

Now go outside and begin measuring. Start with the edges of your property, and measure everything of importance in your existing landscape—a fence line, a wall, the distance between a walkway and a large tree. For very large areas, a walking tape measure (16), as used by professional surveyors, is very helpful. This wheeled tape measure is held in a canelike fashion and rolled along the ground, making it easy for one person to measure even long distances. If you have a big property or intend to do a lot of landscaping or construction work, it is a definite labor saver. For smaller properties or less ambitious landscaping schemes, a good-quality 100-foot contractor's tape is all that is necessary. For visually impaired gardeners, tactile tape measures (101) in both 12- and 20-foot lengths are available with Brailled foot and inch readings. Be as accurate as possible; a mistake in inches can throw off the entire plan by feet later on. As you complete a measurement, jot down the figure on your rough sketch.

SCALE DRAWINGS

Use your rough sketch and the measurements you took to create an accurate scale drawing of your existing landscape. To do so, you will need large sheets of graph paper, tracing paper, pencils, erasers, a T-square, a right-angle triangle, a compass for drawing circles and curves, and a ruler. For those with severe visual impairments, a raised-line drawing kit for creating tactile drawings on special polyester film sheets is available through the American Association for the Blind. The kit, which retails for under $25, includes a rubber-coated drawing board, a package of polyester sheets, and a pen-type stylus. If you are visually impaired, it can be an invaluable aid to planning your garden.

You need to convert the actual measurements into whatever scale measurements will fit on your paper; a scale in which 1 inch equals 4 feet is best for most yards and gardens and easiest to work with because you can get graph paper that is marked off in 4 grids per inch.

On a piece of graph paper, mark off the outer boundaries of your site, measured to scale. Now draw in all the existing trees, shrubs, walks, and other features of your site, and transfer the figures you jotted down on your rough sketch to the appropriate places on the finished scale drawing. Mark which way is north, so that you will be able to determine where sunlight and shadows may fall on the garden throughout the day. Make photocopies of the finished drawing to work from, and keep the original safe so that you won't have to redraw the basic boundaries and permanent features as you experiment with different garden layouts.

Lay a piece of tracing paper over one of your photocopies, and begin sketching in the location of walkways, planting beds, and other features you want in your garden. This is the fun part, so don't be afraid to try out any new ideas that occur to you. Sketch in whatever you like, then go get a cup of coffee and ruminate for a while. Consult with other members of your family. Page through a few landscape or garden design books. Then come back to your plan and see if what you've drawn still seems feasible.

If you are planning a landscaped area, special graphic symbols are commonly used by landscape architects to denote specific types of permanent plantings and building materials. Templates of these shapes are available at most good art-supply stores; these templates make it easy to quickly draw in whatever you want in the garden plan. Just be sure that the size of the template shapes fits the scale of your overall drawing.

For vegetable and flower gardens, you can order a sticker kit of shapes that will allow you to "plant" your garden on paper again and again, rearranging everything until you get it just the way you want it. You can make your own such kit with a smooth lapboard or tabletop, self-stick notes, and round, peel-off price stickers, which come in many different colors.

If you are computer literate, several software programs, like Sprout!, Landscape!, and Compleat Vegetable Garden DRx, are available to help you design or retrofit an on-screen landscape, flower, or vegetable garden, as well as compute best planting times, planting locations, color schemes, and vegetable yields. Sprout! and Landscape! are available from Abracadata Inc., (800) 451-4871; Compleat Vegetable Garden DRx is available through Gurney's Seed and Nursery Co. (70).

GARDEN CONSTRUCTION

Planning the garden on paper was relatively easy and enjoyable. Now comes the hard part: actually creating the garden, with all the time, effort, and expense that this may entail.

Once you have finally decided upon the placement of the permanent features of your garden, use stakes and strings to lay out the changes to your existing landscape and the locations of new planting beds, paths, and other features.

Begin by placing stakes where you anticipate the edges of any paths, beds, patios, or lawn areas will go. Hammering plain wooden stakes into the ground can be difficult, so you may want to have a helper or make a dozen or so special marker stakes from either 3- or 4-foot lengths of doweling or stiff wire with a bit of rag attached as a high-visibility flag. Once the stakes are in place, run string from stake to stake to show the outline of the entire feature you are laying out.

Gently curving lines can be most easily laid out with a length of garden hose; the hose is lightweight enough to be easily moved into whatever shape you want, yet stiff enough to hold a curve without shifting while you mark its location by inserting stakes alongside it.

If the landscape area you are laying out will be either square or rectangular, such as a patio or planting bed, make sure the corners are perfectly square. There are two ways to do this. The first, which you should use if you are laying out a fairly large area, requires a simple geometric formula: In a right triangle, the square of the hypotenuse equals the sum of the squares of the two sides. If one leg of a right triangle measures 3 feet and the other 4 feet, then the hypotenuse is 5 feet ($9 + 16 = 25$, the square root of which is 5).

To check a corner for square using this method, mark a point 3 feet along one side, and a point 4 feet along the second side. Extend your tape measure between these two points; this diagonal measurement must equal 5 feet. If it does not, move your corner markers in or out until the diagonal equals 5 feet. Repeat this process at each of the four corners of your site.

If the area you are laying out is fairly small—a 4-by-4 planting bed, for example—you can use a quicker method to square the corners. First, place your stakes at the corners of the planned bed. Attach the end of a tape measure to one corner stake to hold it securely in place. Run the tape measure to the stake diagonal to the first. Repeat this diagonal measurement for the other two corners of the garden. When the corners are squared, these two diagonal measurements will be equal. For accuracy, remeasure the finished boundary lines.

GETTING THE WORK DONE

After planning and layout are complete, actually constructing your dream garden may be beyond your strength or physical abilities. If this is the case, you will have to either enlist the help of family and friends or hire a reliable landscape contractor.

Before you make any significant changes to your home or land-scape, such as the removal of buildings or large trees, or the addition of ramps, fences, walls, or other structural features, always check with the local governing body for any existing zoning laws and building codes that may have a bearing on the work you plan to do. If your plans violate the regulations in any way, but you feel you can justify the alterations you wish to make in terms of your disability, ask for a variance or special allowance. It may require some negotiation, but most municipalities are eager to help handicapped homeowners make their properties more accessible.

If building a special-use garden will stretch your financial resources a little thin, check into low- or no-interest loans and grants through various agencies specializing in aid to the physically challenged. (Note that if you do receive aid from nonprofit, governmental, or insurance agencies, you may be required to have most if not all construction work done professionally.)

State and local housing authorities often provide loans and grants to their residents for accessibility remodeling. Contact your state or municipal government to see if the work you propose is covered under their funding guidelines. If they do not have funds available, ask for other sources of possible funding; often a variety of state and local agencies may provide the money you need.

In addition, many communities that have home weatherization programs will also help with accessibility modifications around your home. To find out if your community offers such a service, contact the local Energy Conservation Corps or a local area agency or council on aging or handicapped accessibility.

Several federal agencies also provide low-interest loans and grants for accessibility remodeling. The Farmers Home Administration (FmHA) provides 502 or 504 loans for low-income homeowners over age 62 to build and repair their homes; if you are disabled and need to make accessibility modifications or repairs to your property, you may qualify for such funding. The Department of Veterans Affairs (VA) also provides similar low-interest loans to veterans to modify their homes.

The U.S. Department of Housing and Urban Development (HUD) distributes money to localities to be used to develop accessible features for the physically challenged; each local government decides how to best use these funds, and sometimes funds are available to help residents remodel or repair their homes and property. Contact your local government to find out if such funds are available.

Most private organizations aren't able to provide large sums of money to individuals, but the following foundations may be able to offer you some financial (or physical) assistance, especially if you or someone in your family is a member: Muscular Dystrophy Association; Multiple Sclerosis Society; Easter Seals Society; Cerebral Palsy Society; American Association for the Blind; Knights of Columbus; Rotary Clubs; Lions Clubs; local Chambers of Commerce; B'nai B'rith; Shriners Clubs; Sertoma; 4H Clubs; Masonic Lodges; and your own church, temple, or synagogue.

Most agencies and foundations will require you to submit your request for funding in writing. A two- or three-page letter with support documents is the strongest approach to many of these agencies and associations, although some may have their own application forms. In your letter, detail the reason you want to make modifications to your property, the work you propose, and an estimate (prepared by a contractor) listing the itemized breakdown of the total cost of the work proposed. Also include a short letter from your primary-care physician certifying that you are physically challenged and that garden-related therapy would be of benefit to you.

The Internal Revenue Service (IRS) allows you to deduct equipment, furnishings, and permanent changes for access to your home as medical expenses if you are itemizing deductions. Keep itemized receipts for all work done so that you can verify these deductions.

If you decide to have the work done professionally, it is more economical to have as much done at once as possible. Have a carefully thought-out master plan for your contractor to follow.

Selecting a contractor who understands your special requirements and will work with you can be difficult. Get recommendations from others who have had landscape or garden-related construction done. Try to find landscape contractors who are members of the American Society of Landscape Architects, the National Landscape Association, or the Associated Landscape Contractors of America. Local nurseries and garden centers can often recommend good landscape contractors in your area. Get at least three written bids on work to be done. Make an itemized list of exactly what you want done, and submit the same list to all candidates. Ask for start and completion dates in writing as well, and hold your contractor to these dates once the work is under way. Be sure that the contractor you hire understands exactly what you want and why you want it before the actual work begins.

On large projects, you'll probably be asked to provide some money up front. If you arrange to make payments throughout the period of construction, pay 30 percent before work begins, 30 percent at the halfway point, and the final 40 percent when the work is completed to your satisfaction.

If the garden is to be created or converted with the help of friends and family members, consider spreading the work out over a period of time. Many great gardens take years to fully develop and mature. You might put in just a few essential paths and planting beds the first year, and add other features later, as time and finances permit and as your growing experience as a gardener suggests improvements and innovations that will make gardening easier or more productive. If you decide to have the work done gradually over a period of time, it is still essential that you have a firm master plan from which to work, to ultimately avoid an ill-considered hodgepodge effect.

Garden Construction

Building permanent features for your garden can be the most challenging and rewarding aspect of your plan. As with most endeavors, plan carefully and be ready to modify your ideas to fit both your needs and the requirements of your chosen site.

PATHS AND PATIOS

Pathways in the accessible landscape should follow the most comfortable and natural routes through the yard and garden. If you have for years cut across the lawn to get to the mailbox, for example, consider placing a pathway there. Keep pathways as level as possible, with a grade of no more than 5 percent wherever practical. Steep grades and sharply canted pathways are extremely difficult for gardeners using walkers or wheeled mobility aids and may present problems to ambulatory gardeners as well.

Definite pathways are also of great help to blind or partially sighted gardeners, by clearly delineating the garden and gardening areas. Although winding pathways and partly obscured areas lend beauty, mystery, and romance to a garden, if you or other gardeners have visual impairments, or tend to become confused or disoriented on occasion, lay out paths that are as straight and direct as possible, with definite starting and ending points, and preferably with clear visibility to some large, easily recognized structure such as a toolshed or the house. Large, permanent items like benches, raised planting beds, or arbors along pathways can serve as further indications of location and distance. If the garden will see night use, make sure that all pathways and patios are well lit (see chapter 10).

From Dr. Gus Van Der Hoeven, extension specialist, Landscape and Environmental Horticulture, Kansas State University:

" A walk doesn't have to be gravel. It can be grass unless it has a lot of traffic. And what if you are living in a wheelchair? Then you'd better provide a more permanent walkway. You should be able to go for a walk every morning. You can take the same walk every morning for the rest of your life and always see different things.

"Landscapes don't have to be just flowers. You also need space. Make a landscape interesting to explore. Plan for the wheelchair to go everywhere in the landscape. Provide space to sit where people can watch the flowers grow."

In choosing surfacing materials for walks and patio areas, function and beauty must go hand in hand. Use your imagination and ingenuity to strike a happy compromise.

Poured concrete is the surfacing material of choice if you are faced with mobility problems. It is extremely durable, relatively inexpensive considering its longevity, easy to maintain, and virtually skidproof. On the down side, the initial cost of installing concrete is high, but it will pay for itself over the years in low maintenance and repair costs and may add considerable value to your home. Its unrelieved gray surface can be made more attractive with a variety of coloring and texturing techniques that can be employed while the concrete is still wet. For most applications, concrete slabs should be 4 inches thick, over a 6-inch gravel bed. You may need to increase the thickness of both the concrete and the gravel bed if your paved area will be regularly subjected to heavy wheeled traffic like cars or trucks.

Rough-Surfacing Concrete
A rough texture can add both traction and visual appeal. Working a trowel or stiff-bristled broom across the concrete before it hardens will produce an interesting pattern of grooves and swirls. The rougher the trowel or coarser the broom, the deeper the resulting grooves will be. To produce a checkerboard pattern, trowel or sweep each adjoining section in alternate directions.

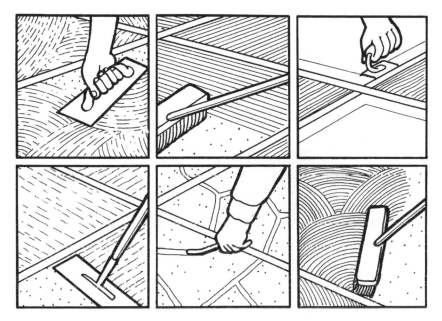

Wet concrete can be surfaced in a number of ways to improve both appearance and traction. Aggregates and colorants can also be added to the concrete mix to produce beautiful, durable, one-of-a-kind custom concrete.

Keystoning

A keystone finish is produced by first brooming a coarse texture into the surface, then spattering on ridges of soft white cement and sand mixed in a 1:2 ratio. As the mortar begins to harden, use a trowel to smooth it down over the rough background surface.

Exposed Aggregate

The rustic, high-traction surface of exposed aggregate concrete can be achieved by either pouring concrete with the chosen aggregate mixed in it and then scrubbing away excess concrete as it hardens, or pouring plain concrete, "seeding" aggregate over the liquid surface, and pressing or screeding it into the base with a trowel or float.

Aggregate comes in many colors and sizes, from big, round river pebbles to fine, angular granite chips. Smaller, rougher aggregates will add to the traction of a concrete surface, but large, smooth aggregates tend to make the surface more slippery, especially when wet.

Patterned Concrete

A mason's joint strike can be used to score wet concrete into geometric shapes and patterns that resemble flagstone, brick, or pavers. Special rubber molds can be used to stamp concrete with textures resembling brick, cobblestones, wood grain, or other paving materials. Patterned concrete provides much better traction than smooth concrete.

Colored Concrete

Prepared powdered dyes can be sprinkled over the top of poured concrete. Interesting granitelike or marbleized effects are possible. When combined with patterning, especially to resemble flagstone, the effect can be lovely and hard to tell from the real thing.

Concrete Pavers

Cheaper than poured concrete and available in a wide range of colors, textures, and shapes, precast concrete pavers set in a firm sand or mortar base are another good choice for durable, slip-proof pathways. Joints between pavers should be narrow and shallow to avoid catching wheelchair or scooter wheels or the rubber feet of walkers or canes.

Concrete "Cobblestones"

A simulated cobblestone pathway can be made from poured concrete with easy-to-use plastic forms (34, 67, 84, 114). You level the soil surface, place the 2-by-2-foot plastic form in place, fill it with concrete, and trowel it smooth. As soon as the concrete is firm, remove the form and start on the next 2-foot section. Walk Maker can make any size or shape you want, and because the surface level of the "cobbles" is uniform and the spaces between relatively narrow, the resulting path is quite safe and comfortable for both wheelchair and walker use.

Brick

Unless salvaged materials are used, brick can be expensive, and it will require seasonal maintenance. If you use brick for your garden walks or patio areas, you have the bonus of a wide range of textures, colors, and patterns from which to choose. Reserve elaborate designs like circular patterns and basketweave for large areas where the full effect can be appreciated; use simpler designs like running bond or herringbone for pathways. Choose one basic pattern for your pathways and stick to it. Varying brick patterns is like mixing too many plaids and prints; a little variety is attractive, but too much becomes confusing. Common building brick, although durable and serviceable, will not withstand the rigors of a severe climate or use by wheelchairs or wheeled-vehicles as well as brick made especially for paving. Paving brick is available through most masonry contractors.

Wood

Wooden walkways can be attractive, but they can also be expensive, labor intensive to maintain, and—if planks are used instead of end-cut wooden blocks—very slippery when wet. If you do use wood, use pressure treated lumber, which will resist insects and decay and is much less expensive than naturally resistant woods such as cedar or redwood. Do not use pressure-treated pathways near food-growing areas, however; the heavy metals and arsenic found in pressure-treated or CCA wood can leach into the soil and be taken up by plants. For pathways near vegetable gardens or orchards, use either a nonorganic path material or an untreated, rot-resistant wood like cedar or redwood.

Flagstone

Flagstone, especially if you are lucky enough to find it free for the taking, is a good choice for pathways, but only if it is fairly even surfaced and is firmly set in a sand or (preferably) mortar base with very narrow joints between. It can be slippery when wet, wobbly underfoot, and encourages the growth of moss and lichen, which can add to traction problems. If the joints are spaced too widely, wheels, canes, and walker feet can become wedged between the stones.

Tile

The rich, earthy tones of clay or slate-colored tile complement almost any garden area, but because tile becomes extremely slippery when wet, it should be used only as accent edging or as surfacing material for areas with very little foot traffic. Wheelchair and scooter gardeners, however, may find tile quite suitable for their use.

Asphalt

Asphalt is not usually a good choice for garden walkways. It tends to develop a slippery oily sheen when wet; it softens, oozes, and can become painfully hot in full sun; and it develops cracks after freezing. The smell that asphalt exudes on a hot summer day—somewhere between tar and camphorated oil—is also particularly offensive to many gardeners.

Crushed Stone
Finely crushed stone or gravel, which compacts well, makes an excellent path and walkway material. It must be poured over a fairly impermeable barrier like weed-block fabric or plastic, or weeds will sprout and grow through it. A 4- to 6-inch layer will make a good, durable walk. Water and tamp the freshly laid crushed stone well before using it for wheeled traffic; freshly spread, it can really bog down wheelchairs.

Loose Fill
Loose fill materials—coarse gravel or "bluestone," rustic bark chips, sand, pine straw, smoothly rounded pebbles—are very attractive and fine for ambulatory gardeners, but wheeled traffic tends to bog down in loose materials. In wheelchair-accessible gardens, save these for mulch and accents in areas that will not see wheeled traffic.

Portable Paths
Several brands of portable paths (34, 15, 146) are on the market. Strips of wood or plastic lath are lashed together with cord to form a flexible, car-petlike, roll-out path. Excellent for temporary duty, portable paths provide good traction for wheelchairs, scooters, and walkers over muddy, slippery, wet, or unstable ground, allowing the gardener access to all parts of the garden or landscape. Portable paths are tough, but are not durable enough for permanent installation. Save them for wet-weather days when you simply *must* get into that hard-to-reach back corner to plant.

SAND-BASED PATHS AND PATIOS
A pathway or patio area paved with brick, flags, or pavers set in a firmly packed sand base creates a beautiful, durable, and skidproof surface that will survive intact the freeze and thaw cycles that would crack or heave concrete or asphalt. Sand-based paving is durable enough to take heavy foot traffic but may begin to show ruts from continuous wheelchair or scooter use. If this happens, however, it is usually a relatively simple job to lift and adjust any out-of-level pavers. If your walkways will see heavy wheelchair or scooter use, you may prefer to set the bricks firmly in a concrete base.

The real bonus of sand-based paving is that it is easy: Only a few inches of soil need to be excavated, layers of crushed stone and sand are spread, surfacing material set, and more sand added.

One of the real benefits of using bricks, flags, or pavers for surfac-ing material is that you can devise any number of patterns, from simple to complex, to enhance the overall design of your garden. Plastic grid-

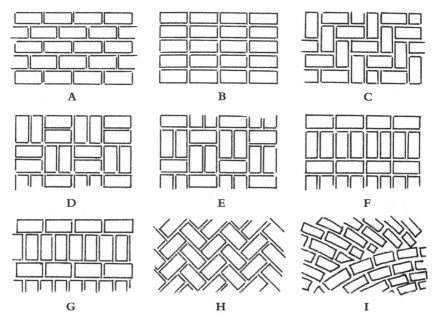

Brick patterns: (A) running bond, (B) stack bond, (C) herringbone, (D, E) basket weave (two variations), (F) capped herringbone, (G) running and stack bond mixed, (H) diagonal herringbone, and (I) scalloped. Bricks, with their natural texture and colors, can be used as a unifying design element in any garden, formal or informal.

work systems make it even easier: Simply place the grids and insert the bricks; the pattern and spacing are already set for you.

Any pavers should be treated once every year or so with a water-proofing solution. Not only will this treatment keep them looking better longer, but it will also prevent chipping and cracking from frost, and discourage the growth of slippery moss and lichens.

RAMPS AND STEPS

Ramps make an easy transition from one level of a sloping garden or living area to another. Whether ramps are permanent or temporary, solid construction and high-traction surfaces are essential.

Gentle gradients of 1:20 or 1:25 are negotiable by most persons in wheelchairs, especially if they have good upper body strength or are using a powered chair. Handrails must be installed for the entire length of the ramp and should extend for 1 or 2 feet beyond both the top and bottom of the ramp. If you must cover a distance of more than 30 feet, install level landing spaces at 15-foot intervals so that the wheelchair or walker user can pause and rest if necessary. Landings should be no smaller than 5 by 5 feet, to allow a comfortable turning radius for wheelchairs.

For gardener's with visual impairments or who wear bifocal lenses, mark the beginning and ending of each ramp, as well as all handrails, with high-visibility white or yellow paint.

Try to position ramps so that they face southward, especially if you live in a climate with winter snow and ice. A southward-facing ramp will heat up and shed snow and ice more readily than ramps oriented away from the sun.

Portable ramps and ramp cleats (2, 15, 16, 34, 40, 42, 73, 84, 109, 126, 146) are a good solution to a temporary mobility problem. Ramp cleats, which attach at the top and bottom of sturdy 2 by 6 planks, are used to create a do-it-yourself portable ramp option. The cleats clip firmly to van door edges or pickup truck beds and provide an excellent way to get wheelchairs or even heavy riding mowers in and out of vehicles.

Concrete Ramps

For a permanent ramp, poured concrete will yield the best, most durable results. Because of the gentle gradients required by special-use ramps, you will have to allow for a lot of room and, consequently, a lot of concrete: A 1:25 slope means that if you are negotiating a rise of only 2 feet, you will need 50 feet of ramp. To prevent the solid concrete slab from sliding slowly downhill, footers must be installed at the top and bottom of the ramp and at any landing. These footers should extend downward from the slab to below the frost line. (Check with local building codes for the frost-line depth for your area.)

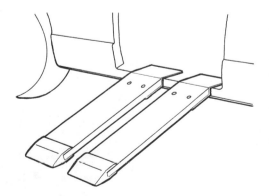

Ramp cleats, available at hardware stores or through specialty supply houses, make quick, inexpensive temporary ramps sturdy enough for loading and unloading lawn tractors, tillers, garden carts, and wheelchairs. The tough metal cleats bolt to 2-by-8 or 2-by-12 lumber, locking anchor pins secure them to the vehicle, and nonskid rubber bottom cleats keep the ramp from moving. Loads up to 1,400 pounds can be moved safely using these ramp cleats.

For safe footing and easy wheelchair use, a roughly broomed surface is essential; to further increase traction on fairly long or steep ramps, set flush wooden treads made of rot-resistant pressure-treated lumber at 1-foot intervals along the length of the ramp before the concrete is poured. Textured rubberized coatings, applied after the concrete is cured and dry, can also dramatically increase the traction of concrete ramps, especially when they are wet.

Wooden Ramps

Wooden ramps are best reserved for relatively short distances and for gardens where the additional seasonal maintenance required by exposed wood will not place an undue burden on the gardener.

Building a wooden ramp is much like constructing a wooden deck. Always use pressure-treated lumber and noncorrosive (galvanized) nails and bolts. Note that although pressure-treated posts can be sunk directly into the ground to support the upper end of the ramp, setting the posts on poured concrete piers will result in a firmer foundation that will not wobble under the weight of a wheelchair or a slow-moving walker.

To increase the traction of wooden ramp surfaces, paint them with exterior enamel paint mixed with sand, at the rate of 1 pound of sand to 1 gallon of paint. Alternatively, you can use rolled asphalt roofing material securely tacked down to the ramp to provide a good nonskid surface for both walking and wheeling. Wooden battens, or small strips of wood nailed to the surface, can also provide additional traction, especially when the ramp is wet or covered with ice or snow.

STEPS AND STAIRWAYS

Well made garden steps can be used as retaining walls to help hold back soil on steep slopes as well as to lead from one level of the garden to another. Solid concrete or brick set in concrete makes the best skid-proof steps, but solid wooden steps can be used if you treat all tread surfaces with a skidproof surfacing material.

When planning steps for a special-use garden, allow enough room for a long, fairly shallow flight of steps rather than a short, steep one. Determine the total rise (height) the steps will ascend and the total run (length) they will traverse. Decide upon an appropriate riser height and tread width, then calculate how many steps it will take to cover this gradient.

Step riser height can vary widely, but a height of about 4 inches is best for outdoor garden steps. Treads should be no less than 13 inches wide; a tread width of up to 25 inches is not excessive. Wide treads will provide the additional safe footing necessary for those using canes or walkers and also blend more naturally with the surrounding landscape.

It is important that all steps be exactly the same height and width; uneven steps invite stumbles and falls. Additionally, avoid open-riser wooden stairs or steps with nosings or overhangs, which can catch at the toe and cause tripping.

All steps should be clearly marked with high-visibility paint for those with vision problems. Check the local building codes for any other requirements for steps and stairways that may exist in your area.

HANDRAILS

Handrails are essential to the safe use of all ramps and stairways. They should be installed on both sides of the ramp or stairway so that anyone with strength on only one side of the body will have adequate support when going up or down. If the ramp or flight of stairs is very wide, consider installing a handrail down the center. All handrails should extend a foot or two beyond the top and bottom of the stairway or ramp to provide users additional support in getting on or off.

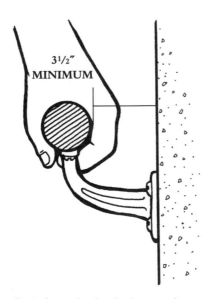

3½″ MINIMUM

Design handrails so that they can be easily gripped between the thumb and forefinger; a smooth, round handrail about 1½ inches in diameter is easier to grip than one that is square or rectangular. For outdoor handrails, smoothly sanded wood is the best choice, as metal tends to get too hot in direct sunlight. All handrails should be well marked with high-visibility paint.

Mount handrails about 3½ inches away from walls to provide adequate space for knuckles and fingers. Don't skimp on support posts or attachments—a handrail must be able to support at least 250 pounds at any point without snapping or coming loose from its supports. Keep handrails in perfect condition at all times to avoid accidents.

Round, wooden handrails, set at least 3½ inches away from walls to prevent scraped knuckles, are more comfortable than metal tubing, which tends to heat up in the sunshine. Use high-gloss exterior paint or varnish to keep handrails smooth and splinter-free.

Handrails for ramps should be set about 32 inches high. This is a good average height for both wheelchair users and those on foot. Along stairways, a handrail height of 30 inches is adequate; raise this to about 34 inches at landings.

When attaching handrail supports to a concrete ramp or flight of concrete steps, make sure that the supports are set firmly into the structure before the first concrete is poured. If it is necessary to attach supports after the concrete has hardened, drill holes into the concrete and install attachment brackets using long masonry anchors and screws.

Handrail supports for wooden ramps and steps must be attached to or be an integral part of the underlying structure of the ramp or stairway, not just attached to the treads themselves, to provide safe, adequate support.

GRAB BARS

Sturdy, well-mounted grab bars (14, 40, 42, 43, 55, 61) should be placed wherever they may be necessary in and around the garden. Grab bars can provide a secure emergency grip to prevent a bad fall, make it easier to arise from a seated position, and help in moving from a wheelchair or scooter to a garden bench or raised-bed seating ledge. Grab bars outdoors should be made of weatherproof wood or plastic; metal bars will get too hot in direct sunlight. If you must use metal, cover it with duct tape or other highly grippable, non-heat-conductive material.

Good places for grab bars are near water faucets, along the sides of outbuildings or solid walls, at greenhouse or lath house doorways, at the top and bottom of stairs and ramps, and along solidly constructed raised beds.

FENCES AND GATES

Fences add privacy; provide protection from wind, noise, and intruders; help delineate the garden's boundaries; create new vertical growing spaces; and serve as a visual aid to those with limited eyesight. A fence can be anything from a simple barrier of woven-wire mesh to keep out small animals to a substantial masonry wall. The fence and gate you select should be based on your needs, finances, and personal preferences.

Fences

Before you begin building any fence, especially one that lies along your property lines, check with local building and zoning codes. Many communities specify maximum height, distance from property lines and streets, and even materials that you may and may not use.

From Howard Brooks, former therapist at Institute of Rehabilitation Medicine, New York City:

" One of the great advantages of gardening is that it is not a static activity: There is always something happening—a new sprout, shoot, or leaf is forming, a flower is opening or fading and has to be removed. Then the cycle begins all over again. For many severely incapacitated people who are totally dependent on others for assistance in even the smallest tasks, having a living thing depend on them for care and sustenance can give them the will to go on and an interest in the future."

Fences less than 3 feet high should be avoided, as they can become tripping hazards. Also avoid fences with sharp top edges, such as picket fences; a fall against these can be very dangerous. All fences and fence materials should be as sturdy, stable, and splinterless as possible, in case they are fallen against or leaned upon. Allow at least 6 to 8 inches of clear space between a fence and the edge of any pathway that runs beside it to provide maneuvering room for wheelchair and walker passage.

If your fence will traverse a slight slope, you can simply let the fence line follow the decline. If the slope is steep, however, "step" the fence down the hill, setting each section lower than the one preceding it.

For wooden fences, posts should be of ground-contact-grade pressure-treated lumber. Bottom rails should also be of pressure-treated wood of top-quality redwood or cedar; top rails can be made of less expensive grades of rot-resistant lumber. Use only hot-dip galvanized nails, screws, and hardware for any fence construction.

Lightweight fencing posts, such as those used to support a chicken-wire barrier fence or to provide intermediate support for a woven-wire fence, can be set directly into the ground. Special galvanized post-support spikes can be purchased at most hardware stores; these make the job of installing light-duty wooden posts very easy—you simply hammer the post-support spike into the ground and attach your wooden post to it. For ultimate security and strength, however, it is best to set each post on its own footing of concrete and gravel.

When using lightweight or temporary fencing, as is sometimes necessary to keep small animals out of the vegetable patch, make sure that all posts and fence lines are clearly visible, especially if you or another gardener has impaired vision. Tie or weave bright-colored tape along the top row of fencing fabric, and paint posts an eye-catching shade of red, pink, or orange.

Gardeners who experience spells of dizziness or who tend to fall easily may want to use bend-away fence posts to hold lightweight or temporary garden fencing. Marketed as posts for driveway markers (15, 97) that will bend out of the way if hit by a car and then spring back up, these bend-away posts can be used as fence posts too, with reflectors attached for added visibility. If someone falls against one, bend-away

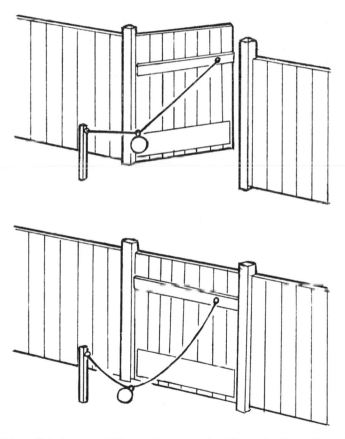

A primitive self-closing gate. This simple system of weights and pulleys allows the gate to swing open easily with only the slightest effort and swing shut again just as easily. Once the gate is swung open and released, the weight drops and pulls the gate closed. A kickplate has been installed to prevent damage from wheelchair footrests.

posts greatly reduce the possibility of injury. They should not, however, be used with any permanent fence that may appear to be sturdy and stable enough to use as a support.

Gates

If your fenced-in garden will require a gate, it must be at least 4 feet wide to provide clearance for wheelchairs, power scooters, and walkers, as well as for wheelbarrows, garden carts, and other wheeled equipment. Allow an unobstructed clearance of 18 to 24 inches beyond the latch so that the gate can swing fully open. If possible, use a sliding gate rather than a swinging one; sliding gates take up less room and are less likely to injure gardeners with vision impairments.

Gates at the top or bottom of stairs or ramps must also have an adjacent landing (level area) of at least 5 by 6½ feet so that walker or wheelchair users can move back out of the way when the gate opens toward them.

Hinges on basic garden gates that do not open on ramps or stairs should allow the gate to be swung open wide from either side, to prevent having to back and maneuver wheelchairs and scooters through the opening. Snap-back hinges, which act as self-closers for gates, are excellent for the accessible garden gate, but make sure the hinges are not so stiff that they slam the gate shut so fast or so hard that fingers can be pinched.

Gate hardware should be of heavy-duty, outdoor-grade, galvanized steel or brass. Latches should be of an easy-open variety, especially for those with restricted finger or hand mobility.

If the gate will see a lot of wheelchair or scooter passage, install a metal kickplate or guard along the bottom to protect the gate frame from excessive wear caused by pushing the gate open with wheelchair footrests. The kickplate should extend up 12 to 16 inches from the bottom of the gate.

CHAPTER THREE

Raised Beds, Containers, and Trellises

Raised beds and containers can aid those with limited mobility or reduced visual acuity by bringing the plants up closer rather than requiring the gardener to bend down to them. And containers can make growing plants possible for bedridden persons or those whose living quarters have no space for a garden.

Raised beds are also of great benefit to the visually impaired gardener. By lifting plants closer to eye (and nose) level, it's much easier to determine what needs attention and to appreciate the colors, scents, and textures of plants growing in your garden. Also, because of the more clearly defined shapes of the beds and because all plants are up above foot level, it's impossible to inadvertently step on a plant.

As a further aid to blind gardeners, a 1-by-2 post inserted at the corner of each raised bed can hold a plastic or metal tag that describes in Braille what is planted in that bed. Individual rows within a bed can also be marked, using Braille-labeled 2-foot stakes at the beginning and end of each row. These same stakes, with a stout cord strung tightly between, can serve as spacing guides during planting time.

RAISED-BED CONSTRUCTION

Raised beds and containers allow much of the work in a garden to be done from a seated position on the ground, on permanent built-in ledges, or from portable chairs, wheelchairs, benches, or scooters. A height of only 9 to 12 inches can greatly ease the bending strain on back, hips, and legs. If you use a walker, a height of about 3 feet will allow you to reach the level of the garden soil without bending or straining. Wheelchair gardeners are limited to a maximum side reach of about 30 inches and a maximum frontal reach of about 48 inches. The lowest easy reach from a seated position is about 9 inches to the sides and 12 inches to the front, so raised beds should be no lower than 9 to 14 inches above ground level.

From Julia Beems, HTR, Craig Hospital, Englewood, Colorado:

"Raised beds may be constructed out of many materials. Raised beds should allow for front wheel projection of the wheelchair beneath the growing area. It is inconvenient to work sideways.

"In planting a raised bed, the types of plant materials are important. A 30-inch height on a bed works well for adult quadriplegics or someone who can't bend over only if short crops are grown. A 24-inch raised bed works well with higher quadriplegics if medium-height crops such as tomatoes and eggplants are used."

Reaching the center of the bed should not be a strain. Beds with access on just one side should be no wider than 2 to 3 feet; beds with pathways all around can be 4 to 5 feet wide, depending on the gardener's reach and upper-body and arm strength.

Try to incorporate wide, level, smooth ledges on which you can lean, kneel, or sit comfortably while gardening. If you extend these ledges outward a few more inches at widely spaced intervals, wheelchair users can use them as easily accessible work tables along the garden paths. Gauge the height of walls and ledges to the height of wheelchair seats, and wheelchair gardeners who have sufficient upper-body strength will be able to lift themselves from wheelchair to ledge, thus substantially increasing their reach distance into the garden beds.

Raised beds can be any shape or length you wish, but keep the overall design of your garden in mind. A series of small rectangular or square beds, perhaps in a subtly staggered arrangement, looks nicer than one or two very long beds running the length of the garden. Straight lines and gentle curves are easiest to navigate; avoid serpentine shapes and narrow, sharp angles. If necessary, recontour existing beds to make them easier to move around.

Constructing many large, permanent raised beds can be an expensive undertaking. Besides the material used to build the bed itself, you must consider the cost of filling the bed. Drainage pipes, gravel, and topsoil will have to be trucked in, and even a relatively small bed can hold a large amount of fill. A raised bed 4 feet wide, 6 feet long, and 2 feet high will hold 48 square feet of soil—roughly 20 bushels of material. If you have decided to convert your entire garden to raised beds, start with temporary beds of straw bales first, and build permanent beds year by year, as finances allow. You may find that by altering your growing techniques, using intensive spacing and trellising, you will not need as many square feet of garden space as you thought.

Unedged Beds
The most basic type of raised bed is achieved by simply raking or hoeing garden soil up into a leveled-off heap. Barring torrential rainstorms, most unedged raised beds will last through the growing season without collapsing, unless your soil is very sandy. The height of such a bed can range anywhere from 3 to 9 inches; anything much higher than that will tend to spread out and sink down closer to the level of the surrounding earth.

The size, shape, and position of an unedged raised bed can be changed from season to season to fit the needs of whatever you wish to

TABLE 3-1:
Raised-Bed Size Guide

Gardener	Maximum Height	Maximum Width
Men		
Ambulant	39–40 inches	36 inches
Seated, but able to get up from chair	30	25
Chairbound	24	16
Women		
Ambulant	35–37 inches	36
Seated, but able to get up from chair	27	21
Chairbound	24	16

grow there. You can tailor the height of the soil mound to the type of plant you're growing: Warm-soil plants like tomatoes, peppers, egg-plants, peanuts, melons, and okra will thrive in higher beds where the sun can strike the sides of the bed and warm the soil more thoroughly; cool-soil plants like lettuce, potatoes, cabbage, broccoli, and cauliflower will do better in lower beds, where soil temperatures are correspond-ingly cooler. Because of the solar-heating advantages of the raised bed, it may be possible to start your garden earlier in the spring, keep it going longer in the fall, and successfully grow varieties that are not nor-mally hardy in your USDA zone.

The primary disadvantage of an unedged raised bed is its lack of permanence. Each spring the beds must be reshaped and built up again. Also, because the height is limited to less than a foot, these beds are not of great benefit to persons who find bending or reaching difficult.

Semipermanent Beds

For those who have good upper-body mobility and reach, an easy, inex-pensive semipermanent raised bed can be constructed of bales of straw (not hay—it will sprout), excelsior, or unshredded sphagnum moss. The width of the bales will decrease the usable soil area of the bed contained within them. But if you can comfortably work from a sitting position on the bales, you can reach quite far into the center of the bed.

Depending on the height you want, lay the bales flat, on edge, or on end and fill in the center of the bed. When making very deep beds, to save on fill, lay in a few more bales to raise the bottom to within 12 to 18 inches of the top. The bales will slowly decompose and provide additional nutrients to the plants. Bale dimensions vary considerably throughout the country, so be sure of the size you'll be working with early in your planning. Baled sphagnum moss is usually available through large garden-supply stores or through commercial nurseries and greenhouses. It can be fairly expensive, so reserve it for small beds. Gardeners in rural areas can usually obtain baled straw from local farms or farm-supply stores or through classified ads. In urban and suburban areas, hunting shops or archery-supply stores may carry straw or excel-sior bales, which are frequently used as backing for targets.

Small, straw-bale raised beds are a perfect place to grow potatoes. Arrange four bales edgewise in a square. Fill the space to within a foot of the top with compost or loose garden soil. Place two or three potato pieces, each containing an eye from which the plant will sprout, on top of the compost. Cover with compost and add a thin layer of straw. As the potato plant grows, fill around it with more compost and straw until the medium inside the square is level with the top of the bales. Harvest your crop by simply toppling one bale over and scooping out the potatoes.

Baled goods are surprisingly long-lasting, but over the course of several years, they will slowly decompose and have to be replaced with either more bales or more permanent materials. As bales break down, add them to the compost pile or scatter the contents over the garden as mulch.

Permanent Beds

Permanent raised beds can be constructed out of any material that is durable enough to withstand constant humidity and strong enough to hold back the considerable weight of soil behind it. Kit beds (34, 67,

Trash bag gardens were developed by Duane Clupper of Kingman, Arizona, as a way to reduce the amount of water he used in his backyard garden. The idea caught on, and such gardens have been used successfully to bring the benefits of homegrown agriculture to gardeners around the world. Inexpensive and amazingly durable, double-ply trash or leaf bags filled with compost or potting soil can be used to grow just about anything. The plastic bags provide water-conserving and weed-suppressing mulch, heat the soil for faster germination and growth, and make sturdy, roomy containers—all in one. For more information, write to Garbage Bag Gardens, 1651 Packard Street, Kingman, AZ 86401.

103, 111, 128, 138) are easiest to make. "Planks" or "logs" made of durable, UV-stabilized PVC snap together to form square or rectangular beds. Several sizes are available, and many come with edge or drip irrigation systems built right in. One such kit that is great for gardeners who have difficulty bending is the Living Wall Garden, which consists of stackable plastic units, either round or square, that can be filled with planting medium and stacked to the desired height, up to about 5 feet.

From Robert Haugh, a wheelchair gardener following the development of a brain tumor, Hagerstown, Maryland:

" I had to learn to do things all over again. I never gardened before. I worked in masonry, as a construction worker. We moved into this house in 1972, and I began gardening then. I have raised flower beds, about 40 feet long and 7 feet wide, that I can reach from the chair. I use short-handled shovels, rakes, and other tools because they're easier to reach with.

"I'm very particular about weeds. I try to spend a few minutes every day or so to keep ahead of them. And I use lots of mulch, especially grass clippings. That really keeps the weeds down!

"When people say I can't do something, I have to prove them wrong. I'm independent and I like to do things on my own."

Wooden railroad ties, landscaping timbers, or pressure-treated lumber can also be used in raised-bed construction. Wooden members can simply be stacked for low beds or spiked, nailed, or screwed together for taller beds. Old tires, stacked to a comfortable working height, are another inexpensive and easy way to construct small raised beds. Very large tires, like those on tractors and trucks, can be used to create a raised bed large enough to hold a generous number of plants and with a rim wide enough to sit on comfortably. No matter what material you use, always leave spaces for water drainage near the bottom of raised beds; waterlogged soil can exert tremendous outward pressure.

Important note: Pressure-treated or chemical-treated (CCA) wood should not be used for any raised beds or planter boxes containing edible crops. The chemicals (copper, chromium, and arsenic) used to make the wood resistant to rot and insects can leach into the soil and be absorbed by plants growing there. Limit the use of CCA-treated wood to beds and containers for flowers and ornamentals. For vegetables and fruits, use naturally rot-resistant woods like redwood and cedar or inorganic materials like masonry or stone to build up your beds. New recycled-plastic products are also safe to use as raised beds and containers for food plants. Do not use chemically treated wood for tables, benches, or playground equipment either, because the arsenic in the wood can easily rub off onto hands. (For more information—and some very frightening reading—on the questionable safety of pressure-treated or CCA-treated woods, see the Bibliography.)

Masonry or stone raised beds can be most easily constructed by stacking unmortared bricks, blocks, or stones up to the desired height and backfilling with soil. Leave some space between the bottom course of bricks and blocks to allow for the drainage of water, and limit the height of unmortared walls to about 2 feet. Anything higher may be too unstable to be safe. Concrete blocks are less expensive than brick or stone but can be unattractive in a garden setting; brick and cut stone are expensive, but they are beautiful in nearly every setting and only get better looking with age. If your raised bed is in an out-of-the-way area and is primarily used for practical purposes, such as growing vegetables for the table or as a nursery for young transplants, then go with the less expensive concrete block. For landscaping beds, use brick or stone, or opt for a well-made lumber wall instead of masonry.

Masonry walls may present too rough a surface for wheelchair or power scooter gardeners should they bump or rub up against it. Besides scratching paint or metalwork, rough masonry walls can also scrape elbows and knees. Padded "bumpers" may be installed on the armrests and wheel mounted grips of wheelchairs to avoid this hazard.

Drainage

With enclosed raised beds, you need to ensure good bottom drainage. Put down a layer of coarse gravel, broken rock, or sharp sand, then fill the beds with any good garden soil, to which has been added the appropriate amendments. Drainage is essential, not only to the health of your plants, most of which will rot in waterlogged soil, but also to the durability of the raised-bed wall. Open materials, like timber, stacked dry stone, or unmortared blocks or bricks, will allow a good deal of water to drain through them unaided. Solid walls, however, will retain water, and the pressure of waterlogged soil can be tremendous. Without adequate means to drain off excess water, solid walls will bulge, crack, and eventually fail.

In mortared block or brick masonry walls, leave narrow gaps as drainage holes near the bottom; in solid concrete walls, install short pieces of 2-inch PVC pipe before the wall is poured, to act as drainage holes in the finished wall. To prevent the blockage of drainage holes with soil or debris, screen the inside opening with a piece of medium-grade hardware cloth. If you live in an area with very high annual rainfall, further increase drainage by laying pieces of perforated drainage pipe onto the bottom gravel, then covering with more gravel or pieces of broken rock. The ends of the pipe should protrude through the wall itself.

CONTAINER GARDENS

Containers and pots allow you to have a garden even if your space is limited to a tabletop beside your bed, a windowsill, or a corner of the porch or patio. Plan the container garden as carefully as you would any other garden. Try massing houseplants or bright flowering annuals that have similar cultural requirements in several large containers rather than planting single plants in small individual pots. They're easier to tend, take up less space, look less cluttered, and give you more of a feel of working in a garden. You can create miniature landscapes within these larger containers, complete with attractive mulches, rocks and stones, and figurines if you wish.

Except for large trees and shrubs, anything that grows in garden soil can be grown in a container. You can have a portable rose garden, a miniature fruit orchard, a strawberry barrel on wheels—the possibilities are endless, as is the selection of containers you can use: clay or plastic pots, terra cotta drainage tiles, hollow cinder blocks, open-patterned decorative bricks, wooden barrels, laundry tubs, old boots, coffee pots, even clean and painted tin cans.

Anything that will hold soil can be used as a container for growing plants. Important criteria for selection of a container are its depth and width, and drainage. With a few exceptions, the essential root depth of plants is roughly equal to two-thirds their height above ground. Hence, to grow sweet corn, which can reach over 6 feet in height, you would need a container of no less than 4 feet deep. To grow pansies, which have a mature height of less than 8 inches, a 5-inch-deep container would be sufficient.

The width of the container should be roughly equal to the farthest spread of leaves on the mature plant. For example, a potato plant will be about 2 feet wide and 3 to 4 feet high at maturity; thus a potato barrel should be about 24 inches wide and 2 to 3 feet deep.

From Charles A. Lewis, horticulturist, Morton Arboretum, Lisle, Illinois:

"In a world of constant judgment, plants are nonthreatening and nondiscriminating. They respond to the care that is given them, not to the physical capacities of the gardener. It doesn't matter if you are healthy or handicapped; plants will grow if you give proper care.

"Plants take away some of the anxiety and tension of the immediate by showing us that there are long, enduring patterns in life. There is a certainty in knowing that a rose is a rose is indeed a rose—at all times and in all places."

Drainage is also important. Few plants will thrive in perpetually soggy soil; most will die of root rot. Like most living things, plants need fresh air to survive. Plants breathe through their roots as well as their leaves, so it is essential that the soil surrounding those roots be light and open enough to admit the minute amounts of air required. Tightly compacted soil will lack sufficient air; waterlogged soil will contain almost no air at all.

Be sure that the container you choose provides adequate bottom drainage. This is best accomplished simply by making a hole or two in the bottom of the container and placing a few pebbles or shards of broken pottery in the bottom before adding soil and plants. A thin layer of drainage material or even a single curved shard of pottery covering the drainage hole works as well as a thick layer of pebbles and allows more room for soil and root development.

One of the simplest container-growing tricks I have ever seen was to slit open plastic bags of potting soil and insert the plants, providing soil, container, and protective plastic mulch all in one.

Planting in plastic bags small enough for tabletop gardening is easily done using gallon-size zipper-type freezer storage bags or even old bread bags (double recycled plastic bags for added strength). Fill the bag with potting mix to within a few inches of the top. Seal shut, using staples to reinforce the seal. Place the filled plastic bag, or pillow pack, on its side in a waterproof tray—an old baking sheet is ideal. To aid drainage and reduce the chance for rot, punch a few holes in the underside of the bag. Then carefully slit the bag and insert seeds or seedlings. Small, fast-growing annual flowers, greens like lettuce or spinach, or radishes are best for these small containers. Water thoroughly; in a few weeks, the plants should be growing vigorously.

If your garden area is limited to a patio or sunny windowsill, you can still have a wonderful selection of plants to enjoy. Boxes and pots can be mounted to sills, walls, and deck railings, their height adjusted to the comfort of wheelchair or walker gardeners. A length of sturdy plastic rain gutter nailed to a wall or railing makes an ideal, inexpensive container for small plants. A surprisingly wide variety of vegetables, herbs, and flowers will grow well in these modest-size outdoor containers.

Very large containers, such as those used for potted palms, miniature fruit trees, or large groupings of flowering plants, should be mounted on wheeled trivets for easy movement. For a truly portable garden, place pots holding larger plants like tomatoes, peppers, or azaleas in a colorfully painted child's wagon. You can move your garden to

A wide variety of containers of different heights can be used to make a garden just about anywhere. Old-fashioned metal hay racks, lined with coco fiber (a safer alternative to sphagnum moss) and filled with lightweight potting soil, can be mounted on any waterproof wall. Barrels and half barrels are just the right height for most walker or wheelchair gardeners and can be mounted on wheeled trivets to create "portable" gardens.

take advantage of sunshine or shade, or out of the reach of frost or high winds. If you garden in a hot climate or if your container garden will be subject to direct sunshine, try double potting with a layer of peat moss between the pots to insulate the roots from excessive heat and reduce evaporation. You'll need to water less often.

For gardeners who find bending or sitting for long periods difficult, a hanging garden that can be tended from a standing position may be ideal. And for wheelchair gardeners, hanging baskets and pots that can be easily pulled down to workable levels maximize growing space on decks and porches and in greenhouses. Commercial pulley pots are widely available, or make your own with strong, lightweight nylon cord and a pulley purchased from a hardware store. Cut the cord long enough for the pot to be lowered to within 2 feet of the ground, and mount a hitch to secure the cord to a nearby wall, about 30 inches above ground level.

TABLETOP GARDENS

Wheelchair gardeners or those who are confined to bed may find a laptop garden very rewarding. A sturdy lapboard can be made from 1/2-inch plywood, edged with precut molding to prevent spills, and lined with countertop laminate or waterproof contact paper. For wheelchair use, the lapboard should extend at least 2 inches beyond the outside edges of the armrests so that it is steady and well supported. A gardening lapboard can be of great value when potting up plants, seeding flats, pruning small potted plants, or doing other gardening chores. Add a nonskid kitchen sink liner to it, and you can carry watering pots, harvest baskets, hand tools, and spray bottles easily between house and garden. The lapboard can also serve as a tabletop gardening tray so that you can use the kitchen table or countertop as a potting bench without scattering potting soil and water everywhere.

A larger and more permanent tabletop garden is constructed of outdoor-grade 3/4-inch plywood, framed and reinforced to bear the weight of plants, containers, and potting soil. It is set up on sawhorses constructed to the appropriate height so that a person using a walker can easily reach the top of the garden soil, or a wheelchair or scooter seat can slide comfortably underneath. For a simpler version of this type of garden, an oversize lapboard-type tray can be set on a picnic table raised on blocks to the appropriate height.

Place the tabletop garden on a level, hard surface that won't be damaged by spilled water or soil and in an area that is relatively sheltered from the wind. When filled with plants and soil, the tabletop garden

Any sturdy table can become a garden. The Versatable, available through the adapt-Ability catalog, makes an ideal tabletop garden for the wheelchair or walker gardener. Table height can be adjusted from 29 to 44 inches, and the scratch- and stain-resistant melamine top has a center cutout and a spill-containing rim all around. When not in use, the Versatable can be folded for storage.

will be quite heavy, but strong winds can have extreme lifting power. If the tabletop garden will be located on a deck or rooftop, consider replacing ordinary potting soil with a lightweight soilless mix, composed primarily of perlite or vermiculite, to reduce the overall weight.

PLANTING MEDIA

Once you have a bed or container for your plants, you must fill it with a growing medium. Most garden soils are too heavy, too infertile, and too coarse to be successfully used for potted plants. The nutrient requirements of a plant growing within the confines of a container must be met by the soil in its pot. For this reason, highly fertile, porous potting mixes are recommended for container growing.

Commercially available potting mixes are your best choice. These sterile, nutrient-enriched mixes are inexpensive; free of soilborne insects, diseases, and weed seeds; and lightweight enough that even large containers are relatively easy to move.

An alternative to potting soil mix is a soilless mix, an especially good choice where weight or sterility is critical. These growing media contain no organic material; all nutrients are supplied through chemical fertilizers that are added to the mix and supplemented by the gardener at appropriate intervals. Soilless mixes are composed primarily of lightweight perlite and vermiculite. You also can purchase these two ingredients individually at most garden-supply stores and add them to any potting soil to decrease its weight and increase its water-holding and waterborne nutrient-holding capacity.

When handling potting mixes or any dry soils or amendments, keep a spray bottle full of hot water handy and moisten the soil as you mix. If the medium is very dry, add a small amount of detergent to the hot water to make it absorb more quickly. Dry mixes can generate a lot of dust, so if you have respiratory problems, wear a dust mask or get someone else to handle the dry ingredients for you.

An added precaution: A fungal disease of the skin, *cutaneous sporotrichosis*, has been linked with the handling of sphagnum moss. This is not the brown sphagnum peat moss commonly used as a soil conditioner and amendment. That product is safe, because it comes from deep, airless layers of mature peat bogs and contains no fungal spores at all. The sphagnum moss that may be dangerous is the greenish, thready stuff used by florists and craftspeople to line baskets and disguise the bases of floral arrangements. Cutaneous sporotrichosis is characterized by persistent lesions on the skin and in a few rare cases has proven fatal. If you have diabetes, circulatory problems, skin grafts, a compromised immune system, or chronic skin problems, do not handle or use sphagnum moss. Substitute shredded bark or excelsior.

TRELLISES AND PLANT SUPPORTS

Trellises and plant supports add a third dimension to any garden and can be used to substantially increase the growing space of raised beds and containers.

Just about anything can be used as a trellis or plant support. An old volleyball, badminton, or tennis net can be recycled as a bean trellis; sticks and small branches from pruning jobs can provide support for sweet peas; the understory of a wooden ramp can support a heavy climbing rose or wisteria vine. Take advantage of existing supports by planting vining crops near fences, walls, and ramp sides. For large, vigorous vines like zucchini, pumpkin, or clematis, plant near a sturdy shrub or small tree and let the vines climb up through the lower branches.

Span a garden pathway with an arbor built of strong, lightweight, 1-inch PVC pipe. Plant pole beans, kiwi fruit, or cucumbers along either side of the path and train them to grow up and over the arbor. Adjust the height of the arbor to your needs, and you can pick from inside the arbor from either a standing or seated position. Because PVC is lightweight, sturdy, and rot-resistant, it makes an ideal building material for the accessible garden: no painting, no splinters, easy to assemble and disassemble (no glue is needed), and light enough to move without much effort. Use pipe at least 1 inch in diameter; anything smaller will bend rather easily under the load.

If you have trouble bending, take advantage of vertical growing space by making arbors and trellises from lightweight, durable PVC pipe or bamboo. If you have a bad back, use a back support belt and a leverage-improving arm grip on your rake handle.

To increase your container garden space, fit large containers with simple PVC or wooden trellises. You can make a combination container-trellis by filling a cylinder of fence wire with shredded newspapers, straw, peat moss, and potting soil, and planting through the holes. Make this planter any size you want, from a tiny, tabletop version planted with miniature ferns or African violets to a garbage-can-size cage planted at the top with a vining tomato or cucumber and along the shady sides with lettuce, spinach, or other smaller, shade-loving plants. Sink a length of perforated PVC pipe down the center of the cage to provide for easier watering; keep it capped with a plastic snap-lid recycled from snack or shortening cans to prevent drying.

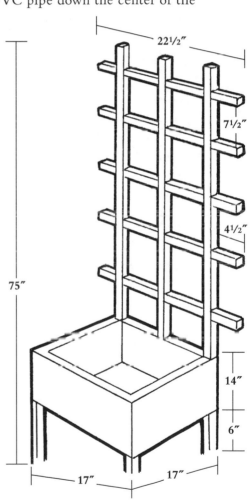

Variations of this design can be used throughout the garden. Planting walls are very popular with gardeners who have bad backs and find bending or stooping painful. To build a planting wall, start by nailing together a simple, sturdy rectangular frame of standard 2-by-6 or 2-by-8 lumber. The frame can be any size you want, but 3 by 6 feet is a good average size that takes advantage of standard lumber lengths. Use galvanized metal corner pieces to reinforce the corners and make nailing easier.

Cover both sides of the finished frame with wide, open-weave fencing, and fill the space between with coarse, unmilled sphagnum moss or excelsior. Water well and allow to settle for a day or so before planting. Use well-rooted seedlings with generous balls of soil attached to their roots. To plant, simply poke a hole into the sphagnum, and push the root ball into the space. Pull the moss back around the plant and water gently to set it in.

A simple planter box with trellis attached, for gardeners with carpentry skills. Vary the dimensions to suit your needs.

TABLE 3-2:
Intensive Spacing for Vegetables

You may be surprised to find out how much you can grow in limited space.
Intensive spacing cuts down on watering and weeding by reducing the
amount of bare ground around plants.

Crop	Spacing	Crop	Spacing
Beans	4–9 inches	Melons	24–36
Beets	2–6	Okra	12–18
Broccoli	15–18	Onions	4–6
Brussels sprouts	15–18	Parsley	4–6
Cabbage	15–18	Peas	2–6
Carrots	2–3	Peppers	12–15
Cauliflower	15–18	Potatoes	10–12
Chinese cabbage	10–12	Pumpkins, squash	24–36
Collards	12–15	Radishes	2–3
Corn	18–22	Spinach	4–6
Cucumbers	18–36	Sweet potatoes	10–12
Eggplant	18–24	Swiss chard	18–24
Kale	15–18	Tomatoes	18–24
Leeks	2–6	Turnips	4–6
Lettuce	6–9		

Mount the planting wall either horizontally or vertically against a
fence or wall. Vertical walls are best for plants that can be planted at the
bottom and trained to grow up over the wall, like peas and beans, or for
plants that can be planted at the top and allowed to trail downward, like
cucumbers and tomatoes. Freestanding planting walls, although providing the maximum planting area, topple over easily.

PLANT SELECTION AND INTENSIVE SPACING

Using raised beds or containers may decrease the overall square footage
in which you garden. But because the soil in the raised bed or container
can be made very rich, friable, and moisture-retentive, you can grow
more in less space. You can double-crop most vegetables as well, tuck-
ing lettuce, spinach, herbs, even flowers in between tomatoes, peppers,

and cabbage. Pole beans and squash can be interplanted with sweet corn, and tall trellised plants like cucumbers can shade a row of cool-weather greens underneath.

Do not allow long, trailing, vines to spill out over the edge of raised beds or containers. Although cascading tendrils of foliage and flowers look attractive, vines sprawling across walkways create tripping hazards and are easily tangled in walker supports, canes, and wheelchair and scooter wheels. Keep vines snipped off neatly before they reach the ground or, better, grow them up a trellis. You will increase your garden space, and if you have trouble bending over, growing things at eye level makes tending and harvesting much easier, as well. If overhead reaching is difficult for you, switching from traditional vine crops to bush hybrids may be the answer to growing old favorites. Bush beans, cucumbers, peas, and squash will all provide bountiful harvests of full-size vegetables without your having to contend with all those vines.

Soil Testing and Preparation

An important first step in any gardening or landscaping venture is a soil test. Understanding exactly what type of soil you have will help you make informed decisions on what will thrive there. If you are growing fruit or vegetables, you need to know just how fertile your soil is and whether it contains toxic elements. Healthy soil grows healthful foods, and a clean, balanced, nutrient–dense diet is important to anyone faced with ongoing health problems.

TEXTURE

Use a simple squeeze test to determine whether your soil is clay, sand, silt, or loam. Scoop up a handful of moist soil and gently squeeze it in your hand or, if it is easier for you, roll it back and forth against a smooth, hard surface like a tabletop or lapboard.

- If the soil forms a compact, sticky ball, it is mostly clay.
- If the soil will not ball up at all and feels gritty, it is sandy.
- If the soil forms a compact ball but feels silky smooth, rather like finely milled flour or talcum powder, it is silt.
- If the soil forms a loose, crumbly ball that breaks easily at a touch, it is loam.

If you lean toward the scientific, you can use fractional analysis to test more precisely the exact components of your garden's soil. You will need a clear, 1-quart glass jar, 3 cups of warm water, 1 cup of finely sifted garden soil, 1 teaspoon of nonsudsing automatic-dishwasher detergent, and a stopwatch or timer.

Mix the soil, detergent, and warm water in the jar, shaking it vigorously. Let the jar stand undisturbed for several days, until the solids set-

From Dr. Karl Menninger, Kansas State University:

" I believe strongly in therapy that brings the individual close to the soil, close to Mother Nature, close to beauty, close to the mystery of growth and development. Gardening is one of the simplest ways to make a cooperative deal with nature for a prompt reward."

tle out and the water is clear. Sand particles are the heaviest and will settle to the bottom of the jar. Silt will form the next layer, followed by clay. Use a crayon to mark the dividing lines between layers, then measure the layers and compare. Clay soil contains about 20 percent sand, 60 percent clay, and 20 percent silt. Sandy soil will be about 60 percent sand, 20 percent clay, and 20 percent silt. Loam will contain about 40 percent sand, 20 percent clay, and 40 percent silt.

IMPROVING SOIL TEXTURE

Loam soil occurs naturally when rotting plant material incorporates itself with the underlying earth. Gardeners can achieve similar results simply by adding organic matter, or humus, to the soil.

Humus is composed of rotted vegetative material. A prime example of humus is the fine, spongy, black carpet found under the fallen leaves in a forest. Humus is alive with microorganisms—fungus, bacteria, and mold—whose life processes release enzymes that free up minerals in the soil for absorption by plant roots. In addition, the small, fibrous bits of wood, bark, and leaves that compose the humus form a loose, water-absorbing material that roots can easily penetrate.

Organic matter for your garden can come from many sources: grass clippings, leaves, peat moss, straw, pine needles, vegetable scraps, coffee grounds, animal manure. Compost (see chapter 5) is made of a balanced mixture of mostly rotted organic matter that closely resembles the forest-produced humus.

Two other texturing amendments widely used in gardening are perlite and vermiculite, natural products produced by the heating and expansion of certain types of volcanic rock. The addition of perlite or vermiculite to sandy soil will enhance its ability to retain water and nutrients; in tight-structured clay or loam soils, they loosen the soil and aid air and water penetration.

By working peat, perlite, vermiculite, compost, or other organic material into the soil, you can quickly improve its texture, water-holding ability, and fertility.

PRESERVING SOIL STRUCTURE

Avoid working in your garden while it is either very wet or very dry. Tilling or digging waterlogged soil, besides being heavy work, may result in rock–hard lumps after the soil has dried out, or the formation of a layer of impenetrable soil known as hardpan a few inches below the surface. Working extremely dry soil can also be very difficult, and disturbing dry soil invites wind erosion and exposes more soil surface to the drying effects of sun and air.

Knowing when your soil is ready to be worked takes a certain amount of gardener's instinct, but a good, simple guide is to take up a handful and squeeze. If the soil forms a ball and oozes water, even a tiny amount, it's too wet; if it leaves your hand dusty, it's too dry. If the soil clumps up but crumbles, it's safely workable.

There is also some controversy as to whether turning the soil over—either by hand or with a tiller or plow—is truly a good gardening practice. By disturbing the naturally occurring layers or zones of the soil and subsoil, we may be doing more harm than good. With the exception of very heavy, unimproved clay soils, it may be sufficient to merely loosen and aerate the soil structure before planting

The Dutch rocking fork allows you to loosen and aerate large amounts of soil without bending and lifting. To use, push the tines deeply into the soil, pull back on the handlebar, rock the fork several times to break up subsoil, then draw it out and move forward 6 or 8 inches, and begin the process again.

with the use of a special rocking fork or digging bar. This is certainly easier on the back, hips, and arms than spading or forking soil in the traditional manner. Amendments to the soil should be applied thinly and frequently to the surface of soils prepared in this manner.

TAKING SOIL TEST SAMPLES

Soil can be tested at any time of the year, provided it's not too wet or hard with frost. Late autumn is ideal, because most annual vegetation is gone, soil-dwelling creatures have retreated below the frost line, and fertilizers and other amendments applied during the summer have had time to disperse evenly through the soil.

To get accurate test results, take several samples of topsoil from different locations within the garden area to be tested. For a raised bed garden, take one or two samples from each bed; for a lawn or large landscaped area, take ten to fifteen widely spaced samples.

If you are testing separate use areas of your property, don't mix samples taken from different areas. Have separate tests done on each area to determine its specific characteristics and deficiencies. A pH of 6, for example, is fine for a vegetable garden but too alkaline for an azalea bed.

To take a soil sample, use an easy-grip trowel, a bulb auger, or a special soil-core tool. Try to get down at least 6 inches so that you have an accurate cross section of the topsoil and, if the topsoil is thin, the subsoil beneath it. Avoid samples from soil that has had recent applications of lime, fertilizer, or other amendments, which can throw off test results.

Mix all samples from one use area together in a bucket, then spread the soil out on a sheet of newspaper to dry for a day or two. Pick out any debris. If there are a lot of hard lumps, either discard them or crush them with the back of a trowel or a rolling pin.

You can buy soil test kits for home use, use a fertility meter (78, 114) or pH probe, or send out your soil to be lab tested. Home test kits and probes are convenient and fairly accurate, but to get a really good cross section of what your soil contains, especially for a new garden, have a professional test done.

PH LEVELS

The soil's pH level refers to its relative acidity or alkalinity. A soil that has a low pH level is acidic; one with a high pH reading is alkaline. Most soils are neutral, with a pH between 6 and 7.5, and most plants grow best at neutral or near-neutral levels.

TABLE 4-1:
Indicator Plants

Weeds can be valuable indicators of soil conditions.

Dry, well-drained, acidic soil, low in nutrients:

Bracken fern *(Pteridium aquilinum)*
Blueberries *(Vaccinium spp.)*
Hair cap moss *(Polytrichum)*
Lichens *(Cladonia spp.)*
Poverty grass *(Danthonia spicata)*
Sweet fern *(Comptonia peregrina)*
Training arbutus *(Epigaea repens)*
Wintergreen *(Gaultheria procumbens)*
Witch grass *(Panicum capillare)*

Moist but well-drained, acidic soil, low in nutrients:

Ground ivy *(Glechoma hederacea)*
Mosses *(Lycopodium* spp.;
   Polytrichum spp.)*
Pearly everlasting *(Anaphalis
   margaritacea)*
Sheep fescue *(Festuca ovina)*
Sheep sorrel or sour grass
   (Rumex acetosella)
Wild strawberry *(Fragaria spp.)*

Wet, poorly drained soil or high water table:

Horsetail *(Equisetum hyemale)*
Reed canary grass *(Phalaris
   arundinacea)*
Rush *(Juncus effusus)*
Sedges *(Cyperaceae spp.)*
Sensitive fern *(Onoclea sensibilis)*
Wool grass *(Scirpus cyperinus)*

Wet soil with standing water through parts of the year:

Cattail rush *(Typha latifolia)*
Marsh fern *(Thelypteris palustris)*
Monkeyflower *(Mimulus ringens)*
Royal fern *(Osmunda regalis)*
Sedges *(Cyperaceae spp.)*
Sweet flag *(Acorus calamus)*

Wet soil with possibility of moving underground water:

False hellebore *(Veratrum viride)*
Speckled alder *(Alnus rugosa)*
Willows *(Salix spp.)*
Witherod *(Viburnum cassinoides)*

Dry, well-drained soil, neutral or alkaline, moderately fertile:

Cinquefoil *(Potentilla spp.)*
Columbine *(Aquilegia canadensis)*
Fragile fern *(Cystopteris fragilis)*
Harebell *(Campanula routundifolia)*

Very fertile, tilled or once-tilled soil:

Barnyard grass *(Echinochloa crus-galli)*
Chickweed *(Stellaria media)*
Crabgrass *(Digitaria ischaemum)*
Lamb's quarter *(Chenopodium album)*
Ostrich fern *(Matteuccia struthiopteris)*
Pigweed *(Amaranthus retroflexus)*
Stinging nettle *(Urtica dioica)*

Compacted soil, poor fertility:
Clover *(Melilotus* spp.*)*
Dandelion *(Taraxacum officinale)*
Field bindweed *(Convolvulus*
   arvensis)
Indian tobacco *(Lobelia inflata)*
Mustards *(Brassica* spp.*)*
Yarrow *(Achillea* spp.*)*
Quack grass *(Agropyron repens)*

Soil disturbed by past human activity or cultivation:
Burdock *(Arctium minus)*
Dock *(Rumex* spp.*)*
Honeysuckle *(Lonicera* spp.*)*
Plantain *(Plantago* spp.*)*
Queen Anne's lace *(Daucus carota)*
Knotweed *(Polygonum aviculare)*

Overgrazed or overcropped pastures and fields:
Canada thistle *(Cirsium arvense)*
Catnip *(Nepeta cataria)*
Bull thistle *(Cirsium vulgare)*
Junipers *(Juniperus* spp.*)*
Vipers bugloss *(Echium vulgare)*

There are exceptions, however. Most evergreens prefer an acidic soil, with a pH of 5 to 5.5. Viburnums, cranberries, blueberries, and bog-type plants also prefer acidic conditions. Certain root vegetables, lilacs, and peonies prefer alkaline soils in the 7.5 to 8 range.

Soil near masonry walls and foundations will tend to be more alkaline than surrounding soil, because the limestone-based mortar may leach out into nearby soil. This can have important consequences for evergreens planted near the foundation. Conversely, soil under the drip line of mature evergreens will tend to be acidic because of the acidic nature of most evergreen needles and leaves.

You can test soil pH at home with a store-bought test kit, or you can let a soil-testing facility do it for you as part of a complete soil work-up. If only the pH level concerns you, then get a home test kit; it's quicker and cheaper than sending samples out to be tested.

Analog and digital readout pH meters (16, 46, 67, 70, 78 95, 114) use two needlelike, mildly electrified metallic probes pushed into the soil to measure acidity. If you have limited use of your hands or have impaired vision, these meters are a wonderful alternative to taking soil samples and reading pH charts. The meters give a numbered readout instantly, and the numbers and color charts are usually clear enough to be read by gardeners with somewhat impaired vision.

To neutralize acidic soil, apply ground limestone or dolomite; to neutralize alkaline soil, apply ground sulfur. Use the following guidelines, depending on your soil types.

To raise the pH level (increase the alkalinity) of acidic clay soil, apply 7 to 8 pounds of limestone per 100 square feet; of acidic loam or silt, 7 to 10 pounds; of very sandy acidic soil, 3 to 6 pounds.

To lower the pH level (increase the acidity) of alkaline clay soil, apply 2 pounds of ground sulfur per 100 square feet; of sandy alkaline soil, 1 pound.

The addition of compost will tend to neutralize the pH level of any soil, because most finished compost is nearly neutral. Organic materials that are acidic, such as pine needles, sawdust, and peat moss, will lower the pH level, and those that are alkaline, such as wood ashes, bone meal, eggshells, and crushed oyster shells, will raise the pH level.

NUTRIENTS

Three major nutrients are vital to plant life: nitrogen (N), phosphorus (P), and potassium (K). An additional thirteen elements are also essential to plants: carbon, hydrogen, oxygen, sulfur, calcium, magnesium, boron, manganese, iron, copper, molybdenum, zinc, and chlorine.

From Dr. Richard Mattson, HTM, Department of Horticultural Therapy, Kansas State University:

"Yes, it's okay to sweat! It's fashionable to do aerobic exercise. It's okay to eat vegetables and healthy foods that we grow in our own gardens. In addition to physical exercise, the garden can be used as a place for meditation or stress reduction. I frequently find that I can reduce my blood pressure by working in the greenhouse or hoeing in the garden.

"The minerals, vitamins, and fiber content of fresh fruits and vegetables grown in our gardens enrich our bodies. Exercise increases aerobic conditioning and muscle tone, and can regulate stress and cardiovascular conditioning. Meditation and peaceful relaxation in a garden setting increases our ability to relax, to think more clearly, and to find solutions to many of life's problems."

The "Big Three," nitrogen, phosphorus, and potassium, are vital for good plant growth and are found in most commercial fertilizer mixes. The relative amounts of each of these nutrients are expressed in ratio form, such as 5–10–5 or 10–10–10, in which the order of the nutrients is always N–P–K. Many home kits that test for pH levels also include tests for N–P–K levels. In plants, nitrogen is essential for producing top-growth leaves and stems. Phosphorus is important to the development of stems, blossoms, and fruits. Potassium is necessary for strong root development. Lettuce, a leaf crop, requires high levels of nitrogen; tomatoes will set better crops in phosphorus-rich soils; root crops, such as carrots and turnips, will grow best in soils with adequate potassium levels. Poor performance in most garden crops can be traced to low levels of one of these three nutrients.

The arguments for and against the use of chemical fertilizers abound. Personally, I believe that to produce healthy plants, the earth itself must be healthy. Soil can be thought of as a living creature, one that needs air, water, and food to maintain its vigor. Gardeners and farmers are becoming more aware of the hazards of chemicals, including manufactured fertilizers, and are using natural alternatives instead. A 1994 survey of American gardeners showed that 45 percent used organic fertilizers rather than chemical, three times as many as in 1987.

If you are already an organic gardener, spread the word. Teach by example. Show how by feeding the earth, you feed yourself—and others. Give away your excess produce; supply local churches and hospitals with flowers; tell everyone who will listen that natural ways are best in the garden.

Chemical fertilizers can do wonders to increase the size, yield, and blossom, but they feed only the plants, not the soil. Though this may suffice for a few years, the all-chemical gardener soon finds the need to apply more and more fertilizer to achieve the same results; plants become less weather-hardy, and disease and insect problems increase. These are all symptoms of depleted soil. No matter what type of soil you have, the key to its health and fertility is humus.

Forming humus is the job of a host of microorganisms called actinomycetes. About ninety species of these tiny half-mold, half-bacteria creatures are found in the first few feet of topsoil. Their primary job is to eat dead stuff: bugs, fallen leaves, overripe fruits and vegetables. In the process of digesting this organic material, they free up the chemical compounds present in all living tissues and produce enzymes,

TABLE 4-2:
Soil Nutrient Deficiencies

Check pH levels first; many deficiencies are most easily corrected by adjusting the pH level of the soil, thus freeing up minerals that have been chemically "locked away" from plants by too-acidic or too-alkaline conditions.

Deficiency	Symptoms	Treatment
Nitrogen	Slow growth; slender, fibrous stems; pale, yellowing foliage	Manure, cottonseed meal, bloodmeal, fish scraps
Phosphorus	Slow growth; undersides of leaves turn reddish purple; fruits slow to set and mature; immature fruits and flowers drop from plants.	Bone meal or phosphate rock powders
Potassium	Poor growth and vigor; leaves turn ashen, curl, then turn bronze; root development poor; plants easily pulled up	Green matter such as grass clippings, kitchen wastes, seaweed, wood ashes
Boron (Rare, especially in organic gardens)	Slow growth; terminal buds die, producing unusually bushy but sickly plants; fruits, tubers, and roots crack and discolor	Granite dust, manure, compost
Calcium	Slow growth characterized by thick, woody stems; terminal buds and young leaves deformed; roots blacken	Limestone, oyster shell, gypsum
Copper (Much less common than copper toxicity)	Usually confined to peaty or black mucky soils; growth is retarded, terminal buds and new growth die back	Compost, manure
Iron	Spotted, colorless areas on young leaves; yellowing leaves, especially on upper parts of plant; soil that is too alkaline, or has had too much limestone applied, will exhibit signs of iron deficiency	Discontinue the application of lime and acidify the soil with pineneedles or sulfur; if symptoms persist, add manure and bloodmeal

Deficiency	Symptoms	Treatment
Magnesium	Immature fruits are slow to mature or drop from plants; leaf tissue yellows, while veins remain bright green	Seawater, seaweed-based fertilizer, or dolomitic limestone
Manganese	Slow growth, poor maturity of fruits and flowers; leaf tissue yellows, while veins remain green; highly alkaline soils are most susceptible	Discontinue application of limestone and acidify soil with sulfur, pine needles, or oak leaves
Zinc	Leaves abnormally long and yellowed, mottled with dead areas; usually also iron deficient	Manure, phosphate rock

which unlock the soil's basic mineral nutrients and make them available to plants.

Applying heavy doses of chemical fertilizers, most of which are in a mineral salt or chlorinated form, kills these beneficial actinomycetes. Without actinomycetes to unlock the mineral content of soil, the soil becomes in effect sterilized, and plants are unable to absorb the elements they need from it, even though those elements may be present in abundance.

A good landsman must learn to think of the microscopic life in his soil needing his care just as a pet does. In return for a good diet rich in organic matter and low in chemical salts, your actinomycetes will work hard to reward you with fertile soil.

TRACE ELEMENTS

Of the remaining thirteen elements, another three—carbon, hydrogen, and oxygen—are found so plentifully everywhere that they can be ignored by the gardener.

The last ten—sulfur, calcium, magnesium, boron, manganese, iron, copper, molybdenum, zinc, and chlorine—are known as trace elements, and they may not always be present in adequate amounts for good plant growth.

To accurately test for the presence of trace elements in the soil, a lab test is needed. Lab testing for these elements can be expensive, and because most reasonably fertile soils have sufficient trace elements present, it is usually much simpler to observe the way plants grow and diagnose any deficiencies.

To remedy any trace-element deficiencies, apply compost, manure, or seaweed- or fish-emulsion-based amendments. Seaweed is especially good because ocean water contains each necessary trace element in abundance.

With the exception of adding sulfur or calcium to correct pH levels, never apply individual trace elements to the soil unless advised to do so by a qualified soil scientist. Too high a level of one or more substances can be just as harmful to your plants as a deficiency.

CONTAMINANTS

In addition to the essential elements, nonessential and even dangerous elements in the soil can be taken up by plants. Soils contaminated with large amounts of heavy metals—lead, arsenic, cadmium, mercury, chromium, or nickel—should not be used to grow any type of crops for human or animal consumption.

If you suspect that your soil may be contaminated with heavy metals, oil, industrial chemicals, pesticides, or herbicides, it is essential that you have the soil specifically tested for these dangerous, even deadly, elements. Most soil-testing laboratories will analyze samples for contaminants for an additional fee.

Garden sites that are at high risk for contamination are those that are near old buildings or on the site of former buildings, where lead-based paints may have been used; near busy roadways; on the site of former commercial orchards or cropland (old-time pesticides relied heavily on arsenic); on or near former or present industrial sites; near open garbage dumps or covered sanitary landfills, where runoff can occur; or where the soil has received applications of sewage sludge as fertilizer.

This last instance is the most controversial. In some communities, sewage sludge is acceptable as fertilizer for food-growing soil because strict testing and regulations exclude the presence of heavy metals. In other communities, especially urban, industrial areas, heavy-metal contamination of sewage is a common, virtually uncontrollable problem. Discuss the use of sewage sludge fertilizer with your county agricultural extension agent before using it on food-growing gardens.

If your soil is contaminated with heavy metals, petroleum-based products like gasoline or motor oil, chemicals, or pesticide residues, abandon the site as a food-growing area or construct raised beds filled with fresh, clean soil.

Despite lumber company assurances to the contrary, do not use pressure-treated lumber to build containers, raised beds, fences, or any other structures near or in soil that will be used to grow food crops. The chemicals found in pressure-treated lumber may leach out into the soil and be absorbed by plants. Soil samples taken from near pressure-treated lumber may test high in arsenic, copper, and other contaminants.

For chemically contaminated non-food-growing areas, like lawns or flower beds, try incorporating half-rotted wood chips into the soil. The white, threadlike fungi found on rotting wood have been discovered to excel at consuming and breaking down certain dangerous chemicals and petroleum-products. They will not, however, affect heavy-metal contamination.

CHAPTER FIVE

Easy Composting

Compost serves many purposes in the garden. It can be used as a fertilizer, to improve tilth, to adjust the pH, and to replenish the topsoil. Compost is also the basic foodstuff of earthworms and other soil dwellers. When present in the soil, it inhibits disease organisms yet encourages the growth of actinomycetes, beneficial soil microbes that produce essential enzymes that free up minerals and make them available to plants. In a humusy, microorganism-rich soil, plants grow and bloom to their maximum potential and are more resistant to diseases and insects. Additionally, fruits and vegetables grown in compost-rich soil have greater nutritional value.

All composting techniques, however simple or complex, are based on one premise: Stuff rots. Anything that was once alive—orange peels, apple cores, grass clippings, autumn leaves—will, when dead, begin to decompose because of bacterial action.

Decay-promoting microorganisms are found all around us, in the air, soil, and water. Although there are many different species of these microorganisms, including bacteria, mold, and fungi, they can be roughly divided into two groups: aerobic and anaerobic. Aerobic organisms thrive in the presence of air, anaerobic in the absence of air. Aerobic bacteria, including most of the various actinomycetes found in topsoil, are more beneficial in a composting operation, because they work quickly, require only a little moisture to keep them active, tend to heat up the organic material they are digesting, and produce only small amounts of by-product gases.

Besides microorganisms, larger creatures like sow bugs, earthworms, ants, and centipedes also play an important role in breaking down organic matter into compost.

From Charles A. Lewis, horticulturist, Morton Arboretum, Lisle, Illinois:

"What is so special about plants? Why are plants therapeutic? They are alive, living. They are growing, changing, not static. We also are alive, growing, and changing. Both plants and people live and die. We share a life rhythm, and that is an important commonality. No piece of pottery, no piece of woodwork can of itself change like a plant can.

"Many plants have a clear life cycle—shoots, stems, leaves, buds, flowers, fruit, death are the usual progression of the plant, and are predictable. But death is a part of life. Without death, there cannot be life. If the plant becomes part of a compost pile, its nutrition goes back into the earth. Death is not an end point, but part of a total cycle."

For organic matter to begin decomposing, or composting, the only essential ingredients are the organic material, microorganisms, air, and moisture. The relative amounts of these essentials merely determine how fast a pile breaks down. A "hot" pile—one with the ideal ratios of organic material, bacteria, air, and moisture—will decompose rapidly; a "cold" pile will decompose more slowly.

To save time and effort, add ground limestone, soil amendments, and pH adjusters to your finished compost before you distribute it over the garden. The amendments will be spread evenly and automatically as you apply the compost.

LAYER-AND-TURN PILES

A traditional compost pile is constructed by layering various materials to achieve a balanced ratio of organic material, bacteria, air, and moisture. To give aerobic bacteria the oxygen necessary to keep them working in high gear, periodic stirring or turning is required. A regularly turned, well-balanced compost heap will often literally cook, reaching temperatures in excess of 165 degrees Fahrenheit as aerobic bacteria produce large amounts of heat energy while they digest organic material. A pile this hot will kill weed seed, insect eggs and larvae, and most disease-causing bacteria and fungi. It will also be ready to use in just two to six weeks.

The types of organic material in the pile will also determine how quickly the pile decomposes. Soft, green, wet materials like grass clippings, lettuce leaves, and raw manure are very high in nitrogen and low in lignin, a tough, carbon-based structural component that gives plant cells their shape. High-nitrogen materials will decompose rapidly, but unless turned very frequently to incorporate air and reduce the moisture content, they will also tend to compact, forming a dense, cold, airless mass that encourages the growth of foul-smelling anaerobic bacteria. (Anyone who has left a pile of fresh grass clippings standing in the hot sun for a few days only to find that it has turned into a smelly, slimy green lump will understand the action and by-products of anaerobic bacteria.)

Low-nitrogen materials, like straw, twigs, dry leaves, and paper, contain high levels of tough, fibrous, carbon-rich lignin and therefore, decay very slowly. Because of the stiff, brittle nature of these items, a pile composed solely of these high-carbon items will often dry out, depriving microorganisms of the moisture they need to survive and halting decomposition entirely. If your pile is composed of a lot of dry materials or if you live in a dry climate, try spraying the pile with soapy water to enhance its activity. Soap acts as a surfactant that enables dry matter to absorb moisture more quickly and retain it better. Don't use bleach-containing laundry detergents or antibacterial soaps, or you'll kill your friendly bacteria.

To achieve an optimum level of aerobic bacterial action, a balance must be struck between carbon- and nitrogen-rich materials. Complicated formulas have been worked out for the mixing of these items to achieve a perfect balance, but there is and easy yet effective method for achieving a good carbon-to-nitrogen ratio. I call it the "crunch or squish" method of analysis. Anything that crunches, like autumn leaves or straw, is probably high in lignin (carbon); anything that squishes, like overripe tomatoes, is probably low in lignin. Mix the crunchy and the squishy material about three to one, and you'll have the beginnings of good, workable compost. If your compost just sits there, add more squishy. If it begins to smell bad, add more crunchy.

A word of warning: Don't add meat scraps, grease, dairy products, or dog and cat droppings to your compost. The first three will produce odors and may attract rodents or insects, and the last may contain potentially dangerous parasites. Eggshells, bird droppings, and liquid waste from aquariums are safe to add and make excellent high-nitrogen composting materials.

To save kitchen scraps for the compost pile without odor prob-

lems, keep them in an empty milk carton in the freezer. When the
carton is full, add the frozen scraps to the top of your compost pile.

Don't bother adding commercially produced compost-making
microorganisms or activators. These products do not hasten the decomposition process greatly enough to be worth their cost. All the actinomycetes and aerobic bacteria you need are present in the soil of your
garden. Tossing a few scoops of soil into the pile will distribute millions
of these microorganisms through the organic material; simply leaving
some soil attached to the roots of pulled-up plants placed on the pile
will do the same.

Do consider adding small quantities of dried blood, fish, or bone
meal; alfalfa or cottonseed meal; dehydrated or fresh manure; or dried,
fresh, or emulsified seaweed products, especially if your pile doesn't
seem to be doing anything productive. The trace elements and nutrients found in these natural products will feed the decay-producing
microorganisms in your composting operation and make them work
even harder at breaking down the materials given them.

NO-TURN PILES

If you don't turn it, a traditional compost heap will take longer than a
turned pile to produce usable compost—six months to a year for an
average 3-by-3-by-3-foot pile. Some weed seeds, pests, and disease

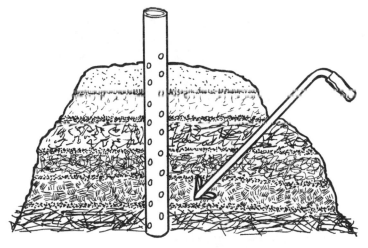

A traditional compost heap is composed of alternating layers of wet, green material; dry, brown material; manure; and garden soil, with a sprinkling of lime or bloodmeal thrown in. Air is essential to fast decomposition. You can use a compost aeration tool to stir the pile's interior without turning it, or insert a length of 3-inch perforated PVC pipe into the center of pile to provide an aerating "chimney."

organisms may survive the process, and you may lose some nutrients to the leaching action of rainfall, but the end result will be good compost.

To speed things up a bit without additional labor, there are several ways to get air into the center of the pile, which will increase bacterial activity. Placing moderate-size branches or brushwood in layers throughout the pile, or inserting perforated PVC or corrugated drainfield pipe either horizontally or vertically through the center of the pile, will allow air to reach the interior. Compost prods (15, 67, 70, 78, 97, 114, 165) also help mix the pile and introduce air to the interior. The tool, which resembles a cane with collapsible blades attached near the tip, is inserted into the pile and jiggled around. As it is withdrawn, the blades open up to catch and stir the material. Prods require a good grip, as well as considerable upper-body and arm strength. A simpler alternative, which works almost as well, is simply to poke a stick or length of pipe into the pile and wiggle it around to create air tunnels.

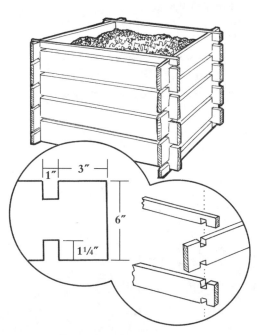

By varying the size of the boards, the basic design of this home-built, "snap together" compost box can be enlarged to form a raised bed or reduced to form individual planter boxes.

COMPOST BINS AND CONTAINERS

A wire-mesh or slat-sided compost bin allows air to circulate more thoroughly through the pile and reduces or eliminates the necessity of turning it.

Many gardeners build two, three, or even more compost bins side by side. Raw materials go into the first bin and begin decomposing. When they are partially rotted they are transferred to the second bin, being inverted and aerated in the process. Decomposition continues for another few weeks, and then the contents of the second bin may be tossed into a third bin where they become finished compost. This multibin system allows a high volume of organic material to continuously process into finished compost.

Emptying and transferring the contents of one bin to another is very hard work, however. If you wish to use a multibin system, you can substantially reduce the work involved in transferring material by constructing slide-out or lift-out side walls on the bins. Remove the end wall of bin one to load it with raw materials. To transfer the compost from bin one to two or two to three, remove the inside walls of the bins and simply push or rake the compost from one bin to the other. Remove the end wall of bin three to empty it of finished compost. You can add block-and-tackle arrangements to make lifting the walls out as easy as tugging on a cord.

A simple cylinder of wire fencing about 3 feet in diameter, set on the ground, will also serve as a good, well-aerated compost bin, as will a ventilated galvanized or plastic garbage can. Set the can up off the ground on a couple of bricks or boards, adjusting its height to your reach. Layer in organic material. If animals are a problem in your area, securely fasten the top to the can. Without stirring, can compost will be ready in six to eight months.

Newly developed biodegradable compost bags (67) produced by Stone Container Corporation look like brown paper shopping bags but are lined with a special cellulose material that prevents tears and leaks and allows air to penetrate to the interior. You simply drop the filled bags directly into your compost bin or stand them in a shady place in the garden to compost on their own. In a week or two, bag, contents, and all will have decomposed into rich, dark compost.

Commercially made compost bins are also available. The NovaWood is made entirely from recycled plastic that looks like silvery gray, weathered wood. It is easily assembled with nails and plastic tie wraps. The advantages of using plastic rather than wood bins are that they won't rot, crack, splinter, or warp; their light weight makes them easy to assemble, disassemble, and move; and you don't risk contaminating your compost, soil, or plants with chemicals from CCA- or pressure-treated wood.

Compost containers like the Soil Saver (15, 67, 165) are attractive choices for gardens, if you wish to avoid open and obvious compost bins or piles. Made of heavy, black, recycled plastic, with a tight-fitting lid and trapdoor, the Soil Saver has a 12-cubic-foot capacity and requires no turning. It is 30 inches tall, so it can be loaded easily through the top even from a seated position. It unloads at ground level (it's bottomless for drainage) through a slide-up door, which could pose problems for gardeners who can't bend over that far or who are gardening from a wheelchair or scooter. This can be overcome, however, by placing a tarpaulin or piece of plastic in front of the unloading area, opening the slide door with a bent wire coat hanger, and scraping out the compost with an old hockey stick or golf club. Because the Soil Saver traps solar heat, compost decomposes rapidly and is ready in about six weeks.

The Green Cone (15) is an innovative design that acts more as a food waste digester and vermicomposter than a straight composter. An 18-inch underground basket collects food wastes and allows earthworms to enter, and a 28-inch aboveground plastic cone acts as a solar trap to accelerate decomposition. The Green Cone quickly reduces kitchen wastes—including meats and dairy products—to virtually nothing. An airtight lid keeps out pests, and the manufacturer guarantees no odors are emitted. This device is more appropriate for those who are interested in disposing of kitchen wastes in an environmentally sound manner than for making large amounts of compost, however, because little is left after the earthworms and bacteria have eaten their fill.

COMPOST TUMBLERS

Tumblers make mixing organic materials, air, and microbes easier, while eliminating the sometimes untidy appearance of a pile of rotting matter plunked down beside the garden shed.

The Compact ComposTumbler from the PBM Group (96) has a gear-drive assembly and a large, side-mounted, crank handle that makes turning its steel-reinforced plastic drum easy, even when full. The vented drum holds about 12 cubic feet of material and has a hinged door for adding and removing material. It is easy to fill, easy to dump, and sits low enough to the ground to be reachable from a wheelchair. The unit also comes with an optional sifting screen. Assembling the ComposTumbler involves lots of nuts, bolts and small pieces; you may need to enlist the aid of a helper and devote an entire afternoon to putting it together. It's fairly permanent once set up, so decide where it will sit ahead of time.

The Garden Way EZ Spin composter (64) works on the same premise as the ComposTumbler, but it is bigger (it holds about 13 cubic feet of material) and sits about 3 feet off the ground, making it easier to dump the finished compost into a wheelbarrow or garden cart. Its height makes it comfortable for anyone in a standing position to load, turn, and empty but may pose problems for wheelchair gardeners or those with limited reach. The EZ Spin has steel grab bars that run across the length of the outside of the drum rather than a crank-type handle; if you have limited upper-body or arm mobility, you may have trouble turning it. If you have a good grip, however, the EZ Spin's grab bars may be easier to use than the motion required by a hand crank, because you can throw your weight into the turning motion. Its black color absorbs heat and speeds decomposition, and its two large access doors make filling and emptying relatively easy. You may need help assembling the EZ Spin, and its size and weight means it will occupy a permanent position in your garden.

Both the Green Magic composter (67) and the CanDo spinning barrel composter are top-fill, garbage-can-shaped tumblers mounted on simple, sturdy frames. When ready to turn, you simply grab the handles and give a shove to rotate. Their biggest drawback is that they may become unbalanced and stick in a horizontal or upside-down position; you may have to rock the drum a few times to right it. Because they tilt easily, however, these barrel composters are easily accessible from both standing or seated positions. They are easy to assemble and, when empty, light enough to move to different locations around the yard.

The TumbleBug (114) is a roll-on-the-ground recycled-plastic container that resembles a big, flat-faced beach ball. The TumbleBug comes in 12- and 20-cubic-foot versions; I recommend the smaller, simply because it's easier to roll over. The twenty flat, triangular pieces that form the ball are assembled with long screws that protrude well into the inside to provide additional mixing action when the Tumble-

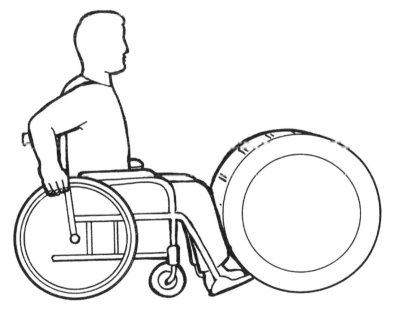

The Enviro-cycler rollover compost bin is made of recycled plastic that holds about 7 cubic feet of materials. By eliminating the curved base, the bin can be rolled by pushing against it with the footrest of a wheelchair. No assembly is required, and the 33-inch height is ideal for access from both standing and seated positions.

Bug is moved. To turn, simply grab the knobs on the outside and push it over, alternating from side to side. Because it has flat faces on all sides, you can also roll it over by pushing a wheelchair's footrest or the base of a cane up against the TumbleBug until it topples over. To unload, simply tumble it to the desired location, open, and pour. The TumbleBug sits right on the ground, however, so if you cannot bend over, you may find it difficult to position and empty. I'd suggest emptying this (or any other ground-level composter) onto a tarpaulin and then dragging the compost to its final location. The Envirocycler (34) is a similar roll-around plastic composter that requires no assembly.

The ultimate in no-work composters are the Swisher solar-powered tumblers (156), which hold from 12 to 23 bushels of material and feature a solar-powered electric motor and battery system to automatically turn the big green metal box for you. Quiet, efficient, and very durable, these sun-powered machines can produce a lot of compost very quickly. All models sit about 23 inches above the ground, making them wheelchair accessible.

COMPOSTING IN PLACE

If you have a small garden or don't want a visible compost pile, bin, or tumbler in your yard, there is another way to produce compost that requires even less effort.

In trench composting, you dig a shallow trench or hole and gradually fill it with organic matter such as kitchen scraps, eggshells, and discarded plant material, then cover it thinly with soil. Because you dig the trench wherever there's open ground, you can add compost to any area of your garden that needs it. You can open up a fairly long trench in the autumn and can compost right through the winter by filling and covering sections of the trench at a time. With the decomposing material buried, little nutrient content leaches away below the level of plant roots, earthworms benefit greatly from the underground feast you provide, and there is no problem with odor, insects, or animals disturbing the cooking compost.

The greatest drawback to trench composting is having to dig and then cover the trench or hole. Some rotary tillers have optional trenching attachments that can make the job easier, but if your garden is small or formed entirely of containers or raised beds, sheet composting may be the answer.

Sheet composting is composting the way nature does it. Organic material is simply spread over the earth and left to rot. It is the method of choice for any gardener who wants big returns for little effort. In his 1943 book, *Plowman's Folly,* Edward Faulkner outraged the agricultural world by denouncing plowing, advocating instead sheet composting for all arable fields and gardens. He practiced what he preached and was able to maintain a successful garden for many years by simply spreading yard and garden wastes on the ground each autumn.

Sheet composting offers an ideal way to add organic material to any area of the garden or landscape, whether idle or actively growing. You can simply tuck potato peels, coffee grounds, and old tea bags under the concealing canopy of leaves provided by growing plants or beneath a layer of attractive mulch. And because the material decomposes on the spot, little nutrient value is wasted, earthworms and actinomycetes proliferate, and the finished compost is right where it will do the most good—all without turning, forking, hauling, or spreading.

Allow a layer of composted kitchen scraps, leaves, manure, or what have you to mingle with the underlying earth, and you will have gone a long way toward correcting soil structural problems as well as adding fertility to the soil.

COVER CROPS

An adjunct to sheet composting is cover cropping. A cover crop is a fast-growing, usually annual plant sown after the regular garden crop is harvested. Grasses like annual rye, wheat, or oats; broad-leaved plants like rape or buckwheat; and leguminous (nitrogen-fixing) plants like soybeans or peas are all used as cover crops.

To compost cover crops, allow them to grow about a foot high. You can let crops like buckwheat and peas flower, but never let any cover crop set seed or they'll end up as persistent weeds. Plant your cover crop late in the autumn. Once frost kills it, simply leave it in place over winter as a mulch. By spring, the residue will have decomposed enough to be either worked lightly into the soil or planted through directly.

SHREDDING COMPOST

To hasten decomposition, reduce the bulk of the material you are composting. On a large scale, this is most easily accomplished with a gasoline-powered chipper-shredder machine that can chew even fairly large branches down to coarse chips. Smaller, electric-powered shredders will reduce old newspapers, leaves, spent flowers, and cornstalks with ease. When purchasing any shredder, look for easy-start options like pushbutton or key ignitions rather than pull cords. Electric shredders are lighter in weight, quieter, safer, and require less maintenance than gasoline-powered models. They will not, however, handle anything larger or more solid than twigs and corn stalks.

For a small-scale or container garden, a shredder may be more than you need. Use a blender or food processor to grind up kitchen wastes like peelings, eggshells, and apple cores to a semiliquid "sludge" that can be poured directly onto the soil and covered with mulch or a thin layer of earth. Because it decomposes so rapidly, compost treated in this manner generates little odor and is ideal for use around potted houseplants or in small container gardens. For sanitation reasons, keep a separate blender jar just for composting operations.

VERMICOMPOSTING

Vermicomposting is a fancy name for using worms to do the work of composting for you. The squeamish may find the idea of keeping a box of worms under the kitchen sink too awful to contemplate, but vermicomposting is a marvel of efficiency, cleanliness, and ease. For the gardener with limited mobility or strength, it is ideal. You can buy ready-made worm composting bins (67, 114, 140), or you can make your own from any fairly large (about 5-gallon minimum) covered plastic tub or can in which you have drilled drainage holes. Set the bin in a tray to catch any liquid that drains out; this liquid is rich in nutrients and can be used straight as a liquid fertilizer or diluted as a foliar feed.

The earthworms used in vermicomposting are either *Eisenia fetida* or *Lumbricus rubellus,* commonly called manure worms, redworms, or red wigglers. They are not usually found in garden soil, unless large amounts of rotted manure have been recently added. You can purchase red wigglers at a bait shop or order them from local or mail-order worm dealers. Worm dealers are also excellent sources of information for the care and feeding of redworms, but the basics of vermicomposting are simply to provide the worms with bedding (usually damp, shredded newspapers mixed with a little soil), moisture, and food. One pound of red wigglers can eat about 3 pounds of solid organic waste per week; they will thrive on most garden and kitchen wastes, with the exception of meat, fish, grease, and dairy products.

As you add each day's wastes to the worm bin, push it slightly under the top level of bedding or soil, varying the location from day to day to keep the worms active and moving. Keep the bin loosely covered to retain moisture while allowing fresh air to circulate. Finished com-

The ComposterPlus vermicomposter uses earthworms to help digest and decompose yard, garden, and kitchen wastes. You add raw materials through the top and take out finished compost through a slide door in the base. The ComposterPlus, fully vented to provide air and prevent heat buildup, is made of durable plastic, requires only a few minutes to assemble, and can hold up to 11 cubic feet of waste.

post, enriched by the worm's waste matter or castings, is ready in two to three months. Scoop it up, sift out the wigglers, and use the compost wherever needed.

COMPOST TEA

Besides using finished compost fresh off the pile, you can make a foliar feed for plants by brewing a bucket of compost tea. To make compost tea, take a good handful of finished compost and mix it with a bucket of water. Set the bucket in a warm, sunny location, and allow the tea to "steep" for a few days. Then strain out the solid material and dilute the

From Dr. Richard Mattson, HTM, Department of Horticultural Therapy, Kansas State University:

"How does health apply to horticulture? It begins at a very early age in the human life cycle. A child of less than two years is aware of the natural world. He learns about the earth and the things that grow in the earth. He learns that tools can be fashioned from sticks, and that seeds can be planted that grow and become plants in a garden. The shapes and appearances of the earth are reflected in miniature within our gardens. Look closely at the patterns of leaves, their shapes and forms. Discover the simplicity, the beauty, and the order in the universe. Focus on the simple things in life, and be aware of the interrelationships of all living things."

resulting liquid with water until it is the color of weak tea. Spray plants with diluted tea to give them a real boost during the growing season, use it full-strength in irrigation systems as a source of direct-contact soil fertilizer, and use it half-strength as a transplanting solution for newly set seedlings.

No matter which method you choose to use, please do compost. You'll save money on chemical fertilizers and ensure nutritious food crops, as well as doing the environment a favor by reducing and recycling wastes that would otherwise end up in overcrowded landfills.

CHAPTER SIX

Water for the Accessible Garden

Of all tasks in the garden, supplying water can be the most difficult. A gallon of water weighs approximately 8¹/2 pounds, making the lifting, carrying, balancing, and pouring of standard 1- and 2-gallon watering cans beyond the strength of many gardeners. A 50-foot garden hose filled with water can weigh as much as 30 pounds, and its heavy coils can spell disaster if dragged through a bed of tender seedlings or over a newly planted lawn.

For wheelchair and walker gardeners, the problem becomes less one of weight than of balance. Few things are as frustrating as starting out with a full pail of water and arriving at your destination with half a pail and drenched pants.

Fortunately, thanks to new technologies and improvements in the old, there are a number of ways to make watering easier.

XERISCAPING AND MESISCAPING

Before exploring new ways to get water to the garden, let's first consider ways to decrease the amount of water needed in maintaining landscape and garden areas.

The simplest way to decrease the need for water is to plant vegetation adapted to the rainfall of a particular region. Xeriscaping, which specifically selects dry-climate plants like cacti and succulents for use as ornamentals over water-intensive plants, and mesiscaping, which uses indigenous plants that require little water other than rainfall, are newly developed landscaping techniques being successfully practiced in areas where water use is restricted.

Adapting these two techniques to your landscape plan does not mean turning your New England lawn into a replica of an Arizona

From Thelma Honey, Albuquerque, New Mexico:

"Make your garden space as productive as you can: As soon as you pull something out, put something else in right away. I mix fresh compost with the soil every time I plant. You must keep plenty of nutrients in the soil.

"With intensive spacing, you'll find you don't use as much water. There's no bare ground to dry out. You don't have as many weeds, because there's no room for them. There aren't as many insects, either, because by mixing vegetables together, you're practicing 'companion planting'—one plant repels the pests that like the plant right next door. Asparagus and tomatoes are a good example. The asparagus repels tomato hornworms, and asparagus beetles don't like tomatoes. I've watched tomato hornworm moths fly away from my tomatoes into my neighbor's garden!"

desert, nor does it mean turning a formal flower border into an unmown prairie. Simply spend a little time surveying your own and neighboring properties and noting what plants do best receiving nothing more than rainfall. A drive through undeveloped or farm country is an excellent way to observe plants, shrubs, and trees that thrive with little or no supplemental watering. Many of these plants and trees, or similar varieties, are available as nursery stock in local garden centers. The cost of replacing a plant that requires a great deal of supplemental water with one that requires little or none may be substantially offset by the savings in time—and money, if you pay for your water—over the course of a couple of years.

In most regions of the United States, mesiscaping, also known as permaculture or naturescaping, usually means phasing out and replacing thirsty plants like hybrid tea roses with hardier ones like shrub roses. If you live in an arid climate, however, consider xeriscaping your landscape to make maximum use of the natural vegetation of your region. The effort, expense, and environmental impact of maintaining a green lawn in the desert Southwest are great; transforming that lawn into a more natural setting for the many beautiful dry-climate plants available will mean great savings all around.

To further reduce the need to water, group plants of like watering needs together in easily accessible beds. Try to place plants needing fairly large amounts of water closest to the house or the nearest source of water so that you're not forced to carry water or drag hoses any great distance to reach them. Such plants may do best grouped near downspouts, where they can benefit from roof runoff as well as helping to prevent erosion and soggy spots in the lawn.

Another water-saving technique is simply to put off watering houseplants, shrubs, perennials, and lawns until they show signs of water stress. Waiting for signs like slight wilting, graying, or dulling of shiny foliage before watering will not harm plants and will encourage them to become hardier and more deeply rooted. Do not do this with your vegetable garden, however; to produce well, most vegetables need a constant steady source of moisture. Even brief periods of wilting and water stress, especially in plants like tomatoes, peppers, and eggplant, can reduce yields.

Use mulches and ground covers wherever possible (see chapter 8). These materials prevent the evaporation of water from the surface of the earth, keep the soil cooler, and reduce the need for watering. If you use a drip irrigation or soaker-hose system to provide water (discussed later in this chapter), mulches and ground covers also protect your system from ultraviolet deterioration.

RAIN GAUGES AND TIMERS

Using a rain gauge to determine the amount of natural precipitation that has fallen in a given time period is another good way to avoid

---

From Charles A. Lewis, horticulturist, Morton Arboretum, Lisle, Illinois:

"Something is inherently beautiful in plants. To me, they speak of a sense of orderliness, or progression, a kind of sanity. There is more than visual beauty in plants; there is a sense of peace. Not only are they peaceful, but they confer peace upon the people who work with them.

"Plants provide a way of getting back into the world. They are nonthreatening, because they do not talk back. Gardening activities can be selected to match your energy mood. Pull weeds to remove anxiety. Depending on how hard a day you have had, you decide how hard you will work."

unnecessary watering. The E-Z Read Rain Gauge (15, 67, 78, 95, 97, 114), with its large, yellow numers and bright red float, is an excellent choice for the accessible garden.

Moisture meters (67, 84, 114), which signal with a buzz or blinking light when soil moisture has dropped below a preset level, are a real help if you have widely scattered container-grown plants that you tend to forget about.

Automatic, programmable electronic watering timers (34, 49, 67, 84, 147, 165), which attach easily to an outdoor faucet, are wonderful time and water savers. You can set them to water at exactly the same time every day or vary the schedule for each day of the week. These devices run on battery power, so the only attention they require is a periodic check to make sure the batteries have not run down. Most feature a small pushbutton panel and LCD display that can be hard to manipulate and read, especially in bright sunlight, so you may need help making the initial settings. Once the timer is set, however, you can virtually forget it for the rest of the season.

An electronic rain gauge like the RainSensor II (67, 114) is a timer accessory that overrides the water-on setting when rainfall is adequate. Thus your lawn sprinkler will not run during a rainstorm.

FAUCETS AND HOSE BIBBS

Having a ready source of water is essential to the accessible garden. If your home is equipped with only a single outdoor faucet or hose bibb, consider having extra faucets installed in locations close to gardens, patios, and driveways. This will save steps and eliminate the need for hoses snaking over the lawn and garden, causing tripping hazards and getting in the way of lawn mowers.

If adding more faucets is not feasible, make one faucet do multiple duty by using a tap distributor. There are several two-, three-, and four-way distributors (16, 26, 67) on the market. When selecting one for the accessible garden, look for easy-turn knobs or lever-action toggles that regulate the flow to any or all of the hoses attached to the tap distributor. Snap-on-and-off hose connections are another good feature. For even greater convenience, the Hydro-Zoner two-way distributor (67) has a built-in timer that will automatically switch the water supply on or off to either hose.

A faucet hidden behind foundation shrubbery can make access difficult. Add a hose extender (16, 34, 67, 84, 97, 114) to bring the faucet out to you. Most extenders consist of about 5 feet of sturdy garden hose with a wire-wrapped section to prevent crimping, a spigot attachment, and a stake or support to hold the spigot up off the ground. The stake provided with these extenders is usually short (12 to 18 inches), so to make the faucet more convenient, you may want to replace it with a taller support post. For walker or wheelchair gardeners, 24 to 36 inches is ideal.

Indoors or out, turning faucets on and off can be difficult if hand mobility is impaired or if you have a weakened grip. To make it easier, add easy-grip, easy-turn faucet handle covers (9, 10, 14, 40, 42, 43, 55, 61, 77, 108, 109, 149). These slip-on covers provide a large lever that can be turned easily, even by arthritic gardeners. Other options are the popular "tip-tap" faucets (30, 109, 110, 162), which operate by lever action, and electronic-sensor faucets (107), which turn on and off at the touch of a finger. These last two options are expensive, though, and require you to remove and replace existing faucets and hose bibbs.

Every outdoor faucet or hose bibb should be equipped with a vacuum breaker or backflow preventer (16, 49, 84). Vacuum breakers screw onto the faucet and prevent water in hoses or drip-irrigation tubing from being sucked back into the house's water supply by back pressure. Back pressure is a common problem in areas where water pressure is low, but it can occur in any water system under certain conditions. It can pose a real hazard when hoses are used with in-line canisters to distribute fertilizers or pesticides.

HOSES

Cheap hoses are no bargain; they deteriorate quickly, kink, crack, and usually need replacing within a couple of years. Invest in a good one. One of the very best is the Flexogen (15, 16, 84), a crack-, break-, and kink-resistant, lifetime-guaranteed hose from Gilmour Products. These lightweight, sturdy hoses remain flexible even in cold weather, and if anything ever happens to it—the dog eats it, the lawn mower shreds it—the Gilmour company will replace it free of charge.

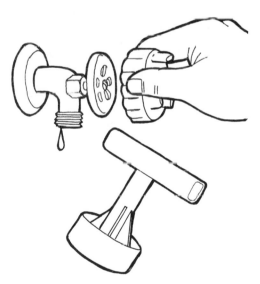

No knob in your home, garden, or greenhouse should be without one of these easy-turn faucet covers. They snap on and off and provide a big, comfortable grip for weak or arthritic fingers. They're an ideal, inexpensive way to make watering easier.

Another good hose choice for the accessible garden is the Claber Company's lightweight, high-visibility orange hose (67), which can be used to transport potable drinking water. It is *not* safe to drink water from ordinary garden hoses, as the chemicals used in their manufacture can leach into the water in minute doses. Weighing half as much as an ordinary hose, the Claber is strong and flexible even at below-zero temperatures, easy to coil, and easy to maneuver when full of water.

To keep hoses from crushing tender plants, use hose guards to gently guide the hose through the garden. You can find these in most catalogs and hardware stores, or make your own by placing 1-foot lengths of 2-inch PVC pipe in strategic locations.

If you're a wheeled gardener, dragging a hose from place to place is much easier if the last 3 or 4 feet are rigidly attached to a length of broom handle, dowel, or other stout stick. With the end held rigidly, there is less chance of the hose dribbling on you or becoming tangled in the wheels of your scooter or chair. Use twist-ties or thick, soft rope to attach the hose to the handle so that you can free it easily.

Quick-connect hose-end attachments and connectors (16, 26, 49, 67, 84) have no threads to screw together and tighten, making it easier for gardeners with impaired vision or reduced hand strength and mobility to add extra hoses or attach accessories. In addition, many snap-on-and-off attachments include a water-stop feature so that you can remove and replace attachments without having to run back to the faucet to turn off the water.

Watering wands extend your reach and make it much simpler to water potted plants throughout the house and garden using a hose rather than an awkward watering can. You can make your own watering wand by taping the last 2 or 3 feet of your hose to a length of wood or a cane; this arrangement also helps keep the hose from getting tangled in wheelchair wheels when you're carrying the hose around the garden.

To extend your reach, several manufacturers produce watering wands (16, 34, 49, 114, 147), lightweight, rigid brass, copper, or plastic tubes that are attached to the end of a watering hose. Most have a squeeze-type, hand-trigger control and shut-off valve at the base of the wand. The best is a 36-inch-long, all-plastic wand with a flexible neck end that bends up to 150 degrees, allowing you to adjust it to whatever angle is most comfortable. The wand is slightly over an inch in diameter, making it easy to grip comfortably, and the locked-on trigger-action control lever requires only a gentle squeeze to set, another to disengage. Wrapping a piece of foam rubber over the wand, which may become slippery when wet, will greatly improve the grip.

To make the watering wand easier to use, attach a U-shaped telephone handset holder (13, 40, 55, 110, 130) to the shaft of the wand with duct tape. The handset holder provides enough control for one handed operation.

You can make your own hose-end extender by fastening the last few feet of garden hose to a cane with twist-ties. Adjust the nozzle to whatever spray pattern or intensity you need, turn on the water, and go to work. This may not be the ideal solution for overhead watering situations, as water will trickle down the cane, but to extend side reach from a wheelchair or walker or to allow you to get close to the ground without bending, it may be all you need.

Winding up a long hose when you've finished with it can be difficult. Hose carts (15, 16, 34, 67), which provide a wind-up reel and a wheeled storage base, are convenient, but only if you have free hands and good mobility. Get the best hose cart you can afford. Look for a cart that feels heavy; it may be a little harder to pull, but it won't tip over as easily as the lightweight models. Make sure that the hand-crank lever is big and easy to grip; a rubber bicycle-handlebar grip slipped over the end will give you a more comfortable surface to hold on to. To improve hose cart mobility, replace small, plastic wheels with the larger inflatable wheels and tires commonly used on wheelbarrows or high-wheel lawn mowers. Use as short a length of hose as practical for your needs; having yards of unused hose coiled on the reel adds unnecessary weight to lug around.

Wall-mounted, automatic retractable hose reels (15, 67) can rewind up to 100 feet of average-size garden hose with the flick of a lever, thanks to a powerful recoil spring mechanism. Use care with these recoil devices; although they do not whip the hose back onto the reel with excessive speed, they do work quickly enough to cause a tripping hazard for the unwary.

The Rebounder is a self-coiling hose that straightens out when water is flowing through it, then recoils as soon as water pressure ceases to flow. Available in 25- and 50-foot lengths, it is lightweight and easily stored, making it ideal for patio, balcony, or deck gardens. This hose is

best used on a smooth lawn or unplanted surface; the fairly rapid recoil-
ing action can damage plants that become caught in the coils.

SPRINKLERS

Sprinklers are a great way to water large areas easily, although on hot or
windy days, a good deal of water may be lost to evaporation. Neverthe-
less, if you're putting in a new lawn, they are far better than spending
hours moving a hose slowly back and forth. Of all the many designs on
the market, the Rain Dial (67) high-density plastic sprinkler is probably
the easiest to set if you have limited hand mobility, a weakened grip, or
visual impairments. It has a big, blue body and bright yellow easy-turn
dial with raised shapes molded into it that correspond to the shape of
the spray pattern you want.

Watering a full-grown garden or a bed of densely grown shrubbery
is best accomplished with a hose holder or with a raised-head sprinkler
like the Raintower (15, 34, 114, 165). The Raintower's sprinkler head
is set on a telescoping tripod tower that can be set to either 41 or 71
inches high, thus raising it above the surrounding vegetation. The
sprinkler head adjusts to a variety of spray patterns and can water up to
5,200 square feet.

An inline fertilizer injector (16, 34, 49, 67) will save you even more
time and effort. With one of these canister units attached to your hose,
you can apply water-soluble fertilizer or pesticide through a sprinkler
system or drip irrigation. The fertilizer is automatically dispensed and

---

*From Steward Dickson, chairman of Green Ridge Village
gardening committee, Newville, Pennsylvania:*

❝ As you age, you have to keep active. If you don't, you just
'rust out.' Those who keep active live longer, healthier
lives; those who don't, die. I think gardening is the best way for
older people to keep active, especially if it's something you've
enjoyed all your life. There's no need to just quit. Sure, when
your joints get stiff, you may have to work a little to warm them
up, but gardening doesn't have to be overly strenuous.

"I think the greatest satisfaction my wife and I get from our
garden is that we get to work together at something we both
enjoy—companionship is very important—and we're very
proud of how nice our property looks."

mixed with the water at a preset rate. Always use a vacuum breaker or backflow preventer on any faucet attached to such a device.

DRIP IRRIGATION

Once the exclusive province of big commercial growers and green-house operators, drip irrigation systems (26, 34, 49, 67, 70, 84, 114) are now readily available to any gardener, from small, tabletop systems for watering potted house-plants to large systems that can cover a big garden or snake around a house's foundation plantings.

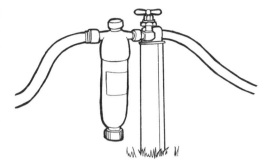

In-line canisters, shown here mounted on a hose-extender post, let you do two jobs at once, by providing a metered dosage of fertilizer or pesticide while you water. Any in-line canister must be equipped with a backflow preventer to keep contaminants from being drawn back into the home water supply.

Once installed, permanent drip systems require little or no additional maintenance, outside of a periodic inspection for blockage or leaks. If you have hard water and find that the tubing blocks frequently, try running a little weak vinegar-and-water solution through the lines periodically. The acid in the vinegar will dissolve mineral deposits without harming plants.

When purchasing drip irrigation systems, opt for the slightly more expensive tubing type, rather than systems that rely on fragile, readily torn flat tapes or ribbons. Many manufacturers offer complete systems in kit form, sized to fit a variety of garden and landscaping needs. If you're new to the concept, these kits are an excellent and inexpensive way to begin.

One of the greatest drawbacks to drip irrigation systems for those with disabilities is that they require quite a bit of dexterity to assemble and install. The tubes, connectors, and emitters can be tiny, and if you have difficulty getting close to the ground, it can be nearly impossible to lay the lines exactly where you want them. Soaker or dew hoses may be a better solution.

Soaker hoses, made of rubber, canvas, or plastic, resemble regular garden hoses except that they ooze water all along their length. Water delivery is not as precise as with drip systems, where emitters can be placed exactly at a plant's roots, but soakers are wonderful for watering long rows of closely spaced plants, such as in vegetable gardens, or in any densely planted area. These systems need no assembly and can be easily laid down wherever you need them, even from wheelchair height. Rubber and plastic hoses are rot-resistant and can be left in place until frost. If you live in an area where temperatures drop below freezing in winter, soaker hoses and surface-installed drip systems need to be gathered up, drained, and stored in a frost-free location.

You can make your own inexpensive soaker hose by punching small, evenly spaced holes in an old garden hose. Cap the end, lay the hose in place, and let it leak water where you want it.

For container gardens, look for capillary matting (67, 114) that sits in a water-filled tray beneath potted plants, and self-watering planters (34, 67, 114) that rely on a water well or reservoir beneath the main pot to provide water to the roots through capillary action. These planters are available as hanging baskets, windowsill planters, and floor-size tubs. Besides providing the root zone with a constant, steady supply of moisture, matting and reservoirs also keep humidity levels high around plants, reducing stress and increasing growth.

A very good material for capillary matting is 5- or 6-ounce urethane-foam carpet padding. You can usually obtain small sections of padding free or for a very nominal cost from carpet stores. Place the padding in a waterproof tray, soak it with water, and then set pots directly on top of it. Replenish the water every few days. Flat-bottomed pots with rather large drainage holes work best with capillary mats. Avoid pots with holes that are recessed or raised above the bottom of the pot.

One of the simplest of all capillary watering devices is a length of pure cotton clothesline, with one end in a full glass of water and the other coiled on the surface of a flowerpot. As water is absorbed into the soil, more water will be drawn up the clothesline by capillary action.

WATERING CANS

Many gardeners still find that a traditional watering can (15, 46, 67, 97, 148, 165) is the simplest way to get water to their plants. When selecting a watering can, choose one that is lightweight, durable, and well balanced. The finest are the famous Haws watering cans from England. They are expensive but worth every penny. Less expensive imitations abound, but test a can carefully before you buy by balancing it by the handle on your finger. If the can hangs fairly level while empty, it will be easier to carry and pour when full. Haws cans (165) and other good-quality watering cans are available at many gardening stores and through mail-order.

When carrying any liquid-filled container in a wheelchair, use a lapboard covered with a nonslip surface, and fill the container only half

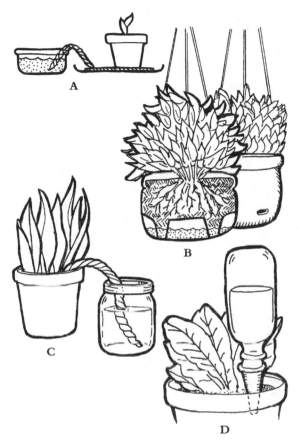

Wherever possible, let your pots water themselves. Self-watering options include (A) a simple capillary matting arrangement; (B) specially designed "intelligent" hanging pots that need refilling only once a week; (C) wicks that draw water up to replenish dry soil; and (D) Aqua-Spikes, which turn soft-drink bottles into efficient automatic irrigation devices for use indoors and out.

full or use one with a leakproof lid. It may take two trips instead of one, but it's better than getting soaked in the process, and if you're carrying anything other than water, it's the only safe way to go. A hook used to suspend paint buckets from ladders may provide a convenient way for walker gardeners to carry buckets or watering cans. Hang the water bucket from the side, not the front, of your walker, and fill the container only half full or use a container with a tight lid to prevent spills.

The visually impaired gardener can use a special liquid-level indicator (101). This handy little electronic device clips to the top edge of the watering can, bucket, or bottle and buzzes or vibrates when liquid reaches the top of the container. These indicators are commonly used in the kitchen and bath, but why not get a couple for use in the garden and potting shed, too?

ADAPTIVE WATERING AIDS

Empty 1-liter plastic soda bottles make wonderful homemade watering devices. Drill a small hole in the cap, half fill the bottle, and use it as a squeeze-type waterer to direct a jet of water at plant roots or leaves.

The commercially available Aqua Spike (67) is a handy gadget made of perforated plastic that is screwed onto an empty soda bottle and inserted into the ground near a plant. Through capillary action, a small, steady amount of water flows from the bottle directly to the plant's root zone.

Conserve water and protect young transplants from the drying effects of wind and sun with lightweight spun-bond garden fabric. To

Take advantage of "dual-purpose" garden accessories whenever possible. This plastic edging incorporates a hose coupling at either end for no-work watering of plants up to 4 feet from the edge of the bed.

protect individual plants, use cloches as miniature greenhouses, or make them from milk jugs or green plastic bottles by cutting off the bottoms, removing the caps, and placing over tender seedlings.

Sink water-filled 5-gallon buckets, with small holes punched in the base, into the earth near water-craving plants. Keep the buckets covered to reduce evaporation. Unglazed clay containers can also be used as underground waterers.

To make overhead watering quicker and easier, mount large coffee cans on sturdy 2-by-4 posts or racks. Pierce small holes around the base of each can. When filled with water, the cans will slowly empty a shower over the crops beneath. Filling a single wide-mouthed can is much easier than holding a hose trained over one spot for any length of time.

WATER CONSERVATION TIPS

Plan your garden for low water needs:

• Small containers dry out more quickly than large ones; where possible, group several plants together in one big container.

• Raised beds dry out more quickly than level earth. If you have to water your lawn once a week, you will probably have to water your raised-bed garden at least twice a week to maintain a healthy level of soil moisture.

• Clay and wood containers dry out more quickly than plastic or glazed ceramic. Plants potted in clay and wood need to be checked carefully and often, especially during hot, dry, windy weather.

• Vegetables and flowers need at least 1 inch of water a week to maintain peak production, either from rainfall or supplemental watering.

• Water deeply. Wait until the soil is dry, then soak it thoroughly. Frequent light waterings encourage fragile, shallow root systems that dry out quickly; watering deeply, then allowing the soil to thoroughly dry, encourages tough, deep root systems and better vigor.

• New transplants need more water than established plants. For transplanted vegetables and flowers, this means religious watering until new growth appears. For trees, shrubs, and heavy-rooted perennials, water daily for the first two weeks, then gradually decrease the amount and frequency to fit in with the rest of the garden's needs.

• Except in extreme drought, established trees, shrubs, and grasses do not need watering, even if they drop some leaves or, in the case of lawn grasses, turn brown. In periods of extended heat and water stress, many plants go dormant; watering them at this time will keep the plant from dormancy and in need of water.

Tools for Accessibility

Gardening tools may present one of the biggest obstacles to persons with physical disabilities. It is difficult to use ordinary, full-size shovels, hoes, rakes, and other implements if you are using a wheelchair, a power scooter, or a walker. If you have limited hand strength or mobility, using trowels, pruning shears, and other small tools can be awkward and even painful.

Special tools are uniquely designed for use by special-needs gardeners, and with a little ingenuity, many common tools can be successfully converted and other objects adapted for use in the garden.

If you have trouble locating tools in your area, get help from Project LINK (Link to Assistive Products), sponsored by the Center of Assistive Technology (CAT) at the University of Buffalo. LINK mails out periodic adaptive tool and assistive product catalogs and manufacturer listings at no charge. In addition, no product endorsements are made, no salesmen will call you, and you are under no obligation to buy anything. Write to Project LINK, CAT/UB, 515 Kimball Tower, Buffalo, NY 14214-3079, or telephone (800) 628-2281.

LEVERAGE AIDS

Most tools depend on the principle of lever action to work. Leverage is often a matter of position rather than strength, and in many cases increasing your leverage is all that is necessary to make an impossible tool work as you wish.

One of the most basic leverage aids is a triangular wooden block. Placed on the ground, with a long-handled tool such as a hoe or rake propped over it, the block acts as a fulcrum, taking the weight of the

From Meta Blue, horticultural therapist, Northview Developmental Center, Newton, Kansas:

"When setting out to design an adaptive tool or device, ask yourself, 'What are the characteristics this thing must possess?' The next step is to find a ready-made object that fits that description and serves that function, or to create one.

"Foot-care and auto-supply departments are good sources of soft, protective materials: foam toe guards, felt, moleskin, sponges, chamois, furry car wax mitts. Bicycle accessories, especially the fancy handlebar grips and crash bar pads, will fit a lot of tool handles to help people who require a larger handle to grip. Housewares can also be useful for gardening: barbecue mitts, tongs, blending forks, spaghetti strainers, and salt shakers, which can be used by gardeners with poor grip strength or poor finger dexterity to sow fine seeds."

tool off your arms and upper back, and allowing you to put your energy into moving the tool rather than into holding, lifting, and balancing it. This block is especially helpful to anyone who is gardening from a seated position, because it reduces the stress placed on the wrists, upper arms, and shoulders by holding the weight of the tool for you. A block of 4-by-4 timber, about a foot long, can be sawn lengthwise to produce two such blocks. Used railroad ties or landscape timbers are a good source for wood, and most lumberyards and millwork operations will saw the wood for you. Don't make the block too big or it will be heavy and hard to move.

Commercial, tool-mounted leverage aids are available from several sources. D- and straight-grip handles (46, 110, 165) that slide onto long-handled brooms, rakes, and shovels make using these tools much easier by providing a more natural positioning of the hands and arms. You don't have to bend over to work the tool back and forth, thus eliminating lower-back strain. The adjustable grip handles attach with a slip screw, so you can move them from tool to tool.

Lever-Aide hand tools (P.O. Box 623, Chanhassen, MN 55317) feature a cushioned, over-the-wrist strap design that allows the gardener to use the muscles of the lower arm, rather than the hand and fingers,

to work the soil. Arthritic gardeners or gardeners using prosthetic
hand or lower-arm appliances
should find the Lever-Aide wrist
strap design fairly comfortable, and
the ergonomic handle precludes
the need for a tight grip on the
tool itself.

Wrist and hand straps (110,
162) like those used to help hold
eating utensils, paintbrushes, and
pencils can also be used to support
lightweight gardening hand tools.
Experiment with Velcro and various wrist straps and splints until
you find a comfortable combination of tool and support.

To help you hold and balance
long-handled tools, you can make a
long arm cuff from the sleeve of an
old denim or heavy-weight fabric
jacket. Sew a loop of Velcro about
3 inches from the wrist and another
loop just below the elbow. Slip the
tool handle into these loops to give
you better leverage and control. To
keep the entire sleeve from sliding
off your arm, attach a strap, like
those used to keep arm slings in
place, to the top of the sleeve. Pass
the strap behind the shoulders and
around the body, back to the top of
the sleeve.

GRIP IMPROVEMENTS
Improving your grip on any tool
will go a long way toward improving your ability to use that tool.
Slippery tools are not only difficult
to use, but they can also be danger-

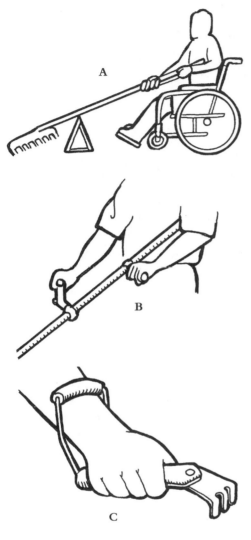

*Increasing leverage increases the ease
with which tools can be used. A simple
lever block (A) can be made from wood;
(B) slip-on D-grip handles can be inter-
changed from tool to tool to make it
possible to rake and hoe without bending; and the over-the-wrist strap of
Lever-Aide hand tools (C) allows gardeners with a weak grip to use hand
tools successfully.*

ous. A tool handle that moves and rubs against the skin of your hand, foot, or arm can cause blisters, splinters, and even open sores if used long enough.

Always wear gloves and protective clothing while gardening; this is especially important if you have diabetes, allergies, or circulatory problems in your hands or feet. Ask your health-care provider about custom-designed hand braces, arch supports, and therapeutic stockings and gloves that can improve circulation and lend extra support to fingers, wrists, legs, and feet.

The color of the clothing you wear is also important. White clothing will help you stay cool in hot weather; dark clothing absorbs the sun's heat and will keep you warm in cool, windy weather. Bright yellows and blues are attractive to insects, and you may find yourself the target of unwanted attention. Stick to dull colors—grays, khakis, and tans.

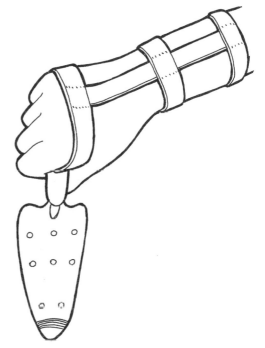

Splints designed to help hold eating utensils and paintbrushes can be adapted for garden hand tools. Holes drilled into the blade of this trowel provide a depth guide for blind or visually impaired gardeners.

In selecting gardening gloves, look for a good fit, rubber or leather palm and finger pads, and tight, smooth seams to keep out dirt. Big, floppy gloves should be avoided, as should very tight gloves, as both can cause blisters. Leather or imitation-leather driving gloves, such as those worn by wheelchair gardeners to improve their grip on the drive wheels of their chairs, can make good gardening gloves, provided you do not make direct contact with wet soil. Carry several pairs of clean gloves with you while you work, and change them as soon as they become very dirty, wet, or damaged.

To further improve your grip on tools, wind self-adhesive Dycem tape (9) strips around handles to provide a nonslip gripping surface, or dip tool handles in a liquid rubber coating material (available in most hardware stores) that hardens to a bright, durable, highly grippable finish.

The brilliant colors of these liquid rubber products also make it almost impossible to lose a tool in the garden's greenery.

To customize your grip on any hand tool, apply a thick coat of epoxy putty (60) to the existing handle. Wearing rubber surgical gloves to protect your skin, take a firm grip of the putty-covered handle, holding the tool as you would in use. The putty will conform exactly to your grip. Before the putty hardens, carefully carve away the excess. It will harden completely in several hours to form a smooth, washable handle that won't slip off the tool or crack under normal use.

Inexpensive slip-on foam rubber sleeves (165) can be moved from tool to tool to provide you with a better grip and to protect your fingers from contact with rough wood or cold metal surfaces. You can make your own slip-on handle covers by recycling foam rubber packing fabric. Cut the foam into strips, wind tightly around tool handles, and tape in place with fabric-faced first-aid tape.

For gardeners who have difficulty closing their fingers into the tight fist required of most hand tools, a child's ball may prove the answer. Find a firm solid rubber ball big enough that you can grip it comfortably. Drill a hole straight through the ball, and slip it down over the tool's handle to just above the tang. Use tape or glue to secure it, if necessary. The ball becomes a spherical, expanded hand grip for you to hold. Clawlike cultivators and small trowels that require a raking motion work well with this idea.

HAND TROWELS AND CULTIVATORS

Trowels are probably the most used gardening tool. For grubbing out stubborn weeds, filling pots with soil, opening furrows for seeds, and planting bulbs and transplants, nothing can beat these short-handled "minishovels."

Short-handled trowels may not be practical, however, if you have a restricted reach or are unable to bend down close to the ground. In this case, long-handled hand tools (46, 67, 98, 106, 138, 143, 148, 165) may be the easiest solution. Several manufacturers produce long-handled equipment, including the SuperGrip (66) line and Gardena's Combisystem (98), which allows you to interchange snap-on tool heads (saw, rake, cultivator, and scraper) on a lightweight, easy-grip telescopic handle that adjusts from 30 to 55 inches in length.

Tool handle extensions (7, 66), such as the Upper Hand, can be slipped onto any tool handle to increase its reach and its balance. A similar effect can be achieved by slipping a length of PVC pipe of the appropriate diameter over the tool handle. Wrap a piece of nonslip tape around the PVC pipe handle to improve your grip.

If you have carpal tunnel syndrome or other hand- or wrist-related problems, the jab-and-twist motion required with a conventional trowel can be painful, if not damaging. Many ergonomically designed trowels and other hand tools are available, including the NoBlist'r (16, 114) padded-handle trowel.

The Planter's Hand (165) is a contemporary version of an ancient trowel. The straight, slightly hollowed blade is set at right angles to a thick, comfortable handle, allowing you to carve out planting holes and furrows with one easy stroke. Because the motion comes from the shoulder and elbow rather than the wrist and fingers, you can avoid the jab-and-twist motion needed with most conventional trowels. The Asian Hand cultivator (97, 165), from an old Korean design, also features an easy-grip handle set at right angles to a triangular blade shaped like a miniature plow. It is excellent for digging, furrowing, and cultivating.

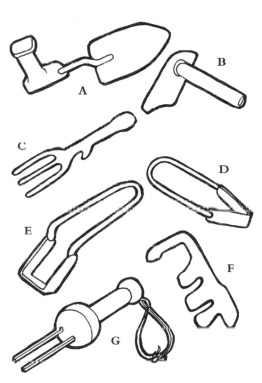

Handform (165) trowels and claws are made of a polycarbonate resin—a sort of high-grade plastic—that is very lightweight, warm to the touch (a real plus if cold metal makes your fingers ache), and easily honed to a sharp edge with a file. Handform trowels are ergonomically designed to fit snugly against the palm, allowing you to push the tool into the soil without a tight grip. These are excellent for anyone with arthritic fingers or carpal tunnel syndrome.

An assortment of easy-grip hand trowels, weeders, and cultivators. (A) Fist-Grip garden trowel; (B) the Planter's Hand Korean hand trowel–cultivator; (C) Trigger Tools hand fork; (D, E) the Vee and Uoo hand weeders; (F) the Handform claw for raking, weeding, and cultivating; and (G) the Appalachian Ball Weeder, which uses leverage to "pop" weeds out of the ground.

Trigger Tools (34, 97, 114, 148) are wonderful for gardeners with a weak or arthritic grip. Made of polished, lightweight cast aluminum, these tools won't rust, bend, or break. They are comfortable in the hand, and a special trigger-type grip makes them easy to hold and use. Plus Four Hand Tools (148) are similar ergonomically designed, lightweight, polished aluminum tools with an extremely comfortable hand-fitting grip. Both Trigger Tools and Plus Fours can be improved with a nonslip liquid rubber coating on the handles.

Fist-Grip hand tools, manufactured by the Peta Scissorcraft company in England, are ergonomically designed, lightweight, stainless-steel tools, each of which is fitted with a plastic, lever-style handle, positioned at right angles from the tool's head to provide maximum leverage with minimum effort. These are excellent for gardeners with weak hands or severely restricted hand movement.

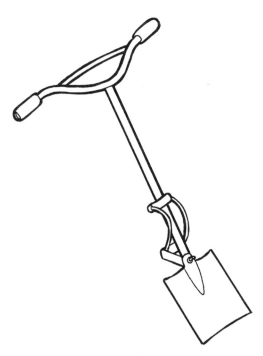

A pedal spade requires less leg strength than a regular spade to push into the ground; it also lets you dig deeply without excessive bending.

DIGGING TOOLS

Digging holes and turning soil are hard work, but there are several spades, shovels, and scoops available to make the job a little easier.

Ergonomically designed "back-saver" shovels (143) are made of lightweight aluminum, with curved or angled handles that allow you to remain upright while scooping or shoveling snow, dirt, or other debris. They are not designed for digging or spading work, but if you routinely need to move manure, snow, or compost, a back-saver shovel will save your lower back considerable stress. This same back-saver design is also available in brooms and rakes.

If you can find it, the British company Wolf Ltd. makes a uniquely designed garden spade known as the Terrex. It has a long, adjustable shaft and bicycle handle-bar-like grip. The gardener uses a foot pedal to push the blade into the ground, and then pivots the shovel to throw soil up and out. There is no need to bend down while using the Terrex spade. Another British company, Wilkinson, produces a telescopic gardening fork, also with an adjustable handle.

If full-size tools are too heavy, too awkward, or just too big for you, invest in a set of good-quality children's tools (46, 67, 74, 97, 148, 165). Don't buy the cheap plastic variety found in most discount stores; they will invariably bend or break with any sort of hard use.

The best children's tools are miniature versions of full-size tools. Sheffield Pride makes a set of top-quality forged steel, ash-handled tools that are scaled-down versions of their full-size spade, fork, rake, and hoe. The spade and fork have an overall length of 30 inches; the rake and hoe, 40 inches. You'll pay more for these tools than you would for toy tools, but these are sturdy, serious garden tools, not toys. They'll pay for themselves many times over.

Sheffield Pride also makes a yard-long, small-bladed shovel known in Europe as a rabbiting tool, because it was once routinely used to dig out rabbit warrens. The T handle construction and short length make it a perfect shovel for the seated gardener working in containers or raised beds.

A professional planting bar, which is a cross between a shovel and a long-handled trowel, is another excellent back-saving tool. The 4-inch-wide blade, with generous, extended footrests on either side, is just big enough to open the soil for bulbs or transplants, and the 42-inch, T-type handle allows you to work without bending.

Correct technique will also go a long way toward saving your back while spading. Stand up straight. Drive the spade or shovel into the ground using one foot only; never jump onto the shovel blade. Push down firmly, rocking the blade slightly if necessary to force it no more than three-quarters of the way into the earth. Bend at the knees, not just at the waist, to lift the full shovel. Slide one hand as far down the shaft as comfortable, so that one hand and arm act as a fulcrum for the load. As you lift, straighten your knees and tighten your stomach muscles to take the strain off your back. Work at a slow, steady pace. Take frequent breaks; after every three spadefuls or so, straighten up, place your hands on your hips, and gently bend backward and from side to side. It adds only a few minutes to your work time, and you will finish the job feeling better and less exhausted.

Avoid double-digging. Although beneficial in breaking up hard-pan, adobe, or compacted soil, it's backbreaking work and in most cases unnecessary. Instead, apply a thick, continuous layer of mulch and compost to attract earthworms and others of nature's soil tillers. Let them do the work for you.

Using a trowel to dig out planting holes for bulbs and transplants can be exhausting if you have more than just a few bulbs or plants to place. A fine alternative is an earth auger (15, 16, 34, 70, 78, 95, 97, 114), a sort of gigantic drill bit. Two versions are available: One fits most electric hand drills and is especially useful in hard, compacted soil; the other is hand-powered, has a large T-shaped handle, and is operated similar to a corkscrew. If you have a good grip and sufficient arm strength, both versions can be operated with one hand.

Somewhat similar are bulb planters, which come in both short- and long-handled versions (16, 46, 95, 114, 165). The long-handled versions have a built-in step bar to allow you to use your weight to punch the can-shaped planter head deep into the soil. Don't reserve these tools only for planting bulbs; they are excellent work-saving devices when taking soil samples, planting small transplants, removing deep-rooted weeds, and opening holes near trees and shrubs for deep feeding.

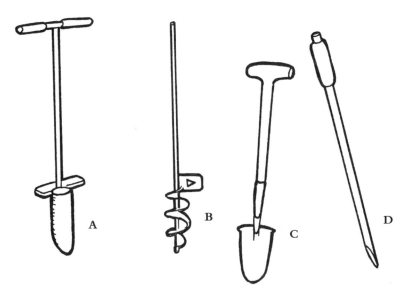

Digging tools. Use a long-handled bulb planter (A) or an earth auger (B) for setting transplants, taking soil samples, and opening the ground for deep-root fertilization, in addition to bulb planting. The English rabbiting spade (C) is only 36 inches long, with a 5-inch-wide blade that makes it ideal for use in small spaces; its T-shaped handle is easy to grip and provides additional leverage. A simple dibber or digging tool (D) can be made from PVC pipe, with one end cut at an angle to make a sharpened point. A piece of foam rubber provides a comfortable, nonslip grip.

Dibbles or dibbers (16, 46, 95, 97, 98, 165) are ancient tools that are useful for the gardener with disabilities. These simple L- or T-shaped wooden tools with a pointed, sometimes metal-reinforced tip are fine for poking holes into the earth, scratching out planting furrows, and pricking out small weeds. The wide T-handle provides an easy grip, and because it sits at right angles to the body of the tool, you use your palm and arm muscles rather than your wrist and fingers to propel it. You can make a back-saving stand-up dibble from a 3-foot length of 1-inch PVC pipe or dowel, angle-cut at the end to form a sharpened point. Use another length of pipe or dowel, threaded through a T-shaped pipe joint, for the handle.

If your legs and lower back are in good shape but you have problems with your upper back, shoulders, elbows, or wrists, try the digging bar or rocking fork (46, 67, 165). With this tool, you don't actually lift and turn the soil at all. Instead, you push the five big tines into the soil with the pressure of your foot, grab the wide cross-bar handle, rock back and forth on the tool, withdraw it, and start again a few inches farther on. The digging bar's tines loosen three times more soil per bite than the average gardening fork, all without lifting a spadeful. Because you use your body weight both to press the tines into the soil and to rock the tool back and forth, you save wear and tear on joints, tendons, and muscles.

POWERED TILLERS

Gas-powered tillers, from little cultivators to big, multihorsepower rear-tine models, are fine for any gardener with the strength and dexterity to use them. The small front-tine power cultivators, like the EZ Hoe and Mantis (16, 67, 111), are especially useful in large gardens, but I wouldn't recommend trying to use them in a high raised bed from a seated position.

Big power tillers are classified as either front- or rear-tine. Other than very small power cultivators, don't buy a front-tine tiller, because they are difficult to control. The forward motion of a front-tine tiller depends on the rotating digging tines to pull it along. In soft soil, you may be able to hold back on the tiller and steer it fairly well, but on hard ground or turf, it's easy for the tines to lift out of the soil and "walk" across the surface, dragging the operator behind. Also, because the tines are mounted at the end of the handlebars, the vibration and lurching motion of the moving machine is tremendous—and very uncomfortable.

Rear-tine tillers, on the other hand, have powered wheels that are geared just like a car. You control the forward and reverse speed. Because the tiller blades are mounted behind the motorized "tractor" and spin independently of the wheel motion, the tilling action is much smoother. And because the tines don't supply the forward motion, they rotate much more rapidly and tilling is much faster. Rear-tine tillers are more expensive than front-tine because you're paying for a fairly sophisticated drive shaft, transmission, and engine, but the extra money is well worth it, both for ease of use and because many rear-tine tillers may be fitted with accessories that transform them into cutting bars, snowblowers, chippers, log splitters, and riding mowers.

If you are contemplating a powered tiller purchase, don't rely on slick magazine or mail-order advertisements to tell you what you need to know. Visit several dealerships and ask to try out the tiller before you buy. Look for features like electronic key start rather than a pull-cord starter, a "dead-man" or operator-presence switch that deactivates the tiller when you let go of the controls, adjustable handlebars that can be raised or lowered, easy stopping and maneuvering features, and transport wheels that allow you to roll the unpowered tiller easily to and from work sites. Vibration and noise that seem inconsequential during a short test run can be unbearable under actual operating conditions, so look for equipment with good mufflers and antivibration designs. Don't be content to watch someone else run the machine; insist on trying it out for yourself, under real working conditions. Only then can be you be sure whether the machine will be a labor and time saver.

To make tilling easier, learn to guide and control your rear-tine machine with one hand only, walking beside the machine rather than behind it. This is the recommended technique for power rotary tiller operation, because you are less likely to be struck by any debris kicked up by the revolving tines, the chance of a foot slipping under the tines is greatly reduced, and you are prevented from leaning into or lifting and pushing the tiller over rough terrain, saving strain on both you and the machine. If the tines should become entangled and the tiller lurches forward, you're more likely to let go of the handle, thus allowing the operator-presence switch to stop the tines, rather than hang on and be pulled along after the machine.

Walking beside the tiller also keeps the freshly tilled earth behind the tines loose and uncompacted by your footsteps. It takes a little practice and a little more time, since you may have to go back over rough spots a few times, but in the long run both you and your tiller will be less stressed by the experience.

If you are able to use a riding lawn mower or tractor, consider investing in a powered tiller attachment that will allow you to turn over large areas quickly and with little effort (see chapter 8).

WEEDING TOOLS

Nobody likes to weed. My father always said you spend 10 percent of the time in the garden putting things into the ground, and the other 90 percent pulling things out. Mulches, plastic and paper sheeting, and closely spaced (intensive) plantings all reduce the number of weeds, but the occasional opportunistic dandelion or chickweed is still sure to creep in.

From Thelma Honey, Albuquerque, New Mexico:

" Adaptive tools are a big help. I have a weeder that is about 30 inches long and can be used from a wheelchair. You just put the weeder over the weed, push down, and pop the weed out. Cut-and-hold flower gatherers are good, too. I think those are probably two very important tools.

"I use intensive gardening. I have raised a tremendous amount of vegetables in what are basically small—4-by-10-foot—raised beds. A bushel of carrots one year! My beds are made out of railroad ties, stacked two high. I put carpet on the ties and I can sit on the edge to work."

To make the job easier, tool manufacturers and gardeners through the ages have developed a number of weeding devices. The hoe is the simplest of these and has, over the years, evolved into many forms, from the simple, square-bladed Warren hoe to the oscillating-bladed hoe.

Unfortunately, no one hoe is perfect for every gardening task or every gardener. Try out a few different designs. Look for lightweight, solid construction (you don't want the neck to bend if you lean on it), a comfortable handle, and a blade that sharpens easily and holds a good edge. The Precision Weeder (114, 165) has a hooklike blade only 5/8 inch wide mounted on a 60-inch, lightweight handle. It is ideal for wheelchair gardeners or for anyone who needs to get into tight places to cultivate and weed.

For close-in hand weeding, the Appalachian Ball Weeder (8, 165) is an old design that has found its way into modern gardens. A simple tuning fork shaped tool with a wooden ball placed halfway down the handle, the ball weeder relies on leverage action to help pry stubborn weeds out of the ground. You insert the fork alongside the weed, then push back on the handle, letting the ball act as a fulcrum to help lift the weed out.

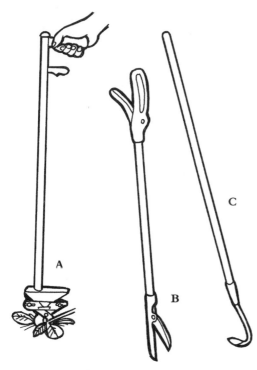

The Uoo and Vee hand weeders (164) are uniquely designed hand tools for thinning and weeding small plants. They have easy-grip handles, weigh only 4 ounces, and depend on a sharp, spring steel blade to cut through surface soil and roots. Their slender, lightweight blades are ideal for use in tight spots.

To weed without bending, there are several varieties of long-handled, mechanical, scissor-action weeders like the Ripper Weeder (34, 67, 164). You position the head of the tool over a weed, step down on the footrest to insert the blades around the weed, then pull on a trigger to pop the weed from the ground, all without bending over. Although these mechanical weeders work well for shallow-rooted weeds, they won't dig deep enough to completely eliminate deep, tap-rooted weeds like dandelion or chicory.

Weeding made easier. The Ripper Weeder (A) and the Firm Grip Weed Puller (B) use leverage action to grip and pull weeds from the ground without bending. The Precision Weeder (C) is a small, lightweight hoe with a blade only ⁵/₈ inch wide that lets you cultivate with ease in narrow places, such as containers and intensively planted raised beds.

An easy-reach tool (42, 52, 110) used to help pick up objects from high or low areas can also be used as a weeder and cultivator, as can a long-handled cut-and-hold flower gatherer (16, 90). Use the cut-and-hold tool to snip off young weeds at the soil line without bending, and the easy-reach tool to gather up the cut weeds and to scrape mulch over the weeded site.

PRUNING AND HARVESTING TOOLS

Pruning, cutting flowers for arrangements, deadheading, and harvesting are all made easier with ratchet-action cutting tools, such as pruning shears, loppers, and clippers. These tools rely on lever action to increase your hand strength. With a relatively light squeeze, it is possible to cut large branches with ease.

Another fine tool for light-duty pruning or gathering is the cut-and-hold flower gatherer (16, 90). Blades mounted at the end of a 31-inch-long, lightweight aluminum handle are designed to grab, then cut and lock onto flower stems or thin branches. This tool is great for extending your reach to the back of a bed or overhead to hanging plants. Its slender design is even thin enough to fit through a 1-inch-wide bottleneck for terrarium use.

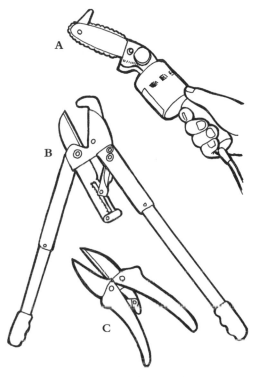

Harvest fruit without ladders or straining with a long-handled, basketlike fruit picker (15, 16, 115, 165). Mounted on a lightweight aluminum or fiberglass pole, the fruit picker acts like an extended hand by gently grabbing the fruit with wire "fingers" and holding the picked fruit in a small wire basket. Fruit pickers are also helpful for thinning fruits, raking out dead flowerheads from thorny rosebushes, and retrieving dropped objects from a seated position.

Electric, rechargeable powered pruners (A) allow you to cut even fairly large branches with little effort. A pole-mounted version can be used to reach high, overhead branches. Ratchet-action loppers (B) and pruners (C) multiply hand strength through leverage power, so that even gardeners with a weak grip can cut easily through tough twigs and small branches.

Telescopic tree saws and pruners (15, 16, 34, 46, 148), with cutting heads mounted on adjustable, lightweight aluminum or fiberglass poles, are fine for doing light tree pruning, up to about 1-inch-diameter branches. Pulley action on the lopper attachment gives a mechanical advantage of 10 to 1, but holding the tool overhead for any length of time is tiring. You'll need very good coordination, upper-body and arm strength, and a sound back to use these tools.

Lumex/Swedish Rehab Corporation (109) makes a wide variety of tools, cutlery, and accessories designed to make life easier. For light pruning and trimming work, the Swedish Rehab scissor-cutter has wide spring handles that snap open when you release your grip.

For delicate work like deadheading, trimming houseplants, or gathering small blossoms, invest in a pair of easy-grip or bonsai scissors (10, 13, 16, 32, 42, 55, 67, 91, 97, 109, 114, 116, 135, 147, 154). Designed with large, comfortable hand grips and small, sharp blades, these lightweight scissors are easy to use, even if you have a weakened grip.

Electric-powered pruners (15, 16) are fine for anyone whose hands and fingers become easily tired with repetitive open-and-close motions, but they are fairly heavy and require considerable arm and upper-body mobility and dexterity, especially if you intend to cut branches or twigs overhead. The hand-held pruner is cordless, powered by a 13.2-volt battery; the long-handled tree pruner plugs into any standard 110-volt AC outlet. Both powered pruners work something like miniature chain saws, so they can be dangerous if used improperly.

English sheep shears (16, 46, 114, 164), virtually unchanged since the Middle Ages (you can see them in old illustrated manuscripts), are made of lightweight, high-carbon steel that takes a razor edge and holds it. Their unique, springy, one-piece design makes them easy to use even without a strong grip, and their wide-open jaws makes deadheading masses of flowers or trimming grass quick work.

SPRAYERS

Even in the most carefully managed gardens, there comes a time when it's necessary to spray to eliminate insect pests or diseases. In the accessible garden, chemical pesticides, herbicides, and fungicides should be strictly avoided. Besides their negative impact on the environment, many of these chemical compounds can do severe damage to the human respiratory, nervous, and immune systems. If you are already in poor health, the danger from chemical pesticides is magnified even further.

Even the use of naturally occurring substances such as baking soda, powdered limestone, diatomaceous earth, *Bacillus thuringiensis* (Bt), sulfur, rotenone, and pyrethrum should be kept to a minimum. Although these products have no prolonged residual effect in the garden, they are still, to varying degrees, toxins or irritants and should be handled accordingly.

Protect yourself from direct contact with any spray or dust. Even something as seemingly harmless as baking soda can be troublesome if inhaled. Always wear a dust mask or respirator (16, 114) when applying pesticides. Dress appropriately in a long-sleeved shirt, long pants, gloves, and eye protectors. Spray and dust only on windless days, and stay out of the path of any drift that occurs. When you're finished, change clothes and wash your face, hands, and any other exposed areas of your body thoroughly, even if you think you didn't get any spray or dust on you.

Apply as little product as necessary to get the job done. To spot-apply powders and dusts, use a cotton ball, a powderpuff, or even an old cotton sock to dab the pesticide where it is needed. Lightly misting plants before dusting will help the product adhere better and reduce drift.

A number of home-brewed pesticides made from soap, water, garlic, rubbing alcohol, tobacco, or hot pepper juice have proven effective. Use care when mixing and applying these concoctions, especially those containing nicotine (toxic) or hot peppers (highly irritating, especially to eyes and mouth). Always test a homemade spray on one plant or one leaf before dousing an entire crop; some plants may have adverse reactions. Spray these pesticides only on cloudy or overcast, windless days to prevent drift and sunscald.

For low-growing crops like cabbages and bush beans, make a tap-can duster by attaching an empty can with a plastic snap-on lid, such as a peanut can, to a yardstick or length of pipe with duct tape. Position the can about 18 inches from the bottom of the stick. Punch small holes in the bottom of the can with a tack. Fill the can with BT, rotenone, or whatever other pesticide dust you are using, and put the lid on tightly. As you walk or ride along your garden rows, bump or tap the end of the stick on the ground beside the plants, and a cloud of dust will be shaken out of the can to coat the leaves.

A small, hand-held, rubber-bulb mister-duster is convenient for spraying and dusting small houseplants without the risk of damage to delicate leaves or flowers. The soft rubber bulb is easy to squeeze and comes with a 6-inch extension wand to allow you to get in between leaves. For very small spray jobs, use an ear or nose syringe kept exclusively for garden use.

For small gardens, a hand-held spray bottle may be all you need to apply water-based sprays. Trigger-action bottles can be tiring to use for more than a couple of minutes, so look for continuous-action spray bottles like the PolySprayer, by Olympic (67, 95, 114). A miniature version of the larger, pressurized sprayers used in big gardens, the Poly-Sprayer is pressurized with a few strokes of the pump handle. Lock the trigger handle to the on position, and you can spray continuously for about a minute, in either a jet or a fine mist.

For larger gardens, you may want to invest in a full-size, pump-action, pressurized sprayer (16, 67, 114). These sprayers resemble fat, old-fashioned fire extinguishers, but don't let their size or appearance intimidate you. You can mount the sprayer firmly to the seat of a Scoot 'n' Do with a length of cord or tape and pull it along, or strap it to the side of a wheelchair, walker, or scooter with a leather belt or length of Velcro tape. Once you pump up the pressure, you can spray for several minutes.

Pressurized backpack sprayers (16, 67, 114), which hold up to 5 gallons of liquid product, are heavy, and you may not be able to carry one, but it can be mounted behind a wheelchair and used very easily from a seated position, or placed in a garden cart or child's wagon and wheeled along. Because of their powerful jet-spray action, even the topmost branches of most fruit trees are within reach.

Trombone-style dusters, with a sliding stem action, have been around for years, but I don't recommend their use. Besides being awkward, they usually apply the dust unevenly and in too heavy a concentration, and cannot be used to apply liquids. A recent improvement, however, is the long-reach Spritzer (70, 164). This dust and spray wand allows you to spray at ground level without bending, and because the barrel is almost 30 inches long, you don't risk contact with the drift.

The lightweight, easy to hold Dustin' Mizer (16, 67, 70, 78, 114) is a good choice for accessible gardens. This hand-cranked duster is comfortable enough to be held in your lap, if you are a wheelchair gardener, and it has a long nozzle that can be directed at specific areas of the garden. A wide outlet opening ensures a fine, even application.

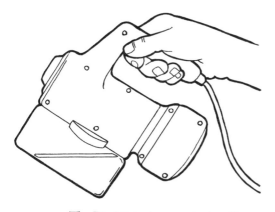

The Bio-Mister is a completely self-contained electric-powered sprayer that releases a fine mist of organic pyrethrin pesticide and water. Its light weight and easy-grip handle make it a good choice for the accessible garden.

SEEDERS

Planting seeds can be trying to those with limited visual acuity or reduced manual dexterity. Don't be too concerned with spacing seeds exactly; plant with a lavish hand and thin the seedlings later. Don't worry about straight rows, either. Wide-row and bed plantings, where seed is broadcast over a large area, are much easier, and close-spaced plantings require less weeding, watering, and mulching than do regularly spaced rows.

If you have trouble seeing small seeds, try mixing them with a little flour or powdered limestone before planting; the bright white powder is highly visible against dark earth. Use the back of your hand to cover or press seeds into the earth; it's easier than using your fingers, and you'll be less likely to poke seeds too deeply underground.

For tiny, fine seeds, use a syringe-type seed dispenser (67, 70, 78, 97) or a Seedmaster trowel (70, 95, 114), which has a dispenser built in. You fill the compartment with seeds and use your thumb to turn a small wheel that dispenses the seeds at a set rate. You can make your own seed dispenses by drilling small holes into a child's flat-bladed, plastic sand shovel. Gently shake the shovel over the prepared bed to broadcase fine seeds such as lettuce, beets, and carrots.

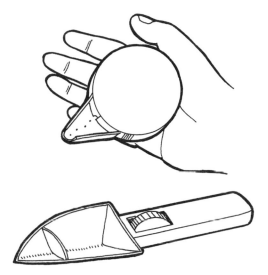

Sowing small seeds can be made easier with the use of seed dispensers that meter out the correct number of seeds per inch as you move down the row.

Seed tapes are another real time saver. Burpee's Seed Company (36) offers a wide variety of popular flower and vegetable seeds on tapes. You can make your own by cutting 1-inch-wide strips of paper towel. Dot the strips with a thin flour-and-water paste, sprinkle on seeds, wait a few minutes for the paste to set, and then shake off the excess seeds. The paper towel will disintegrate once it's planted in the earth. Use an EZ Reach tool to help you position the seed tape.

Another alternative is to make a gel from 1 tablespoon of cornstarch and 1 cup of water. Simmer the mixture over low heat until it becomes the consistency of thick honey. Allow to cool, then stir in seeds. Pour the mixture into a sealable plastic bag. Cut off one corner of the bag and use it as you would a pastry bag to squeeze out the seed-and-gel mix.

For visually impaired gardeners, a notched seeding stick makes seed and transplant spacing easier. You can make one from a wooden, raised-mark ruler or yardstick (101). Cut out small notches at 1-inch intervals all along the measuring stick, and use these notches to evenly space larger seeds like corn, peas, beans, beets, or okra along a row. Make every third notch a little bigger and you will not have to count each notch to figure out your spacing.

If you have a large garden and are able to get around fairly easily, you may want to invest in a wheel-type seeder (16, 67, 70, 78, 114), a sort of miniature wheeled plow that cuts a furrow and deposits seed with one motion. Several interchangeable plates are available to meter out the seeds according to their size and spacing requirements, helpful for the visually impaired gardener who may have trouble judging seed spacing. These seeders are best used in soft, loose, already-tilled soil, not as sod-busters. Improve your grip by wrapping the handlebars in foam rubber, and keep the furrow-cutting blade as sharp as possible to save effort.

ADAPTED TOOLS

A planting tube can be made from PVC pipe. Begin by measuring your hand's reach from the ground when you are in your normal gardening position (seated or standing). Cut a length of large-diameter pipe to match this distance, then cut one end at a 45-degree angle.

To use your PVC planting tube, scoop out a hole or dig a furrow where you wish to place seeds or small transplants. Position the angled end of the tube where you want the seed or transplant to go, pop a seed

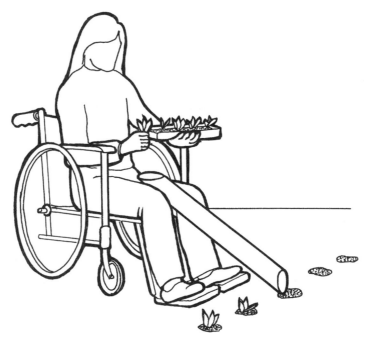

Wheelchair gardeners can use a planting tube made from large-diameter PVC pipe. Angle-cut both ends, and slide transplants or seed down the tube to prepared planting holes.

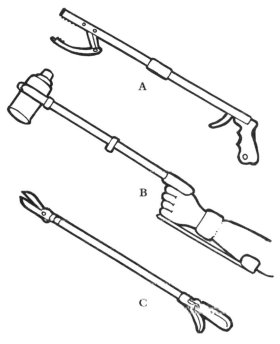

Reachers (A,B) provide the extra few inches of reach necessary to get to hanging pots, planters, overhead shelves, or the back of garden beds. The Winchester reacher (B) features a removable arm brace that makes it easier to lift and balance heavy objects. Seated gardeners can use cut-and-hold flower gatherers (C) as weeders.

or plant into the top end of the tube, tilt, and let it slide down the pipe and into the ground. If you have the dexterity to manage it, you can even use the angle-cut lower end of the pipe to cover the seed or firm the soil around the transplant. Use a funnel at the top of the tube to apply liquid or granular fertilizer.

For container or small-area gardeners with hand problems, consider buying a set of flexible cutlery (9, 40, 42, 47, 55, 57, 109, 110, 162) to use exclusively around your potted plants. These specially designed knives, forks, and spoons have big, soft, easy-grip handles and heads that can be bent up to 90 degrees in any direction to make them easier to use. In the kitchen and dining room, they make eating much easier, and in the garden, they can do the same for small-area weeding and cultivating. Even ordinary cutlery can be adapted, with a few judicious bends and kinks, to serve as specialized tools for the container gardener.

If you routinely use a long-reach gripper to help you around the house, then also keep one by your side while you work in the garden to help maneuver such things as bottles, sprayers, and small potted plants. The Winchester Reacher (9) has a handy locking mechanism that eliminates the need to squeeze the trigger to hold on to an object. It also features a removable arm brace that increases your strength when lifting or maneuvering heavy objects, and a clip to secure it to a wheelchair or walker when not in use. Look for reacher-grabbers with claws that close down to a size small enough to pick up even tiny, thin objects like dropped seed packets. Magnetized tips are another useful feature for picking up such things as twist-ties, tacks, and metal plant tags.

MOBILITY AIDS

Golf carts are excellent mobility aids for the accessible garden because of their simple controls, quiet and economical operation, and the ease with which they can be entered and exited. Check with local golf courses for sources of new carts, or ask if they have an older one that they might sell you.

If using a standard single-wheeled wheelbarrow is too much for your back, switch to a two-wheeled garden cart (15, 16, 46, 64, 67, 90, 114). These carts are designed with large, bicycle-type wheels mounted on a wide axle directly under the center of the load. This puts the weight of the load on the wheels, not on your arms and lower back, and you'll be able to move heavy loads—up to several hundred pounds—with amazing ease. The roomy, square body of most garden carts is also much better designed to carry bulky items like bags of leaves, bales of straw, or sacks of peat moss. When buying a garden cart, look for sturdy wheel and axle construction, sliding dump panels that make emptying the cart easier, strong but lightweight aluminum framing, and a weather-resistant exterior-grade plywood or plastic body. If storage space is at a premium, a collapsible design (34, 41, 44, 62, 92, 93, 157) that can be folded up for winter is another plus.

Electric Mobility Corporation (53) offers a two-wheeled garden cart that can be attached to the rear of any three-wheeled scooter or wheelchair alternative to form a sturdy, load-hauling trailer to transport large or fairly heavy items.

A garden scoot (15, 34, 42, 44, 67, 70, 78, 84, 114, 165) such as the Scoot 'n' Do is an invaluable aid when working in the garden. This comfortable small bench mounted on wheels allows you to sit down to garden and roll yourself along without much effort. Several models are available. The best feature a metal frame and wide, heavy-duty wheels. Added features include padded seat covers and saddlebags or compartments to carry tools and supplies. Most wheeled garden scoots sit about

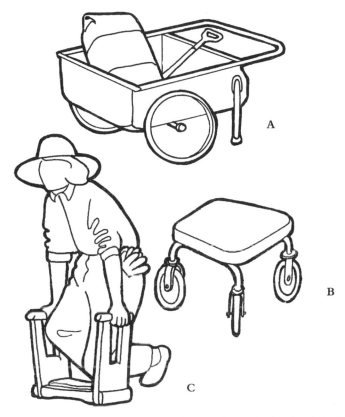

Garden carts (A), wheeled garden scoots (B), and reversible kneeler-benches (C) all make gardening easier on the legs, knees, and back.

10½ inches from the ground. If you cannot safely bend that low, you might be better off gardening from a lawn chair, with lightweight, long-handled tools. To keep the chair from sinking into soft soil or tipping over as you bend, attach 1-by-4 planks to the bottom of the legs. These runners will also allow you to slide the chair along the ground to move it.

Reversible kneeler-benches (15, 34, 44, 67, 70, 78, 97, 114, 148, 165) allow you to garden from either a sitting or kneeling position simply by turning the bench over. Its legs can be used as a support while you lower your body. When buying a kneeler-bench, look for a sturdy frame, thick padding, and durable, easily cleaned pad cover. Several brands of kneeler-benches come with add-on wheels to transform them into scooter seats.

If you are unable to garden with your knees bent, try slide boards, pieces of smooth, painted plywood 14 inches wide and 4 feet long with rounded corners so that they won't dig into the earth. Use two at a time, end to end. Place them on the ground where you'll be working, sit on one board, and slide yourself along the row. When you come to the end of the first board, slide onto the next, and leapfrog the first board to keep extending your work space.

Comfortable, heavy-duty kneepads (16, 37, 42, 67, 78, 114, 164) are available from several sources, or you can make your own by attaching pieces of foam padding covered with sturdy fabric to the knees of your gardening pants with velcro strips. These detachable knee pads are easily removed for laundering or re-covering when the fabric becomes worn. Be careful that knee pad straps do not pinch or bind behind the knee.

Make your own tool carrier–seat by wrapping a heavy-duty tool apron or belt (16, 67) around an empty 5-gallon plastic paint bucket. The apron or belt has several deep pockets to hold hand tools, seed packets, and spray bottles, and the bucket can be used as a seat as well as a carrying container. You can add a seat cushion if you wish.

Whenever possible, decrease the number of trips to and from the work site to get tools and supplies. Equip your scooter, wheelchair, or walker with pouches, saddlebags (1, 9, 42, 59, 110, 130, 131, 133, 141, 151), hooks, and clips, or wear a deep-pocketed apron, tool belt, or fanny pack to carry small tools and supplies. Install durable plastic mailboxes at strategic points throughout the garden and use them as tool caches. Use a wheeled carryall cart like those used for groceries or laundry to haul larger tools, buckets, baskets, and bags. Use a child's plastic toboggan or sled (9) to drag heavy loads; you'll be surprised at how easily even a heavily loaded sled moves across grass or smooth dirt.

SAFETY AND HEALTH

Your body is your most valuable gardening tool. Protect and care for it by using back support braces, gloves, hand braces, knee pads, and other protective devices. The following hints can help prevent injury or undue stress when gardening:

• Respect pain. Pain is the body's warning sign that something isn't right. When an activity causes pain, stop. Get help from another person, or try using an assistive tool or device to make the work easier on you.

• Avoid deforming postures or positions. Don't sit slouched over while you work, and don't rest your weight on one leg or one arm while you work. Poor posture and poor joint position can lead to pain, fatigue, and strains.

• Avoid staying in one position too long. Switch tasks often, going from bending jobs like picking beans to reaching jobs like trimming a vine. Bend, stretch, and move around often to avoid stiffness. Repetitive tasks can lead to injury, and overdoing it in the garden—trying to hoe just one more row or pull just a few more weeds—can cause inflammation, tenderness, and pain.

• Use the strongest and largest joints and muscles for the job. Use your legs, not your back, when spading or lifting. Use your forearm and elbow, not your wrist or fingers, when troweling. Use your palms to push levers or tools, not your fingers.

• Pace yourself. You don't have to mow all the lawn in one afternoon, or rake up all the leaves, or shovel the entire walkway of snow. Don't stress yourself to finish any task to schedule. Gardening is a relaxation hobby, not a job.

• Use splints, supports, and assistive devices wherever possible, but only after consulting with your physician or therapist. The wrong splint or support can cause damage.

• Follow all manufacturers' safety tips and instructions. Careless use of tools, or using tools at tasks for which they were not designed, invites injury. When using any tool—and especially power tools—be sure that you understand its operation thoroughly.

• Keep blades sharp, not only on knives and pruning shears, but on shovels, trowels, and hoes as well. Dull tools cause fatigue. Keep a whetstone close at hand, and slick up the edge on your tools as you work. You'll be amazed at the difference.

• Save your fingers. Tools can pinch or cut them, and the repetitive use of a finger, such as in pressing a squeeze-trigger spray bottle, can cause damage to tendons. Alternate finger-intensive activity with less demanding hand tasks, or switch from finger to finger as you work.

• Watch hands and wrists, which are particularly susceptible to tendinitis or carpal tunnel syndrome. Repeated grip-and-release movements, like those used in operating pruning shears, are a prime cause of hand and wrist discomfort. Switch from pruning to less hand-intensive work frequently, or alternate which hand you use.

• Carrying heavy objects like watering cans can also cause hand and wrist injury, especially if handles bite into flesh and cut off circulation. Make sure all handles and carrying straps are thick enough to provide you with a comfortable grip. Add comfortable, nonslip padding wherever necessary.

• Protect elbows and shoulders from damage caused by a lot of twisting and reaching. If you garden from a sitting position, make sure that your work surface is low enough that you won't have to raise your hands above or level with your shoulders.

CHAPTER EIGHT

Lawn Care

Ever since the development of gasoline-powered mowers, American homeowners have considered any landscape without a lush, velvety green lawn somehow deficient. The poor gardener who decides to adopt the live-and-let-live principle of lawn care in an upscale suburban neighborhood, his lawn a colorful carpet of clover and dandelion, is likely to call down the wrath of neighbors and community-action committees.

There are ways to make lawn care easier. The simplest is to hire someone else to do the work of weeding, feeding, watering, and mowing for you. But if you don't want to relinquish your turf to anyone else, there are alternatives you may want to explore.

Replacing some or all of your lawn with nonliving mulches like wood chips or pebbles, or with a living, no-mow ground cover like ivy or pachysandra, may seem like a great idea, but these alternatives pose maintenance difficulties of their own. Studies have shown that the average lawn—mowed regularly but not routinely watered, and fed and treated with pesticides only infrequently—requires far less maintenance time than the same area of ground cover. One hand weeding of a 6,600-square-foot area of English ivy took more time than it would take to mow the same area twenty times a year for sixty years. In many cases, judicious use of hard paving materials may be a better choice, both for low maintenance and higher accessibility.

But don't pave over the lawn yet. A well-maintained lawn enhances the curb value of a home, adding as much as 15 percent to the market value. Lawns serve as natural air and water filtration mechanisms by trapping enormous quantities of airborne dust, pollutants, and runoff from chemically treated gardens and adjacent areas—important to consider if you have allergies or respiratory problems, or get your drinking water from a private well or cistern. Lawns produce oxygen too: A 2,500-square-foot lawn daily releases enough oxygen for a family of four to breathe.

Lawns have a tremendous cooling effect on their surroundings. On hot days, lawns will be about 30 degrees cooler than asphalt or concrete and about 15 degrees cooler than bare soil. The average lawn has a cooling capacity more than double that of the average home air conditioner.

The key to a great, low-maintenance lawn is balance: the right combination of grass, water, mowing techniques, and nutrients. The wrong type of grass, poor watering techniques, under- or over-mowing, and the overuse of high-potency chemical fertilizers, pesticides, and weed killers throw off this balance. Once that happens, we find ourselves reacting to each new problem that presents itself with more quick-fix chemicals, more water, more fertilizer.

Because it takes the natural cycle of growth, dormancy, and regrowth into account, the well-balanced, accessible lawn requires less time and effort to maintain than a high-input chemically maintained lawn. And because it relies on natural methods of fertilization and weed and pest control, it is safe for people, pets, and wildlife.

SELECTING THE RIGHT GRASS

If you decide to establish a new lawn, the most important decision is what type of grass to grow. Whether you are putting in a seeded lawn by yourself, hiring a contractor to do it for you, or having a sodded lawn installed, contact your county cooperative extension agent for detailed information on grass types, cultivars, and maintenance requirements for your area. Every region has a particular strain of grass that does especially well there despite variations in soil conditions, local insect populations, and weather. Don't assume that your landscaper will automatically select the appropriate grass.

Lawn grasses are divided into three broad categories: cool-season, transitional, and warm-season grasses. Cool-season grasses grow best in areas with moderate summer temperatures and rainfall and cold winters. Popular cool-season grasses are Kentucky bluegrass, bent grass, fine fescue, and perennial ryegrass.

Transitional grasses do best in areas of hot, dry summers and cold, dry winters—conditions found in large parts of the American Midwest and high plains. They include blue grama grass, buffalograss, fairway crested wheat grass, and tall fescues. The first two perform optimally in warmer regions, the others in cooler regions.

Warm-season grasses, like Bermuda grass, centipede grass, St. Augustine grass, bahia grass, and zoysia grass, are drought-tolerant and cold-intolerant. They do best in areas of hot summers and warm, frost-free winters.

The best lawns are seeded with mixtures of grasses. This diversity ensures that the entire lawn won't be wiped out by disease or pests. In transitional regions, particularly, these mixes can be quite complex. Again, your county cooperative extension agent can give you the best information on the composition of lawn mixes.

The use of the lawn should also be considered. If your lawn will receive heavy foot or wheel traffic, then a tough sod of fescues, rye-grass, buffalograss, Bermuda grass, or zoysia grass is in order. If it will not get much use, you can plant less sturdy varieties like bluegrass or centipede grass. Shady areas are best seeded with fescues or St. Augustine grass; the other varieties need full sun. When given the choice between an old standby and a new cultivar, opt for the newest cultivars available; these usually have improved disease resistance and slower regrowth characteristics bred in. A lot of research is being done on dwarf and semidwarf grasses, most notably hybrids of native buffalo-grasses and hardy fescues, which may dramatically reduce the frequency of mowing. Two varieties of semidwarf low-mow grasses now available to homeowners are TurfAlive III and Mic 18, both through Gardens Alive! in Lawrenceville, Indiana. These grow much more slowly than regular grass mixtures and require mowing only about half as often to maintain a height of 2 or 3 inches.

Endophytic grass seed is a breakthrough in natural disease and insect resistance. Endophytes are fungal organisms that live in certain grasses. The fungi cause no harm to the grass but poison insects that eat the blades. Webworms, armyworms, aphids, cutworms, billbugs, chinch bugs, and some weevils are killed by endophyte-infected grass. Endo-phytic grass seed is becoming increasingly available across the country; check with your landscape contractor or county cooperative extension agent for sources.

Grass seed is fairly perishable, so check the side or back panel of the package for the germination test date before buying. Last year's seed likely won't come up.

PLANTING THE LAWN

Putting in a new lawn is a big job that requires a substantial amount of time and effort. The traditional method of clearing, leveling, raking, and dry or broadcast seeding is best reserved for small areas. For new lawns or for large reseeding projects, either hire a landscape contractor who specializes in hydroseeding or have a sodded lawn installed. Some lawn grasses, zoysia grass in particular, are established through plugs or sprigs, a job best left to hired help unless the area to be plugged is very small.

Hydroseeding uses a slurry of grass seed, mulch (usually finely ground peat moss or wood shavings), fertilizer, water, and possibly a preemergent herbicide. The slurry is applied to prepared bare ground with a high-pressure hose that can cover a large area quickly. Because several steps are done at one time, hydroseeding is a quick way to get a lawn planted, but because the seed must not be allowed to dry out, hydroseeding, like traditional broadcast-seeding methods, is best performed during the cool, damp weather of early spring or early autumn. It is not recommended for very small areas or very steep slopes.

The sodded lawn is the ultimate in ease and speed and is becoming increasingly popular. Initial preparation for sod lawns is identical to that for broadcast seeding or hydroseeding: Existing vegetation must be cleared, the soil tilled, raked, and leveled. Amendments like limestone or fertilizer must be worked in ahead of time. Never lay a sod lawn over an existing lawn or weeds. Turfgrass sod will not smother all plants growing beneath it, and weeds that survive will be hard to remove. Laying the lawn isn't too difficult—it's much like laying carpet or tile. For small areas, you may be able to do the work yourself; for larger projects, hire a professional.

The sodded lawn needs a lot of water for the first couple of weeks, until its roots become firmly attached to the underlying soil. After that, a sod lawn can be cared for just like any other.

Wholesale plugged or sprig-planted lawns are best avoided. The initial work required to insert small, individual grass plants into the lawn is intensive, and the effect is spotty and uneven for the first few months. Until the plugs spread and create a solid turf, weeds are a constant problem. Exposed areas between plugs allow the ground to dry out quickly, meaning constant watering. Reserve plugging or sprig planting for patching small areas of existing lawns.

MOWING HEIGHT

Each variety of grass has an optimum height at which it will have better root growth, slower regrowth, greater photosynthetic capacity, greater density, and less stress. A tight, healthy turf also helps prevent weeds from getting started, and grass is more disease- and insect-resistant when it isn't stressed from being cut too short. During spells of hot, dry weather, the grass should not cut be as short as during cool, rainy weather. The

TABLE 8-1:
Mowing heights for different grasses

Mowing to the correct height saves time and energy, and the grass will be healthier.

Grass	Recommended Height
Bermuda grass	$1-1^1/2$ inches
Bluegrass	$2^1/2-3$
Centipede grass	$1-1^1/2$
Fine fescue	$1^1/2-2^1/2$
Perennial ryegrass	$1^1/2-2^1/2$
St. Augustine grass	$2-3$
Tall fescue	$2^1/2-3^1/2$
Zoysia grass	$1-1^1/2$

figures presented in the accompanying table are good general mowing height guidelines. Recent studies, however, have found that mowing grass an inch higher than recommended substantially decreases mowing frequency without detracting from the appearance of the lawn. When consistently allowed to put on that extra inch of growth, most lawn grasses regrow more slowly, and the lawn will require less water.

MOWING EQUIPMENT

Self-propelled walk-behind mowers are ideal for small lawns and for gardeners who find walking at a slow, steady pace good exercise. Electric mowers are a better choice than gasoline-powered mowers because they are lighter, quieter, require less maintenance, and emit no noxious fumes. One of the best electric walk-behind mowers for those with disabilities is the cordless, battery-powered Ryobi Mulchinator (144), an easy-starting, self-propelled mulching mower that is lightweight and easy to maneuver, and requires little maintenance.

Make sure the mower you buy is equipped with an operator presence switch that stops blade rotation if you let go of the handle. Most newer models have this feature, but if your mower does not, an emergency shut-off switch can be made using a bicycle caliper-type hand brake and cable. For complete instructions on how to make and install this device, contact the Cerebral Palsy Research Foundation, Kansas Rehabilitation Engineering Center, 2021 North Old Manor, Wichita, KS 67208.

Even if you are a wheelchair gardener, you may not need to hire someone to mow your lawn for you. There are several hand-controlled riding mowers and garden tractors suitable for persons who have little or no use of their legs and feet, provided that they are in fairly good overall condition and are able to use their arms and hands without much restriction.

Walker Manufacturing (164) offers four hand-controlled lawn tractors or mowers. Several different gasoline and diesel engines are available, from 11 to the 25 horsepower. Mowing decks are available in a vacuum-and-bag, side-discharge, or mulching-blade style, in cutting widths from 36 to 62 inches. You can purchase optional attachments to convert the mower into a snowblower, a lawn dethatcher, a rotary broom for sweeping driveways and walks, or a miniature dozer or snowplow.

Because the hand controls are easily moved and operated, even someone with limited hand and arm mobility can safely operate a Walker mower. The mowing deck is mounted in front of and lower than the operator's feet, so the mower can negotiate tight spaces and sharp curves well. Other features include unobstructed forward and side visibility and a wide, comfortably positioned seat that allows the operator to slide easily from wheelchair or walker to mower.

Swisher Mower & Machine Company, Inc. (156), also has several models of riding and tow-behind lawn mowers particularly suited to those with special needs. The Swisher A2 Ride King and Swisher Big Mow are simple, highly maneuverable, hand-controlled mowers. Both

---

From Shirley Woodriff, Grants Pass, Oregon:

" I am a paraplegic, paralyzed below chest level. Before I got a riding mower, I was dependent upon someone else to keep the lawn mowed, a chore that I had always enjoyed prior to becoming wheelchair bound. Not only did the riding mower allow me to resume caring for my lawn, but it also provided me with a multifunctional tool that gives me easy access to the outdoors. Sometimes I get on it just to take a ride out in the field to park and read for a while among the cattle! My dogs think it's the greatest invention, because as I am more mobile, they also get to roam farther with me.

"I know that the mower has vastly improved my life."

Many riding mowers are totally hand controlled, making them accessible to gardeners with limited leg and foot mobility. Look for mowers with good front visibility, comfortable seats that make wheelchair-mower transfers easy, and optional roll bars, seat belts, and shoulder harnesses for greater safety and security.

have wide, padded seats for easy accessibility. The seats have very low backs and no armrests, however, so if you require additional support, you may have to purchase a high-backed seat from another manufacturer and have it mounted on the Swisher mower. Swisher offers baggers, side discharge, and mulching options for each mower.

Swisher Trailmowers are towable mowing units, about the size and shape of a big gasoline-powered push mover, that can be drawn behind any vehicle with sufficient horsepower to pull it, such as a lawn tractor or golf cart. If you have a battery-powered wheelchair of sufficient power, you may be able to use the Trailmower behind it, depending on the sturdiness and maneuverability of your chair; the size, slope, and shape of the lawn to be mown; and the security of the trailer hitch.

Power King (139) produces two small lawn-and-garden tractors that also meet special needs. Power steering is standard on Power King tractors, so they require only a light touch to maneuver. The 162OHV has a fender-mounted hydrostatic drive transmission with all forward and reverse motion controlled by hand, a wide, comfortable seat that is easy to get in and out of, and can be equipped with an optional roll-over protection cage and seat belts. The UT62OHV is similar except that it has foot-pedal forward-and-reverse operation, making it a good choice for someone with limited hand or arm mobility.

Dixon Industries, Inc. (47), makes a hand-controlled, zero-turning-radius riding lawn mower that is accessible to wheelchair gardeners. Push-pull hand levers control forward and backward motion, speed, and braking action. The seat is available in molded plastic or foam padded with armrests.

John Deere Company (93) makes one lawn tractor, the STX hydrostatic drive, that has hand-operated speed and direction control.

If you purchase a bagging-type mower, you may need assistance in removing and emptying the bag when it is full. A better option may be

a side-discharge mower or, better still, a mulching mower that eliminates the need for raking or bagging altogether. Mulching mowers are also better for the environment. High-nitrogen grass clippings will help nourish your lawn, cutting down on the amount of fertilizer needed. And because they form an absorbent, soil-building compost, your lawn will also require less water.

MOWING SAFETY

There are some safety points to remember when using any power mower:

• Do not mow any hillside with a slope greater than 20 degrees on a riding mower. Even the best-made, well-balanced mowers and tractors may tip over, and you could be seriously hurt.

• Before you mow, survey the lawn for stones, twigs, pets' or children's toys, hoses, and anything else that could be damaged or caught and flung by the mower blades.

• Keep pets and small children indoors and away from the area you're mowing.

• Until you are comfortable with your machine and the area being mowed, have someone stand by in case you need assistance.

• Keep your special needs in mind. In the pleasure of self-sufficiency and mobility in the great outdoors, it is easy to forget just how hot the sun can be, especially

For the ultimate in no-work lawn mowing, the Weed Eater solar-powered, no-maintenance robotic lawn mower is an "electric sheep" that quietly and inconspicuously "grazes" your lawn whenever the sun shines. Buried wires and an on-board electric sensor keep the robotic mower within bounds, and its small blades stop immediately on contact with solid objects like hoses, stones, or careless feet. Currently designed for use only on fairly level, moderate-sized ($1/3$- to $1/2$-acre) lawns, robotic mowers should be capable of a far wider range of applications in the future.

for someone whose sweat glands may not be functioning properly or who, because of medication, is sensitive to high temperatures or bright sunshine. Limit your mowing to the coolest part of the day—early morning after the dew has burned off or late afternoon—and mow on cloudy days. Wear sunscreen, protective clothing, and sunglasses. Take frequent breaks in the shade, and drink plenty of fluids.

• When fueling gasoline- or diesel-powered machinery, wear heavy-duty solventproof gloves, eye protection, and protective clothing to prevent getting any fuel on your skin or in your eyes. Refuel only in open air, never refuel a hot machine, and store fuel safely in metal or plastic cans, out of the sun.

• Have a qualified mechanic properly install any modification devices. Do not rig up something yourself in an attempt to turn your present, nonaccessible riding mower or tractor into a hand-controlled or foot-steerable design. Any modifications to power equipment must meet ANSI safety standards to be acceptable, and you could be seriously hurt if the work is not done properly and something goes wrong with you on board.

WATERING THE LAWN
Watering lawns probably provokes some of the greatest controversy among gardeners, homeowners, environmentalists, and landscape maintenance crews. It is a fact that to maintain a lush, green appearance, a constant and plentiful supply of water is necessary. It is also a fact that in most areas of the United States, the rainfall is insufficient to keep lawns green during summer months. In times of severe drought or in areas with chronic water shortages, the whole situation may be further complicated by restrictions on water use.

Grass has evolved to successfully deal with all types of weather conditions, however; there was grass long before the advent of sprinklers. In its natural growth cycle, grass is an opportunistic plant. While water is plentiful, it will make fast, heavy growth. When water is scarce, it will go dormant. Grass will draw moisture and nutrients down from its blades into the dense root system and simply wait out the dry spell. When water is once again plentiful, the growth cycle begins again.

While grass is dormant, it is no longer green. And a brown lawn can be a distressing sight to many people, even though it is part of the natural order of things.

There are two ways around this situation. First, you can simply ignore it. It has been proven that watering a lawn during hot, dry weather often causes more harm than good by encouraging the grass to

---

Special Note to Farmers and Ranchers

Several organizations for physically disabled farmers and ranchers exist to provide information, conferences, workshops, and personal support. Purdue University's Agricultural Engineering Department has created Breaking New Ground (BNG), a clearinghouse for innovative designs to help disabled farm workers regain accessibility to farm machinery. Among the items designed and produced by BNG are the Purdue Lift, a hydraulic chair lift that gives access to tractor cabs and seats, and devices that modify foot pedals to hand-operated controls.

The book *Agricultural Tools, Machinery & Buildings for Farmers and Ranchers with Physical Handicaps,* vol. 2, by W. E. Field, available through the Breaking New Ground Resource Center (33) of Purdue University, describes professionally designed modification devices that convert existing foot controls into hand-operated controls.

Other organizations include the International Conference on Rural Rehabilitation Technology (ICRRT), which compiles the Rural Rehab Technologies Database catalog of inventions, ideas, innovations, and resource outlets of benefit to farm workers and rural residents in general.

The Physically Challenged Farmers of Alberta works to promote the capabilities of disabled farmers and ranchers and works as a network to connect people to resources and support groups.

Family Farm Rehabilitation Management (FaRM) is an offshoot of the Breaking New Ground project that offers free referral services, work-site modification consultations, vocational counseling, job placement, and peer support services to disabled rural residents.

For further information on these organizations, contact them at the addresses listed in appendix B.

---

continue growing when it should be resting. Allowing the grass to become yellow and dormant during drought periods may be the best course to follow, as well as the easiest. Only in the severest drought will lawns actually die.

Recent research shows that during summers of average temperature, with no rainfall, most lawns can be kept unwatered and dormant for up to two months before suffering damage. During spells of extremely hot, dry weather, lawns can stay dormant for only three to five weeks. Giving dormant lawns a light watering of 1/2 inch of water once a week during very hot drought periods will keep the grass alive but will not break its dormancy, which could be fatal.

The second solution to a dry, brown lawn is to water it deeply once a week. Frequent, light watering is a great killer of grass. To be beneficial, you must apply enough water to thoroughly soak the ground— about 1 full inch. For small areas, a hose my be sufficient, but sitting or standing outside, under a hot sun with hose in hand is not what most people would consider an ideal way to spend a summer afternoon. You can purchase hose towers (15, 114, 164) to hold the hose for you, but because they are stationary, most of the water will be applied in one small spot. To cover a wider area of grass, you'll need a sprinkler.

Oscillating hose-end sprinklers, available in a wide variety of shapes and sizes in nearly every hardware store and catalog, can cover fairly large areas of lawn pretty efficiently. In hot weather, however, a great deal of water can be lost to evaporation as the water is jetted high into the air. If you use a hose-end sprinkler, run it during the coolest part of the day—early morning or late afternoon—and never when it is windy. Lawns can be watered during the night, but this may increase the incidence of fungal diseases. Get a good timer (see chapter 6), and set it to run for the time it takes to accumulate 1 inch of water in a cup set on the lawn where the sprinkler can reach it.

By far the easiest and most efficient way to water your lawn is to install a permanent, underground sprinkler system. Primarily an option for gardeners living in a frost-free area, permanent lawn sprinkler systems are the ultimate in accessible watering devices. They are expensive, however, and should be installed professionally. Before installing a permanent system, think carefully about any future landscaping changes you may want to make. The addition of a ramp, walkway, patio, or deck may necessitate digging up and repositioning or eliminating a portion of the sprinkler system. If possible, have the system installed by a landscape design firm that understands your special requirements. They will have the knowledge and expertise needed to advise you on the most effective layout for the system.

FERTILIZING THE LAWN

Chemical fertilizers gradually erode the health of the soil in two ways: by lowering soil pH levels, thereby binding up valuable nutrients, and by slowly killing off the population of soil microorganisms that work to compost plant wastes and free up nutrients. Lawns fed a regular diet of chemicals may look fine and seem to perform well, but they are totally dependent on a steady input of fertilizers, pesticides, herbicides, and supplemental water. Such lawns have no place in the low-maintenance, accessible landscape.

Because most chemical fertilizers are ammonium or urea based, both highly acidic compounds, they lower soil pH levels. And because grass grows best in a neutral or only slightly acidic soil, the use of these chemicals makes it necessary to apply limestone to the lawn. Although you may notice rapid green-up and lush growth for the first several years, with time, if the pH level is not brought up with regular applications of limestone, grass begins to exhibit stress. Low soil pH levels tie up phosphorus, potassium, calcium, and magnesium, making them unavailable to plant roots, and the soil may exhibit patches of yellow or brown, symptoms of aluminum, iron, manganese, and zinc toxicity.

A chemically dependent lawn cannot be cut off overnight from the chemicals on which it depends. You must follow a gradual process, and your lawn will be pretty ragged for a while.

Begin by halving the spring and autumn applications of chemical fertilizer. Finely sifted, well-rotted manure or finished compost is the safest and best fertilizer for your lawn. Apply it twice a year, in early spring and late fall. Apply lightly—just enough to be barely visible over the grass. Use either a broadcast- or drop-type spreader to do the job. If you are a wheelchair gardener, you can use the broadcast spreader held between your knees. Drop-type spreaders are usually light enough to be pulled behind a riding mower, a scooter, or a powered wheelchair, if you can rig a hitch.

To increase the potency of compost lawn fertilizer, add a pound of Epsom salts to a couple bushels of compost before spreading. As soon as you're finished, mix together 2 cups of beer (or a package of dry yeast to 2 cups warm water) and 1/2 cup of dishwashing liquid in a hose-end sprayer jar, and water the lawn thoroughly. Beer contains microorganisms that will speed up the decomposition of grass clippings on the lawn, and detergent will make it able to penetrate more deeply.

Insects and diseases are drawn to weak plants. Once a month, disinfect your entire lawn by adding 1 cup of antiseptic mouthwash when you water. An in-line injector (16, 34, 49, 67) for your sprinkler hose is the easiest way to do this.

To add a steady supply of nitrogen to lawns, sprinkle white Dutch clover seed into patchy areas of your lawn, or add one part clover seeds to every ten parts of grass seed when you reseed. Clover is a nitrogen-fixing legume whose roots draw airborne nitrogen into the soil; the excess is available for other plants growing nearby. Clover's deep root structure will also help open up compacted or heavy clay soils.

If you use a mulching lawn mower, you'll need to water and feed much less often, since the decomposing clippings will add nutrients to the lawn and form a light, water-retentive mulch.

WEEDING

Herbicides are among the most dangerous of yard and garden chemicals on the market. Use them as sparingly as possible, spot-treating weeds rather than spraying the entire lawn. If you use a professional lawn-care service, ask whether a nonchemical alternative is available.

Crabgrass is the bane of both newly planted organic lawns and lawns recovering from chemical dependency. A-maizing, available through Gardens Alive!, is a safe, organic, preemergent herbicide based on corn syrup by-products that works by suppressing the germination of weed seeds in the soil. It won't kill established weeds, but it will stop annual weeds from coming back. As an added benefit, it decomposes quickly and adds nitrogen to the lawn.

To spot-treat lawn weeds, try organic weed killers based on concentrated fatty acid compounds. These will wipe out most shallow-rooted weeds like chickweed and crabgrass, although they won't permanently remove deep-rooted weeds like chicory or dandelions. To deal with these tough customers, you'll have to learn to live with them, dig them out, or spot-treat with a chemical herbicide like Round-Up or Finale. Both kill *anything* green, so be very careful. These compounds break down quickly, however, and have no residual effect in the soil. You can safely plant grass seed a week after treatment.

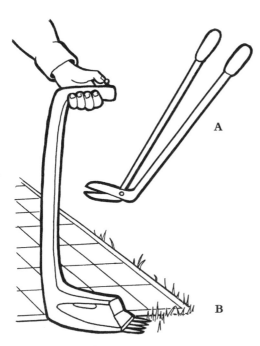

Long-handled clippers (A) and powered long-handled grass trimmers (B) make trimming grass along walls, walkways, and around tree trunks much easier on the back and knees.

> *From Jeff Vining, Griffin, Georgia, a quadriplegic who manages a successful lawn maintenance company and is presently developing a tract of land to be used as a vocational-recreational rehabilitation center for other paralyzed persons:*
>
> "Before my surfing accident, I used to do it all. If the break had been a little higher, I would have been paralyzed from the neck down. A little lower, and I would have total use of my hands. Do as much as you can possibly do. I could sit in the chair and twiddle my thumbs, or make good with what I have."

DETHATCHING

Thatch is formed by dead grass roots that have grown too near the surface, usually because of overfertilization and light, frequent watering during dry spells. It is not formed by accumulated grass clippings. A thick thatch layer will gradually kill grass, because water can't easily penetrate it, it dries out quickly and kills any roots growing through it, and it makes a fine hiding place for lawn-damaging insects and disease spores. Heavily thatched lawns also usually exhibit dense, compacted soil structure just below the shallow root line of the grass.

To remove heavy thatch, you must rake it out with a metal garden rake or buy or rent a mechanical dethatcher. Light thatch can be removed with an organic dethatcher, like Thatch Buster. These products contain high concentrations of the same microorganisms that are used in compost activators. They speed up the decomposition of the thatch layer, then move down into the compacted lifeless soil below and increase valuable microbial action there.

To prevent thatch buildup, follow the mowing, watering, and feeding guidelines presented above.

RAKING LEAVES

If you have deciduous trees growing in your lawn, you have leaves to rake. To eliminate this chore, two solutions exist: cut down the trees or get rid of the grass. By far the more aesthetic and environmentally sound option is to get rid of the grass. Replace lawn areas that fall within the drip line of large trees with mulch or densely planted shade-loving ground covers or shrubs. Leaves falling onto these areas provide natural fertilization, winter protection, and soil-building compost to the plants beneath.

Enormously overgrown trees, especially those varieties whose large limbs tend to break off easily (ash and silver maple are among the worst), may be better removed and replaced. When selecting trees as replacements or as new plantings, opt for smaller, fine-leaved varieties like birch, flowering crab apple, cherry, or dogwood. Not only do these trees produce fewer leaves because of their small size, but their leaves are fine enough to virtually disappear into the lawn without raking. (See chapter 9 for a list of low-maintenance trees for the accessible landscape.)

Some raking may still be necessary to maintain a neat appearance on your property. The easiest way to "rake" your lawn is to mow it. Mowing fallen leaves, even without a vacuum-and-bag system to collect them, will shred the leaves finely enough to all but eliminate them. An added benefit of this shredding action is that it turns the leaves into fertilizer for your lawn, adding nutrients and water-holding humus to the soil.

Hand raking is made much easier with ergonomically designed back-saver rakes (15, 67, 143), with angled handles that allow you to stand upright while raking. Seated gardeners may find ordinary, straight-handled rakes made of lightweight bamboo or aluminum easier to use. You can use your garden scoot when raking, especially if standing for long periods of time tires you easily.

Raking leaves and grass clippings need not be a back-breaking chore, especially when using the new ergonomically designed Back Saver rake and a lightweight, folding leaf cart. which makes it a snap to gather and transport up to 15 bushels of yard wastes to the compost heap.

To gather leaves easily and efficiently without bending and lifting, rake them onto a large sheet or tarpaulin, gather up the corners when full, and drag the leaves away. Better yet, purchase a folding leaf cart (15, 46, 97), an ingenious wheeled device made of lightweight nylon mesh fabric mounted on a folding, tubular framework. To use, you unfold it, rake leaves directly into it, then tilt it up and roll it away. It weighs only 16 pounds empty and will hold several bushels of leaves at a time.

Electric-powered landscape vacuums (15, 16, 67), such as the McCullough Mac-Vac, are another option. Working just like an ordinary vacuum cleaner, these machines pick up leaves, pine needles, grass clippings, paper, and other lightweight debris. They aren't designed to handle hard, nonorganic items like rocks, cans, or broken glass, so don't use them for litter pickup. They are fairly lightweight (about twice the weight of an indoor vacuum cleaner), roll easily over most outdoor surfaces, and are easy to start and use. As with any power tool, try one out before buying.

A corollary to autumn leaf raking is gutter cleanout. Leaves that accumulate in rain gutters and downspouts can cause clogs, leading to roof and siding damage. Consider having mesh leaf guards installed over

Pushing, rather than shoveling, snow out of the way is easier on the back and the cardiovascular system. The Back Saver snow shovel (A) has a bent handle that allows you to push without bending. A wheeled shovel (B) makes pushing easier. The wide-capacity Big Scoop (C) acts like a mini-snow plow to clear large areas quickly. For small driveways and narrow walks, an "electric broom" type snowblower (D) is ideal.

your rain gutters. Failing this, or if the mesh guards become heavily covered with leaves, you may have to hire someone to get up there and clean the leaves away. If you have good arm and upper-body strength, you may be able to clean the gutters from ground level, using a special gutter rake (15). These tools have handles that extend to 14 feet, with a specially curved rake attached to the end that reaches into the gutters.

LAWN ALTERNATIVES

Wildflower Meadows

Many homeowners decide to do away with part or all of the grass around their homes by replacing the lawn with an unmown wildflower meadow. This is very nice in rural areas, especially in places that are particularly difficult to maintain—along ditches, on steep embankments, or in rocky or swampy terrain. Before replacing your bluegrass turf with an unmown meadow, however, talk with your neighbors and consult the local zoning board. Many people find the look of a wildflower lawn unsightly (one man's wildflower is another man's weed), and some communities have ordinances forbidding unmown or "weedy" areas around homes.

Even if a wildflower meadow is acceptable in your community, establishing such a meadow is neither easy nor quick. The existing turf must be entirely removed, either chemically or physically. Once the grass is gone, the earth must be tilled very lightly—no deeper than an inch—just enough to loosen it for the wildflower seeds, but not so deep that dormant weed seeds are brought to the surface to germinate. After seeding with wildflowers, the area must be watered and weeded religiously until the desired plants are well established, usually one full year. Each year, in the late summer to early autumn, you should mow the meadow to help scatter the ripened wildflower seeds. No regular lawn mower will go through such growth; you'll have to rent or hire a "brush hog" mower.

Even with judicious care, the hardiest and most aggressive plants usually will come to dominate a wildflower meadow. Goldenrod, Queen Anne's lace, thistle, and chicory may soon crowd out more delicate cornflowers, poppies, and cosmos. If you can accept this process of natural selection, then by all means plant a wildflower meadow. If you have your heart set on a colorful tapestry of many different types of flowers, be prepared to reseed weaker species and thin out aggressive ones fairly frequently.

Grass and Wildflower Mixes

Lawn-grass and wildflower mixes offer homeowners the best of both worlds: the untamed beauty of a wildflower meadow, with the more civilized aspects of a mown, albeit rather long, lawn. Only low-growing, mow-tolerant flower varieties are used in these mixes, along with hardy grasses. English daisies, yarrow, clovers, buttercups, violets, and other flowers are usually mixed in about a one-to-five ratio with grass seed. If you're adventurous, you can experiment with your own custom blends of grass seed and wildflowers to create an elegant, low-maintenance, subtly colorful carpet for your accessible landscape.

Ground Covers

Ground covers are another popular alternative to grass. As noted above, however, it is often more labor intensive to establish and maintain ground covers than to mow a lawn. Use a ground cover only in areas where grass (and weeds) will not grow, such as under trees or in very shady or dry areas under overhanging eaves. Some ground covers, like Roman chamomile, are hardy enough to stand up to occasional foot traffic—and walking across a bed of chamomile releases a wonderful fragrance into the air. Most ground covers will not tolerate heavy traffic, however, and are best reserved for areas away from the beaten path. When planting ground cover near pathways, select nonvining varieties like lamium, chamomile, speedwell, or thyme. Avoid aggressively viny plants like ivy and pennywort; the vines trailing across pathways can cause tripping hazards or tangle in wheelchair and scooter wheels.

Select ground covers for the amount of sunlight they will receive: full sun, sun to partial shade, or dense shade. A few varieties will do well in all three locations, but most plants are particular. For the least maintenance and the lowest risk of failure, select the best possible plant for the site.

Mulches

Attractive inorganic (nonliving) alternatives to lawns include raked gravel, pebbles, pine-bark mulch, and cocoa hulls. Don't lay these over bare ground, though; you'll have a constant battle with weeds. Areas to be mulched must first be thoroughly stripped of vegetation, using a nonselective organic herbicide or dousing the area with salt and vinegar. Put down a layer of weedproof fabric such as Typar or Weed-X, plastic, cardboard, or paper (HortoPaper or several layers of newsprint). Tape seams and fasten the edges securely so that sunlight cannot penetrate to

TABLE 8.2:
Ground covers for various locations

Choose the appropriate ground cover for the amount of sunlight the area receives.

Full Sun

Ground Cover	Description	Zone
Anacyclus depressus (Mount Atlas daisy)	Daisy-flowered. Heat- and drought-resistant.	6–10
Arctostaphylos uva-ursi (bearberry)	Birds love the berries. Will withstand salt spray.	2–8
Ceratostigma plumbaginoides (plumbago)	Brilliant blue flowers; leaves tinged with purple or red; 6-10 inches tall. Very hardy and reliable; will grow anywhere.	5–9
Chrysanthemum pacificum or *Dendranthema pacificum* (gold and silver chrysanthemum)	Dense mats of 12-inch-tall rich green foliage edged in gold. Small yellow flowers appear sporadically.	5–9
Clematis spp. (clematis vine)	Clematis vines can be allowed to trail down banks to provide ground cover as well as beautiful flowers all summer long. Many colors.	5–9
Conradina verticillata (conradina)	Rosemarylike plant with soft blue flowers to 6 inches. Needs full sun, sandy soil.	6–11
Coronilla varia (crown vetch)	A coarse, leguminous plant, growing up to 24 inches tall, covered with pink flowers throughout the summer. Best used in mass plantings on steep banks or unmowable areas.	3–9
Cotoneaster spp. (Cotoneaster)	Several varieties of low-growing cotoneasters can be used as ground cover. Bright red berries throughout the winter.	6–8
Dianthus spp. (dianthus)	To 12 inches; spicy, fragrant flowers throughout summer.	3–8
Euonymus spp. (euonymus)	A large group of landscape shrubs. Low-growing climbing and trailing varieties, some variegated, make dense matts of evergreen foliage.	5–9
Fragaria 'Pink Panda' (strawberry)	The only ground cover strawberries; covered with pink flowers spring to fall; sets a few flavorful fruits.	3–9

Ground Cover	Description	Zone
Geranium spp. (cranesbill)	The perennial *Geranium* genus, not the *Pelargonium* raised as potted flowering plants. Perennial geraniums are extremely hardy, do well under most soil conditions, and spread freely. Small-flowered pink, white, purple, and blue varieties available.	3–8
Hemerocallis spp. (daylily)	Daylilies form masses of thick, green, straplike foliage and are great for covering large areas or steep banks. Traditional tawny orange daylilies are often seen growing wild; hybridized varieties are in all colors of the rainbow. From 2 to 3 inches tall.	3–9
Mentha spp. (mint)	Many low-growing varieties of mints, including pennyroyal, can be used as ground cover; very invasive, so use barriers.	3–10
Delosperma nubigenum (ice plant)	Drought- and heat-resistant. Good for arid regions; used as a firebreak in some areas.	5–10
Sedum spurium (stonecrop)	Succulent, prostrate, spreading plants form dense mat, covered in late summer or fall with lavender, yellow, or red flower heads. Needs little care.	3–8
Thymus spp. (creeping thyme)	All creeping thymes make good full-sun ground covers. *T. serphyllum coccineus* is red flowered.	5–9
Verbena spp. (verbena)	Fragrant, 10–18 inches tall, pink, purple, white, or lavender.	7–10
Vinca minor (periwinkle or trailing myrtle)	Dark green with soft lavender flowers. 6 inches tall.	4–9

Sun to Partial Shade

Aegopodium podagraria (bishop's weed)	Bright green and variegated varieties brighten dark areas.	3–9
Ajuga spp. (bugleweed)	Green- or purple-leaved varieties, some with pink or white flowers.	4–9
Arabis ferdinandi coburgi (white snowcap)	Clouds of tiny white flowers on 5-inch plants. Prefers alkaline soil.	6–9
Capanula portenschlagiana (dalmatian bellflower)	Dwarf, 6-inch spreading variety, soft blue flowers.	4–9

continued

TABLE 8.2: (Continued)

Ground Cover	Description	Zone
Houttuynia cordata (chameleon plant)	Korean natives with spectacular variegated foliage. Small white flowers on 6- to 9-inch plants. Does best in moist woodland soils.	3–8
Hypericum calycinum (Saint-John's-wort)	Bright yellow flowers on deep green foliage. 12–18 inches.	5–8
Juniperus spp. (juniper)	A number of low-growing, spreading junipers can be used as ground covers. 'Blue Rug' is by far the lowest growing, followed by 'Blue Pacific', 'Bar Harbor', and 'Broadmoor'. 'Prince of Wales', 'Blue Tamarix', 'Blue Chip', 'Green Mound', and 'Blue Star' are also low-growing blue to green junipers. A unique golden juniper, 'Mother Lode', is a yellow sport of 'Blue Rug'.	4–9
Lamium maculatum (dead nettle)	Soft, heart-shaped leaves, some varieties with striking colors. Blue, pink, or white flowers. 6–9 inches.	4–9
Liriope muscari (lilyturf)	Straplike leaves with long panicles of white flowers. 12–15 inches. Best in shade.	6–10
Lysimachia vulgans (loosestrife)	New from China. Yellow-flowered, spreading plant.	7–9
Omphalodes verna (blue-eyed Mary)	Shiny green leaves and tiny blue flowers. 8 inches.	5–8
Phlox subulata (moss pink or thrift)	Forms carpets of dense, brilliantly colored flowers in red, pink, white, purple, or lavender.	2–9
Rosa spp. (rose)	Low-growing, spreading roses like the 'Meidiland' series and 'Sea Foam' can be used as ground covers anywhere they will have room to spread. Fragrant flowers throughout summer. Zones vary depending on variety.	4–9
Shade		
Asarum europaeum (European ginger)	Rounded, fleshy bright green leaves. 6–8 inches. Hardy.	4–7
Chrysogonum virginianum (golden star)	Yellow, daisylike blooms, long bloom season. Tolerates sun in colder climates.	5–9

Ground Cover	Description	Zone
Coptis groenlandica (eastern goldthread)	Spreading mats covered with white, buttercuplike flowers.	3–7
Daphne cneorum (garland flower)	Dwarf, spreading variety. Sweetly scented pink flowers 9–12 inches.	4–7
Epimedium x *perralchicum* (epimedium)	Evergreen foliage, yellow flowers. Does best in moist, woodland soils. 12 inches.	5–8
Erythronium spp. (dogtooth violet)	White, yellow, pink, or purple flowers.	4–8
Euphorbia robbiae (euphorbia or spurge)	Dark, evergreen leaves with large, lime green bracts. Steady spreader, but not invasive.	7–11
Galium ordoratum (sweet woodruff)	Lacy, bright green leaves and sweet, hay-scented white flowers through spring and summer. 6–8 inches.	4–8
Hedera helix (English ivy)	Will tolerate even heavy shade. Good climber, and can be invasive.	5–10
Hosta spp. (hosta or funkia)	Many varieties; bright green, blue, white- or gold-variegated.	3–9
Mazus reptans (mazus)	Low-growing, spreading, very tough. Will withstand some foot traffic. Shell-like lavender flowers.	5–9
Meehania cordata	Heart-shaped leaves and mauve, trumpet-shaped flowers in spring. Hardy native plant.	3–8
Microbiota decussata (Siberian carpet cypress)	Dense, low-growing cypress tolerates even heavy shade.	2–8
Pachysandra terminalis (pachysandra)	Does well even in dense shade. Soft green foliage brightens dark spots.	4–9
Pulmonaria saccharata, P. angustifolia (Bethlehem sage, blue cowslip)	Dense, spreading clumps with pink flowers fading to blue in spring.	4–9
Rhododendron spp. (azalea)	Smaller varieties of azaleas can be planted under trees, especially 'Hilda Niblett'. Zones vary depending on variety.	5–9

stimulate weed seeds to sprout. Use loose, easily dislodged materials like rounded pebbles only on fairly level areas; on steeper slopes, especially near pathways, choose stable mulches like heavy bark nuggets. Keep mulches off pathways to prevent trips and spills.

When buying organic mulches, smell them first; they should smell sweet and woodsy. A strong ammonia scent indicates an early stage of decomposition, and the release of ammonia gas may be harmful to sensitive plants. If nearby plants wilt or turn yellow after mulching, rake it back and allow it to dry in the sun a few days before reapplying.

• CHAPTER NINE •

Accessible Landscapes

L ow-maintenance plants add greatly to the pleasures of the accessible landscape. Take a moment to evaluate your present landscape. Do you spend more time caring for it than enjoying it? Do some areas need frequent replanting to keep them looking their best? Are there particular plants that require constant attention throughout the season? Do some require protection from cold, heat, or sun? You might be better off without them.

A certain amount of emotional fortitude is required to pull up and discard delicate specimens that you've nurtured along for years. You need not replace them all at once. Start with a few plants that you know are not suited to a low-maintenance garden, dig them up, and give them to gardening friends who may welcome the challenge. Successful gardening is a process of evolution and adaptation: no garden is ever complete, no garden is ever static. Gradually incorporate change into your accessible garden, rather than making an abrupt and transition.

Study the microclimates present in even the smallest gardens. Areas of dense shade are cooler than spots receiving full sun; low spots tend to collect cold air and frost; the south side of the house is warmer and more sheltered than the north or west. Boggy spots, rocky hillsides, planting areas enclosed by paving—all these areas present microclimates that may make it easier to look after a particular plant.

PERMACULTURE

Permaculture, or naturescaping, is a way of gardening that works with, rather than against, nature. It drastically reduces the amount of effort needed to sustain any landscape, and it is ecologically sound as well,

From Dr. John O. Dunbar, director of Kansas Agricultural Experiment Station, College of Agriculture, Kansas:

"I have a well-landscaped yard and flower garden, and a houseful of plants. When I go home from work, one of the first things I do is walk around the house and see what has happened to these plants. If it has been an especially frustrating day, I will take another tour to see what I missed the first time, then I'll pull some weeds and see what needs attention. This gets me started. I might spend two or three hours gardening and releasing tensions. I know the value and joys—the therapy—of horticulture."

providing habitat for small wildlife, reducing or eliminating the need for chemical fertilizers and pesticides, and conserving water.

To practice permaculture, observe the natural partnerships, or "guilds," that occur in your region. Note which plants or types of plants seem to consistently grow together, and try to mimic those relationships in your own landscape. A stroll or drive through a woodland will make you aware of one simple fact that we seem to have forgotten: Grass rarely grows under trees. Brambles, ferns, creeping plants, shrubs, and flowering bulbs all grow happily beneath most deciduous trees, and even some evergreens, but not grass. By following nature's lead and planting blueberry bushes or flowering azaleas beneath that birch or maple in the front yard, you'll reduce the amount of effort needed to care for your landscape: When you mow, you won't have to content with bumpy roots and low-hanging branches, you'll no longer have to wrap the tree trunk to protect it from mower bruises, and fallen leaves disappear into the shrubby undergrowth.

Observe an open meadow to see other "guilds" at work. Umbel-flowering plants like Queen Anne's lace, milkweed, and butterfly weed attract bees and other pollinating insects, and fruit-bearing plants like blackberries or wild roses are likely to be found nearby. By encouraging similar plant combinations in the home orchard, berry patch, or vegetable garden, you can improve the pollination—and hence the fruit production—of your crops. Second-year flowering carrots, cabbage, and parsley, as well as dill, thyme, and yarrow, are all good umbel-flowering plants for use in the garden. As an added benefit, predatory beneficial insects like wasps, spiders, lacewings, lady beetles, and praying mantises are also attracted by these flowering plants. The result: instant, all-natural "insecticide."

Design these natural "guilds" into your accessible landscape and you will reduce effort and increase yields.

From Dr. Richard Mattson, HTM, Department of Horticultural Therapy, Kansas State University:

" Our minds must be exercised just as our bodies. We have a need for nurturance: we need to be continually developing caring human relationships. Our gardens also need care and nurturance in order to thrive. We have to assume responsibility for our actions. As our plants grow and respond to our loving care, we feel better about our achievements and ourselves. Our self-image and self-concept are enhanced. We appreciate the value of life and our place in the natural world.

"As we appreciate beauty, we are more content, and happiness is not a rare occasion. We are more tolerant, more accepting, and spiritual needs are met through an increased awareness of a higher order of creation."

TREES

Trees are by far the most visible part of any landscape. They can provide cooling shade, protection from harsh winds, fruit for humans and animals, and springtime bloom or autumn color. The right tree in the right place adds immeasurably to the beauty and value of any property; conversely, the wrong tree can be a constant source of trouble and expense.

Shade Trees

Do not underestimate the mature size of a baby tree. That frail red maple sapling looks so tiny it's easy to forget that in fifteen to twenty-five years it will attain a height of 30 to 60 feet and a spread of nearly 40 feet. If your property is large enough to accommodate great trees like red oak, weeping willow, ash, maple, sycamore, and umbrella pine, by all means plant them. But in most home landscapes, trees should have mature heights of no more than 35 feet. Many beautiful flowering trees fall into this range, as do a number of trees grown primarily for their shape or autumn colors.

Hugely overgrown trees block the front views from this home, make growing and mowing grass nearly impossible around their protruding roots, and dump tons of leaves on the lawn, roof, and gutters, every autumn.

The decision to remove a healthy but overgrown tree is difficult for most gardeners. Yet the alternative decision to top or prune a mature tree in hopes of reducing its size or the quantity of autumn leaves to rake is disastrous. No outdoor tree can be pruned to control its size without sacrificing its beauty and health. A mature tree should be pruned only to remove dead, broken, or diseased limbs; to thin the crown to admit sunlight and air for the benefit of the tree; or to "limb up" a low-growing tree so that it can be walked under. Pruning a tree for any other reason is pointless, unnecessarily costly, and in some cases potentially dangerous.

A tree's main trunk and limbs will continue to grow upward despite drastic, heavy-handed attempts at pruning. Severe cutting back will only result in a malformed specimen prone to disease, insects, or storm

It's a difficult decision to remove large, healthy, trees from the landscape, but the improvement is immediately apparent. Smaller-scale, fine-leaved, ornamental trees like flowering crab apples, paper birches, golden rain trees, or dogwoods let in sunlight and enhance rather than hide the front entrance to the home. Heavily mulching or planting ground cover around their bases make mowing easier.

damage. By depriving a tree of most of its large limbs (and therefore its leaves), you slowly starve it to death. It may produce a flush of new growth in the spring, but this is not a sign of vitality; rather, it is the tree's desperate attempt to survive by channeling all its reserve strength into repairing its damaged crown. Nutrients that should be going down into the roots are forced upward to produce new growth, and the root system is often severely compromised. Roots anchor the tree to the ground; once those roots are weakened, the tree may topple in high winds or under heavy snow loads.

Do not attempt major pruning jobs on sizable trees yourself. Hire a professional. Check out tree services in your area by asking for references, then go out and look at their work. Avoid one-man-one-chain-saw outfits that recommend topping a tree to reduce its size. Hand tools, power tools and chippers, ladders, and cranes mark a high-quality, professional firm. Make sure the arborist you choose is licensed, insured, and bonded in case anything goes wrong.

Once you choose a tree service, discuss the job with the person who will do the actual work. Don't rely on relayed, over-the-phone instructions. Show the pruner your tree's problem areas. If possible, stay nearby (but well away from the actual work area) during the entire operation. Inspect the finished work before the team leaves and before you pay. Look for cleanly cut, short stubs where limbs have been removed, and insist on a thorough cleanup of debris. A good tree service should not damage lawns and surrounding plantings with truck tires, equipment, or fallen limbs. When a tree has been entirely removed, ask that the stump be removed also. In some cases, this may require backhoe work; in others, a mechanical grinder can be used to reduce the stump to sawdust without digging up the lawn.

Reputable arborists may suggest follow-up care for your trees, like fertilization and pest and disease control, as part of a tree-management program. Consider costs versus benefits carefully. Unless a tree is of great value, don't waste time and money trying to save a badly damaged, lightning-struck, or insect- or disease-ridden tree, and avoid tree firms that try to persuade you to do so.

For very valuable or historic trees, cabling or bracing can increase the strength of large limbs under snow or wind loads. Trees that present a lightning hazard to nearby homes can be rigged with grounding cables that will direct electricity harmlessly to the ground in the event of a strike.

If you decide to remove a tree, immediately select a replacement. Consider the new tree's mature height and canopy spread. For low-maintenance, choose trees with small, fine leaves that will virtually disappear into the lawn or surrounding mulch. Avoid trees that drop a lot of fruit, nuts, or seedpods, unless you intend to harvest them or use them as wildlife forage. Site the new tree carefully. Plant away from nearby structures, overhead and underground utility lines, sewer and water pipes, sidewalks, ramps, and driveways.

When removing trees, remember that "We plant flowers for ourselves, but trees for our grandchildren." For every tree you cut down, plant two to replace it—if not in your own yard, then in a park, public garden, or reforestation area. Doing so not only benefits the environment and public good, but it also eases the sting of conscience many of us feel at having to "put down" a big old tree.

TABLE 9-1:
Small to moderate-sized trees for the accessible landscape

These trees all have mature heights of 35 feet or less.

Tree	Description	Zone
Acacia pravissima (oven wattle)	Fine leaves, fragrant yellow flowers.	9–11
Acer ginnala, A. griseum, A. japonicum, A. palmatum (Amur, paperbark, full-moon, and Japanese maples)	Brilliant fall color. Quick growth to full size.	3–8
Aesculus pavia (buckeye or horse chestnut)	Pest and disease free. Red or coral blooms in May.	6–9
Amelanchier spp. (Juneberry, serviceberry, or shadblow)	White spring flowers, followed by red berries. Attracts birds.	4–7
Araucaria heterophylla (Norfolk Island pine)	Christmas tree shape. Good container tree.	7–10
Bauhinia forficata (butterfly tree)	White flowers throughout year.	9–11
Betula nigra (river birch)	Good for wet areas; not subject to borers. Attractive bark.	5–9
Brugmansia spp. (lily trumpet tree)	Pendulous, yellow trumpet-shaped flowers. Fast growing.	9–11
Butia captitata (pindo palm)	Gray-green fronds; good container tree.	9–11
Cercis canadensis (redbud)	Quick growing; good branch pattern. Dark rose flowers in early spring.	4–9
Chamaecyparis obtusa (false cypress or Hinoki cypress)	Dwarf cultivars make good evergreen container plants.	4–8
Chilopsis bignoniacea (desert willow)	Willowlike weeping branches and foliage.	8–10
Chionanthus virginicus (white fringe tree)	Fragrant, pendant white flowers; blue-black berries.	4–9
Chorisia bombacacea (floss or kapok tree)	Palmlike leaves. Fall-blooming, lily-shaped flowers in pink to purple.★	9–11

continued

TABLE 9–1: (Continued)

Tree	Description	Zone
Cladrastis lutea (yellowwood)	Pest-free native; pendulous white flowers in May.	4–8
Cordyline agavacea (cabbage palm)	Slender leaves; fragrant cream-colored spring bloom.	8–11
Cornus spp. (dogwood)	Many varieties, some planted for colorful winter bark color.	3–8
Cotinus coggygria (smoke tree)	Purplish gray clouds of blossoms in spring; fine leaves.	5–9
Crataegus spp. (hawthorn)	Thorny; covered with fragrant pink, white, or red flowers in spring, red berries in fall.	3–8
Cycas revoluta (sago palm)	Glossy herringbone leaves; neither palm nor fern.	9–11
Diospyros virginiana (persimmon)	Beautiful flame-colored fall foliage; edible orange fruits.	5–9
Elaeagnus angustifolia (oleaster or Russian olive)	Silver foliage; birds love black berries. Prune to single trunk.	3–8
Halesia carolina (Carolina silverbell)	Fragrant, white bell-shaped spring flowers.	5–9
Jacaranda mimosifolia (jacaranda)	Fine leaves; trumpet-shaped flowers in lavender, blue, white, or pink.★	9–11
Koelreuteria paniculata (golden rain tree)	Fine leaves; pendant yellow flowers in midsummer.	5–9
Magnolia nigra (purple lily magnolia)	Better frost resistance than some southern cultivars. Pink flowers.	5–9
Malus spp. (flowering crab apple)	Fragrant springtime pink, red, or white flowers; some varieties bred not to set fruit.	3–8
Melia azedarach (Chinaberry)	Deep green leaves, fragrant lavender flowers followed by yellow beadlike berries.★	8–10
Myrica cerifera (wax myrtle)	Similar to bayberry; fruit covered in aromatic wax. Prune to single stem. Good potted tree.★	7–9
Myrtus communis (true myrtle)	Small, shiny leaves; white flowers with showy yellow powderpuff of stamens. Good potted tree.★	8–9
Osmanthus fragrans (sweet olive)	Shiny dark leaves; very fragrant white to pale orange blossoms.★	8–10

Tree	Description	Zone
Oxydendrum arboreum (sourwood)	Likes wet, acid soil. Fragrant white summer flowers; red berries.	5–8
Paulownia tomentosa (foxglove tree or empress tree)	Coarse leaves; orchidlike flowers, cream with purple throat.★	5–9
Pinus aristata (bristlecone pine)	Extremely hardy; grows slowly to height of only 20 feet.★	2–10
Pithecellobium flexicaule (Texas ebony)	Wide crown; fragrant pale yellow flowers in long clusters.★	9–10
Pittosporum phillyraeoides (willow pittosporum)	Willowlike evergreen; tiny yellow flowers and orange fruit.★	9–10
Populus tremuloides (quaking aspen)	Brilliant coinlike gold autumn leaves. very hardy.★	1–6
Prosopis glandulosa 10–11 (honey or Texas mesquite)	Hybrid thornless cultivar. Bright green, fernlike foliage.★	
Prunus spp. (flowering cherry, flowering plum)	White or pink flowers; some cultivars have weeping branches.	4–8
Sapindus drummondii (soapberry)	Big sprays of creamy flowers in spring; fine foliage.★	6–9
Schinus molle (pepper tree)	Half-weeping form. Fine dark leaves; yellow flowers followed by red "peppercorns."★	9–11
Sorbus americana (mountain ash)	Fine leaves; orange-red fruit throughout winter.	4–9
Stewartia pseudocamellia (Japanese stewartia)	Camellialike flowers in spring; prefers moist, acid soil.	5–8
Syringa reticulata (tree lilac)	Fragrant white pannicles in spring.	4–7
Tamarix spp. (tamarisk)	Many cultivars; finely leaved, arching branches covered with clouds of pink or white blossoms.★	6–10
Xanthoceras sorbifolium (yellowhorn)	Creamy flowers with red throats borne on spikes.	4–6

★drought-resistant.

Fruit Trees

Fruit trees in the accessible landscape provide both springtime beauty and a summer or fall harvest. Many standard-size fruit trees are small enough to fit comfortably in most landscapes and, along with semidwarf, dwarf, and miniature fruit trees, present a wide selection of sizes to fit your needs. As a general rule, a standard tree has a mature height of about 25 feet; semidwarf, 14 to 18 feet; dwarf, 8 to 12 feet; and miniature, 4 to 8 feet. For the accessible garden, smaller trees will be easier to pick, prune, and maintain. Dwarfs and miniatures are small enough for containers and allow you to have an entire orchard of apples, peaches, cherries, and other fruits on your deck or patio.

Fruit trees in the accessible landscape have some drawbacks, however, the biggest of which is the fruit itself. It's easy to become inundated by a heavy harvest from a well-grown apple or plum tree, and if every windfall isn't picked up, the rotting fruit may encourage wasps or

You don't need a large yard to have an orchard; you can grow miniature apple, peach, plum, cherry, apricot, and nectarine trees successfully in containers. These trees all produce surprisingly high yields of full-size fruit. Wheeled casters make your orchard portable so that you can shelter them indoors over winter, ensuring that you'll get a good harvest even after harsh winters that wipe out commercial producers' crops.

deer into the garden. Fruit that falls on steps, ramps, or walkways can pose a slipping hazard, so place fruit trees well away from traffic areas.

SHRUBS

Used judiciously, shrubs can add beauty and make your landscape easier to maintain. Used incorrectly, they become time-consuming maintenance problems.

Nearly every American home features a foundation planting—a vegetative border that skirts the house and hides the foundation from view. In many cases, the homeowner spends much time and effort maintaining the appearance of the foundation planting; neglecting to do so would compromise the home's overall attractiveness and value. You can, however, reduce the amount of maintenance required, imperative for the accessible landscape.

Spend some time evaluating your foundation planting. Ask yourself the following questions:

- Does it enhance the appearance of the home?
- Does it obscure architectural details?
- Are windows and entryways shaded or blocked by overhanging branches?
- Are portions of the walls or the foundation kept constantly damp by shading vegetation?
- Do overgrown shrubs make it difficult to perform maintenance on the house?
- Do dense plantings provide possible hiding places for intruders?
- Have certain plants outgrown their neighbors and produced an unbalanced or awkward effect?
- Has the landscape kept up with the times, or does it date your home? Fashions in landscape design, like fashions in clothing, change over the years. Updating your foundation planting is a good way to beautify your home and reduce its maintenance requirements.

Begin planning by photographing your home and foundation plantings. Study other designs. The landscape designs around fast-food restaurants are a great source of ideas. Because anything planted in these high-traffic areas must look good and stand up to a lot of abuse and neglect, you can see what low-maintenance plants do well in your region. Most of these commercial landscapes are done by professional designers; study how they blend texture, color, form, and height to achieve a pleasing effect. Ask for the names of landscape designers who have done an especially nice job; it costs surprisingly little to have a professional design drawn.

Choose plants wisely. Planting yews, arborvitae, or larger juniper varieties as foundation shrubbery is probably the single biggest mistake. These are by nature big, fast-growing, dense *trees,* not shrubs—excellent for formal hedges, allées, or topiary, but unsuitable for foundation landscaping. Where these shrubs are planted away from the house, you can reduce maintenance by allowing them gradually to revert to their natural size and shape. Otherwise, remove them.

Eliminate sheared, geometrically shaped shrubs. Perfect cubes, spheres, and cones are maintenance nightmares and have no place in the accessible landscape.

Replace a high-maintenance foundation planting or island bed with an assortment of manageable varieties such as low-growing or dwarf junipers, azaleas, cotoneasters, barberry, and ornamental grasses. Doing so will cut your maintenance time to nearly zero, add color and lively form to your home, and update your landscape.

Avoid placing close to the house plants that are thorny and rambling, such as roses or pyracantha; tall and spreading, like forsythia or lilac; and invasive or climbing, like some euonymus. These are not necessarily high-maintenance species, but they are best reserved for specimen plantings elsewhere in the garden, where their natural form can develop unchecked.

Common design mistakes include foundation plantings that are too big or too small in relation to the house; monotonous, one-color, one-species plantings; too much diversity; and awkward placement of shrubs. Strive for plantings that lead the eye toward the main entrance, balance the structure of the house with its surroundings, and exhibit a changing palette of color year-round. With a little thought, you can design a foundation planting that is both attractive and easy to care for, no matter where you live or under what conditions you garden. You may choose either a fairly formal arrangement of shrubs, balanced on both sides of the entryway, or a looser, less structured look. Move plants around on paper, grouping and regrouping them until you have a pleasing arrangement. Whether formal or informal, two simple rules apply: Use only three or four varieties of plants, and put low-growing varieties in front of tall ones.

Select shrubs planted away from the house for their low-maintenance characteristics, too. Allow sheared, geometric-shaped plants to return to their natural state, or remove them. Group shrubs together and mulch well, at least 2 feet beyond the farthest spread of their branches. Doing so will conserve moisture and make mowing easier. Use low-growing, shade-loving shrubs as understory plantings beneath trees; this cuts down on maintenance time and provides cover for wildlife.

TABLE 9-2:
Shrubs for the accessible landscape

Shrub	Description	Zone
Aesculus parviflora (bottlebrush buckeye)	Wide, spreading shrub to 8 feet. Spiked white flowers in May. Moist, rich soil. Sun or shade.	7–9
Amorpha canescens (lead plant)	Succulent gray-green leaves, spikes of purple-blue flowers to 3 feet. Very tolerant.*	3–8
Arctostaphylos uva-ursi (bearberry)	Creeping evergreen shrub with round leaves, pink flowers, followed by red berries. Tolerates most conditions.*	1–5
Aronia arbutifolia (red chokeberry)	To 12 feet. Deep green leaves; May flowering in white or pink, followed by red fruit. Exceptional fall color. Tolerates most conditions.	1–5
Befaria racemosa (tarflower)	Leathery, evergreen leaves; dense white flowers midsummer. Tolerates most conditions.	7–9
Callicarpa americana (beautybush)	Open shape to 6 feet; may die back in winter. Softly furred leaves; lavender flowers followed by wine-colored fruit. Sun or shade.	7–9
Cephalotaxus harringtonia prostrata (plum yew)	Evergreen to 30 inches. No known pests or diseases. Good alternative to Japanese yew.	6
Clethra spp. (clethra)	Dense, fragrant, summer-flowering shrubs from dwarf to 8 feet. Moist, acid soil.	7–9
Comptonia peregrina (sweetfern)	Low, branching shrub to 3 feet. Fragrant, fernlike leaves. Poor soil; full sun.*	1–5
Corylus americana (American hazel)	Many varieties from dwarf to 10 feet. Bright yellow fall foliage; edible nuts. Very tolerant.	3–8
Fallugia paradoxa (apache plume)	Semievergreen, to 6 feet. White, roselike flowers in spring.*	6–9
Fothergilla gardenii 'Blue Mist' (dwarf fothergilla)	To 3 1/2 feet. White bottlebrush flowers. Needs moist, well-drained soil; light shade.*	3–7
Hamamelis spp. (witchhazel)	Blooms January to March. Good fall color. Many cultivars. To 15 feet.	4–8
Heptacodium minconiodies	Autumn flowering in white followed by red fruit. Fall color. Exfoliating bark. No pests of diseases.	4

continued

TABLE 9-2: (Continued)

Shrub	Description	Zone
Holodiscus discolor (mountain spray)	To 15 feet. Large sprays of ivory-colored flowers throughout summer. Moist soil; partial shade.	3–7
Hydrangea macrophylla (bigleaf hydrangea)	Slightly acid soil; light shade. Masses of flowers, white, pink, or blue, fading to brown. To 4 feet.★	5–8
Hydrangea quercifolia (oakleaf hydrangea)	Tall, arching habit to 6 feet. White to pale pink conical flowers, fading to brown.	5–8
Ilex spp. (holly)	Evergreen and deciduous varieties; attractive to birds. Good winter color. From 2 to 15 feet.	3–9
Kalmia spp. (mountain laurels)	Many cultivars, with flowers ranging from white to red. All require moist, sandy, or peaty acid soil. Full sun or shade.★	1–5
Lyonia lucida (fetterbush)	Mounding evergreen shrub to 6 feet. Arching branches with pink springtime flowers. Moist, acid soil.★	7–9
Mahonia repens (creeping mahonia)	Creeper to 1 foot. Spiny foliage, yellow flowers April–July, blue berries.★	3–7
Potentilla spp. (cinquefoil)	Many cultivars from prostrate to 3 feet. Pink, yellow, or white flowers throughout summer. Very tolerant.★	3–7
Purshia tridentata (bitterbush)	Loose shrub to 10 feet. Small leaves; tiny, star-shaped yellow spring flowers.★	6–9
Rubus parviflorus (thimbleberry)	Rambling shrub to 4 feet. Sticky leaves; white flowers throughout summer; inedible berries.★	1–5
Sambucus pubens (elderberry)	To 12 feet. Delicious fruits; white flowers in May. Tolerates most conditions.	1–5
Spiraea spp. (spireas)	Many cultivars, up to 6 feet. All have wide, arching stems covered with pink or white flowers in early summer.	4–8
Vaccinium spp. (cranberry, bearberry, blueberry, deerberry)	Large group of berry-producing shrubs. From prostrate to 8 feet. Sun to partial shade.	3–7
Viburnum spp. (viburnum)	Low-maintenance, high-impact shrubs. Evergreen and deciduous varieties. Fragrant flowers; good foliage, bark color, and texture. Berries prized by birds.	4–8

★suitable for foundation plantings.

FLOWERS

With their scents, colors, and graceful forms, flowers are a balm to the senses, and no accessible landscape, no matter how small or utilitarian, should be without them. Flowers attract bees, birds, and beneficial insects to the accessible garden, helping to achieve and maintain a natural balance. Their colors can be used to make a narrow property look wider, a small garden bigger, a shady garden brighter. Studies have shown that the scents of certain flowers have an effect on the human nervous system: roses produce a calming effect; rosemary makes us think more clearly, and lavender helps us sleep.

All flowering plants (including many herbs) can be classed into three distinct groups: perennials, biennials, and annuals. Perennials are plants that, once established, grow back year after year without replanting. Biennials grow one year, die back, then come back for one more season to flower, set seed, and die. Most perennials and biennials are hardy as long as their particular climatic and soil conditions are met. Annuals are started from seed each year and complete their cycle of growth, flowering, seed setting, and dieback within one season.

Perennials and Biennials

A flower border of perennials and biennials (the cultural requirements for both are so similar that we will treat them together) has been a staple of garden design for over a century. Planting once for years of bloom may seem like the ideal, low-maintenance solution to flower gardening, but a perennial border can require a lot of work. Besides the considerable effort necessary to properly prepare a site—removing all weeds and existing turf, amending and fertilizing the soil, providing drainage, and planting—a good deal of upkeep is required to keep the border looking its best throughout the season. Some plants will require staking, others may need periodic shearing to remove spent blooms, and still others may be susceptible to blights or insect damage that will require attention. Some perennials will look good for only a short period, producing a brief flush of blooms, then subsiding into sullen unattractiveness.

For the accessible garden, the perennial border must include only those plants that can virtually take care of themselves and still look good. Keep in mind the mature height; the length and time of bloom; color and scent; texture of foliage; whether the foliage persists after blooming (some will die back and leave a hole in the border); how much water the plant requires; whether it spreads or becomes invasive; and how often it will need to be lifted and divided.

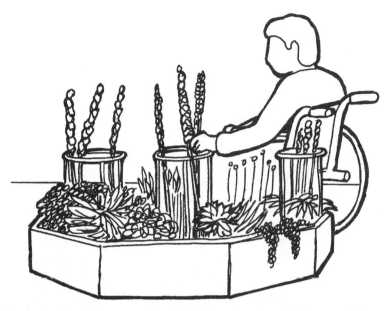

Staking and tying tall flowers can be difficult if you have impaired finger mobility or vision. Try using support hoops instead; simply place them over plants early in the season while they are small, and the flowering stalks will grow up through the supports. These devices can also be used to support top-heavy vegetable plants, such as peppers, cherry tomatoes, bush beans, or peas, and can be draped with plastic or row-cover fabric to make cloches or "minigreenhouses."

It may not be possible to have flowers from spring to autumn, but the border should look neat and attractive even when it is at rest. To get a good idea of what types of plants meet these requirements, observe neighbors' gardens, visit local nurseries, and askquestions. Narrow your choices down to five or six of the hardiest flowering perennials for your area before you buy.

Old cemeteries and abandoned homesites are good places to find out what perennials and biennials do well in your area with little care. Flowers that continue to flourish years after they have been forgotten are excellent for the accessible garden. Do not dig up these plants, however; look for the same species at nurseries instead.

A simple, low-maintenance border based around three perennials—daylilies, bearded irises, and peonies—will provide lots of color and interesting foliage texture. All three come in a wide variety of colors, so any color scheme is possible. Interplant these three with hardy herbs

TABLE 9-3:
Perennial and biennial flowers for the accessible landscape

Flower	Description	Zone
Althaea rosea (hollyhock)	Single and double flowers in shades of white, pink, purple, yellow. Dwarf to 6 feet.	3–9
Aquilegia spp. (columbine)	Tall flower stems above mounded, soft leaves. Many cultivars and colors. Tolerates most conditions.	4–8
Asclepias tuberosa (butterfly weed)	Low, mounding plant with tall flower stalks bearing red-orange flowers midsummer. Full sun.	4–8
Aster (aster or Michaelmas daisy)	Blooms late summer to fall. Moist, slightly acid soil; sun or shade. Drought-tolerant when established. Zones vary depending on cultivar.	1–8
Baptisia autralis (false indigo)	Tall, shrublike plant with blue flowers, April–June. Adaptable to many conditions.	4–8
Buddleia davidii (butterfly bush)	Tall, shrublike plant, to 14 feet. May die back to ground in colder climates. White, pink, purple flower spikes very attractive to butterflies.	
Clematis spp. (clematis)	Rambling flowering vine to 20 feet. Grows upright or prostrate. Many cultivars and colors. Full sun, but cool, shaded soil.	4–8
Coreopsis spp. (tickseed)	Brilliant yellow, daisylike flowers throughout summer. Very tolerant of most conditions.	3–8
Delosperma cooperi (hardy ice plant)	Low-growing, with pink, daisylike flowers throughout summer. Drought tolerant.	6–9
Dodecatheon meadia (shooting star)	White or blue springtime flowers borne on 1-foot stalk. Disappears after flowering.	3–8
Echinacea purpurea (purple coneflower)	Coarse plant with large, daisylike, purple flowers in late summer. Very tolerant.	4–8
Epilobium angustifolium (fireweed)	Blooms of clear pink spring to frost. To 6 feet. Full sun.	1–5
Erigeron spp. (fleabane)	Daisylike flowers on fine-leaved, loosely mounded plant. Summer blooms. Full sun.	3–7
Fritillaria spp. (mission bells)	Tall stems bear green-yellow bell-like flowers. Moist, rich soil; sun to partial shade.	6–9

continued

TABLE 9-3: (Continued)

Flower	Description	Zone
Gaillardia pulchella (blanket flower)	Daisylike, red-and-yellow flowers throughout summer. Slightly prostrate habit. To 3 feet.	3–8
Geranium spp. (cranesbill)	Low-growing, spreading plant. Blue, pink, or white flowers. Very hardy.	4–8
Heliopsis helianthoides (oxeye daisy)	Bushy plant to 3 feet. Yellow flowers with orange centers throughout summer.	3–8
Hemerocallis (daylily)	Great variety of heights, bloom times, colors. Multiplies readily.	3–9
Hibiscus (hibiscus or giant mallow)	Shrublike, large-leaved plants. Huge blooms in pink, red, or white. Moist, average soil; full sun.	7–9
Iris spp. (iris)	Many colors, shapes, and sizes of lightly fragrant, orchidlike flowers. Rhizomes multiple rapidly to form large clumps.	3–9
Liatrus spp. (gayfeather)	Large family of plants, from dwarf to 3 feet. Flower spikes of pink, purple, or white borne in late summer. Full sun.	4–8
Linum spp. (flax)	Diverse group of fine-leaved, blue-flowered plants to 2 feet. Dry soil; full sun.	3–7
Lupinus (lupine)	Many cultivars. Tall spires of richly colored flowers in early summer. Acidic soil; sun.	4–8
Paeonia spp. (peony)	Massive, fragrant, midspring blooms in shades of red, white, or pink. Dark green leathery foliage.	4–9
Passiflora incarnata (passionflower)	Vining plant to 10 feet; purple flowers followed by edible fruit. Average to poor soil; full sun.	7–9
Penstemon spp. (penstemon or beardtongue)	Large group of hardy native plants. From 16 inches to 3 feet. White, pink, or red flowering spires. Very tolerant.	4–8
Phlox paniculata (phlox)	Tall, mid- to late-summer blooms in many colors. Fragrant. Tolerant.	3–8
Physostegia virginiana (false dragonhead or obedient plant)	Vigorous grower. Pink or white summer-flowering spires. Very tolerant.	2–9

Flower	Description	Zone
Rudbeckia hirta (black-eyed Susan)	Coarse-leaved plant with daisylike golden flowers throughout summer. Very tolerant. Treat as hardy annual in severe-winter area.	4–8
Salvia spp. (sage)	Both annual and perennial varieties in wide range of colors and habits. All very tough, tolerant plants.	6–9
Solidago (goldenrod)	Many cultivars, all with deep golden flowers, some fragrant. Can be invasive depending on type. Tolerates most conditions.	4–8
Yucca glauca (spanish needle or soapweed)	Spiky foliage; pendant white flowers borne on tall flower stalks throughout summer. Tolerant of poor soil, drought. Full sun.	3–8

and spring-flowering bulbs, and you'll have a beautiful, easy-care, accessible perennial border.

Annuals

Annual flowers provide big bang for the bucks. They are inexpensive, especially when started from seed, and even when purchased as started seedlings from a nursery or greenhouse, their profuse blooms and long flowering time make them a bargain. Annuals are among the most versatile plants for the accessible garden, doing equally well in pots, hanging planters, windowboxes, and ground-level gardens.

Annuals can be used in the perennial border and vegetable garden to fill in empty spots, camouflage dormant vegetation or leafless stems,

From Meta Blue, horticultural therapist, Northview Developmental Center, Newton, Kansas:

"Perennials may say to a person, 'You know me, I'm the flower your mother grows. You've seen me every time I grew for your mother, and I'll grow for you. I'll be here this year, and I'll be here next year, as long as you take good care of me. You can count on me. I'm dependable. Sure, I go through cycles where I'm ugly. I need watering and fertilizer. But in the spring, you can take part of me and pass my beauty on to someone else.'"

and add color. When left undisturbed, a number of annuals will reseed themselves year after year, especially in areas with mild winters. These "volunteer" species include marigolds, cosmos, pansies, snapdragons, alyssum, larkspur, coreopsis, nicotiana, zinnias, cleomes, and many annual herbs. To encourage reseeding, don't be too tidy around these flowers in late summer and autumn. Let them develop seed heads and shed seeds. Don't disturb, weed, or cultivate the soil around them, either in autumn or the following spring, so that you don't inadvertently remove new young seedlings. Learn to recognize the emerging seedlings of these species so that you can distinguish them from weeds.

Bulbs

Bulbs are probably the best value for your money. Because most bulbs multiply rapidly, a small investment can pay increasingly great dividends over the years.

Naturalizing bulbs into the accessible landscape is a fine low-maintenance practice. Small, early-flowering varieties like crocuses, snowdrops, trout lilies, and chionodoxa can be planted randomly throughout a section of turf, where they will provide welcome color early in the spring. Drifts of daffodils, snowdrops, and grape hyacinths can be used as early-season ground cover beneath deciduous trees. Hyacinths and tulips can bring color to the early-spring perennial border. Daffodils are excellent bulbs for the accessible garden. They spread rapidly yet will not need to be lifted and divided, even after many years. They are hardy and can be planted almost anywhere, except in boggy ground, and they are poisonous, so rodents will not eat them.

THE FRAGRANCE GARDEN

A garden filled with sweet-scented flowers and herbs adds great charm to any setting. For gardeners with impaired vision, scented plants increase enjoyment and may even be used as "markers" throughout the garden, giving scent clues to location. Because many of the newer "improved" hybrids, such as sweet peas, have sacrificed scent for color, bloom size, or other characteristics, heirloom varieties may be better choices for the fragrance garden.

You can't have to many fragrant flowers, especially in an open-air garden. For indoor gardens, however, choose fragrant plants carefully and use them sparingly. In the close confines of a small apartment or enclosed greenhouse, the fragrance of massed hyacinths, jasmine, or other sweet-smelling flowers can easily become overwhelming, especially to persons with allergies.

TABLE 9-4:
Fragrant shrubs, trees, flowers, and vines

Plant	Description	Zone
Calycanthus floridus (Carolina allspice or common sweetshrub)	Glossy leaves, with spidery flowers May–June. Rich soil; sun or shade.	7–9
Chimonanthus praecox (fragrant wintersweet)	Yellow blooms in winter. Shrubs to 12 feet.	6–9
Clematis paniculata (sweetautumn clematis)	Vining plant to 30 feet. Covered with small white flowers late summer.	5–9
Clethra spp. (clethra)	Summer-flowering shrubs from dwarf to 8 feet. Moist, acid soil.	7–9
Convallaria majalis (lily-of-the-valley)	Tiny, nodding cup-shaped flowers borne on spikes to 10 inches. Spring blooming. Sun or shade.	3–8
Daphne caucasica (daphne)	White flowers April to frost; sun or partial shade. To 5 feet.	7–9
Gelsemium sempervirens (Carolina jessamine)	Woody vine to 20 feet. Smooth, shiny leaves; yellow, early-spring flowers.	7–9
Lonicera spp. (honeysuckle)	Twining or shrubby cultivars available. Intensely sweet summer flowers; cream, yellow, or red.	4–9
Matthiola incana (stocks)	Annual flowers in many sizes and colors.	3–8
Monarda spp. (bee balm)	Red, white, lavender, or pink flowers on 3-foot stalks. All parts of plant are fragrant. Attractive to hummingbirds, bees.	4–8
Pancratium maritimum (sea daffodil)	White flowers atop 12- to 18-inch stems in midsummer. Lift and store in cold regions.	7–11
Philadelphus virginalis (mock orange)	Wide, upright shrub to 8 feet. Waxy white blooms resembling citrus flowers throughout summer.	5–8
Phlox spp. (phlox)	Varied colors and heights. Older varieties better scented than newer hybrids.	3–8
Polianthes tuberosa (tuberose)	Waxy white blooms on spikes to 3 feet. Late summer bloom; lift and store in cold regions.	7–10

continued

TABLE 9-4: (Continued)

Plant	Description	Zone
Rhododendron canescens (piedmont azalea)	Open shrub to 15 feet. Spring blooms in white or pink. Spreads slowly to form thickets.	5–9
Stephanotis floribunda (stephanotis)	Waxy white flowers and dark green leaves.	8–11
Syringa vulgaris (lilac)	Tall shrubs; can be pruned to single stem for treelike form. Spring blooms in white, pink, or lavender.	3–8
Trachelospermum jasminoides (star jasmine)	Vining plant to 20 feet. Covered with star-shaped white flowers in early summer. Moist soil, full or partial shade.	7–10
Trillium sessile (toad trillium)	Mottled leaves and maroon flowers with fruity scent. Moist, acid soil; partial shade. Self-sowing.	4–8

Site the fragrance garden where it will be most appreciated: near a patio, porch, or deck; along a sidewalk or ramp; or, especially if someone is housebound, beneath the windows of an often-used room. If possible, position the fragrance garden so that the breezes will waft the fragrance toward you, not away from you. Humidity will usually increase the intensity of fragrance; on particularly dry days, watering in the late afternoon will bring out the fragrance by evening.

Roses are a given in the fragrance garden, as are most herbs, grown for either the flowers or leaves. Lavender, rosemary, and mints, which come in a wide range of scents from lemon to apple, are particularly fragrant. Fruit tree blossoms are usually sweet scented, as are many bulb and rhizome-grown plants such as lilies, peonies, irises, narcissus, and hyacinths.

THE BOG GARDEN

A low-lying, marshy site overgrown with weeds or tall grass but too wet to be mown or cultivated, is one of the most difficult to garden. If you have such an area, first and most important, find out why it's wet. A spring or underground stream may lie near the surface. The water may be an accumulation of rainwater, perhaps runoff from your home's rain gutters and downspouts, that is not able to drain away because of the contours of the land or underlying rock or hardpan. Areas that are marshy from these causes can be safely gardened.

TABLE 9-5:
Bog plants

Plant	Description	Zone
Acorus calamus (sweet flag)	Irislike leaves have sweet scent when crushed. To 3 feet.	4–11
Andromeda glaucophylla (bog rosemary)	Early-summer pink bells; feathery, needlelike foliage. 4 inches to 2 feet. Sun or shade.	1–5
Calla palustris (wild calla or water arum)	Big, heart-shaped leaves; white flowers. Moist soil; will grow in standing water.	1–5
Caltha palustris (marsh marigold)	Golden flowers March to May. Lush foliage. Full sun or partial shade. Will grow in standing water.	1–5
Camassia quamash (camas)	Grasslike foliage to 2 feet. Spikes of bright blue flowers in spring. Full sun.	3–7
Canna spp. (canna)	Many cannas will thrive in wet ground. The Longwood Hybrids are a particularly good choice. To 6 feet.	7–11
Crinum americanum (swamp lily)	Bulb. Tall, straplike leaves to 3 feet. White, spidery flowers. Full sun to light shade.	7–9
Cyperus spp. (papyrus)	From 30 inches to 14 feet, depending on cultivar. Exotic, fan-shaped flower and seed heads above grasslike foliage.	9–11
Cyrilla racemiflora (leatherwood)	Large shrub to 10 feet. Tiny flower spikes in June; red fall color. Full sun or partial shade.	7–9
Eleocharis montevidensis (spike rush)	Low-growing (1-foot) pondside plant; grasslike stems with rounded, tan flower heads.	6–11
Eleocharis tuberosa (Chinese water chestnut)	Upright, reedlike foliage; edible roots. To 3 feet.	7–11
Equisetum hyemale (horsetail)	Stiff, grassy, jointed-stem plant. To 18 inches.	3–11
Eupatorium maculatus, E. perfoliatum (joe-pye weed, boneset)	Deep green leaves, mounding to 4 feet. Pink or white flowers late summer to late fall. Tolerant of drier conditions.	1–8
Helenium autumnale (sneezeweed)	To 4 feet. Yellow or orange daisylike flowers in late summer. Full sun.	3–8
Houttuynia cordata (chameleon plant)	To 1 foot. Ground cover with heart-shaped leaves; variegated varieties in cream, pink, white, or yellow.	6–11

continued

TABLE 9-5: (Continued)

Plant	Description	Zone
Hydrocleys nymphoides (water poppy)	Cheerful yellow blossoms held just above water surface; glossy green leaves.	9–11
Hydrocotyle verticillata (water pennywort)	Small, emerald green leaves form dense mat in shallow water.	5–11
Hymenocallis liriosme (spider lily)	White, fragrant large flowers on 4-foot stalks.	8–11
Iris spp. (iris)	Several species of irises are marginal plants, specifically Siberian iris, Japanese iris, and water iris (*I. pseudacorus*). Bearded iris do not grow well in wet soil. To 2 feet. Flowers May–July. Full sun.	3–7
Itea virginica (Virginia sweetspire)	Mound-shaped to 5 feet. Small, fragrant flowers borne on arching stems. Red fall color. Full sun or partial shade.	7–9
Lobelia cardinalis (cardinalflower)	Brilliant red flowers, 4 to 6 feet. Moist soil, full sun.	7–9
Lysimachia nummularia (creeping Jenny)	Ground cover excellent for edge of pond. Yellow blooms periodically through summer.	6–11
Lysimachia terrestris (swamp candle)	Erect, yellow flowering to 3 feet. Late-summer bloom. Full sun or partial shade.	1–5
Menyanthes trifoliata (bog bean)	Creeper; light green leaves, white flower clusters in June–July. Will grow in standing water.	1–5
Mimulus guttatus (monkey flower)	Bushy plants to 2 feet. Yellow or blue flowers resembling snapdragons May–August. Full sun.	3–7
Myriophyllum aquaticum (parrot's feather)	Lime green foliage trails along water surface. Provides fish spawning habitat.	6–11
Nymphoides crenata, *N. cristata* (snowflakes)	Spring to fall flowers in yellow or white. Interesting brown-and-green leaves.	7–11
Orontium aquaticum (golden club)	To 1 foot. Spring-blooming white spikes tipped with yellow.	6–10
Peltandra virginica (water arum)	Glossy, arrowhead-shaped leaves. To 6 inches.	5–9
Pontederia cordata (pickerel weed)	Heart-shaped, succulent leaves to 3 feet. Purple-blue flowers throughout summer. Will grow in standing water.	7–9

Plant	Description	Zone
Sagittaria latifolia (giant arrowhead)	Aquatic plant with 3-foot-tall arrow-shaped leaves, white flowers. Prefers standing water, but will grow in moist soil. Full sun or partial shade.	5–11
Sarracenia flava, *S. purpurea* (trumpet pitcher plant)	Carnivorous plant with pitcher-shaped leaves and yellow or purple flowers. To 2 feet. Acid soil, full sun.	7–9
Saururus cernuus (lizard's tail)	To 2 feet. Summer-blooming fragrant white flowers on long spikes.	4–9
Thalia geniculata (thalia)	Violet flower spikes may reach 10 feet. Foliage to 5 feet.	9–11
Trollius laxus (globeflower)	Low plant with single creamy white, buttercuplike flowers May–July. Rich soil; full sun.	3–7
Typha latifolia (cattail)	Tall, rushlike foliage to 7 feet. Can be invasive.	2–11
Vernonia noveboracensis (New York ironweed)	Coarse, open plant to 6 feet. Purple-red flowers late summer. Rich, wet soil; full sun.	4–8

Other, more sinister reasons for an area of persistent wetness are leaking water lines, broken or clogged sewer pipes, or a plugged or overflowing septic system. If the area smells bad, or if you suspect a leaking water main, call your local sewer or water authority immediately.

If your property lies within an area designated as a protected wetland, you may need special permission to plant or make any changes to it; check with your county cooperative extension agent's office.

Draining boggy ground requires far more work and expense than the disabled gardener should undertake. Instead, turn your problem area into an asset by working with nature rather than against it. Planted with specimens suited to your climate and soil, bog gardens require little care, growing better and more beautiful as time goes on.

Although most vegetables, bulbs, and fruit trees will not tolerate waterlogged soil, a great number of beautiful flowers, including water lilies and lotus *(Nymphaea* and *Nelumbium)*, which grow only in water, as well as many shrubs, trees, and grasses, will thrive in boggy or marginal land. Some of the most intriguing plant oddities—the carnivorous plants like Venus's flytrap and pitcher plant—will grow nowhere else.

Wildlife of all sorts is attracted to even the smallest of wetlands. Because frogs, toads, salamanders, and other amphibians soon set up housekeeping in environmentally clean marshes, you may be able to reap the benefits of their insatiable appetites for insects in other parts of your garden. Birds, too, will flock to wetland gardens to feed, drink, and nest.

THE ROCK GARDEN

Rock gardens were extremely fashionable a few decades ago, so much so that many suburban gardeners with absolutely perfect deep loam actually had rocks and gravel trucked in to create the boulder-strewn effect of an alpine mountainside. Sadly, the finished effect all too often resembled construction site debris.

If a natural rocky outcropping exists on your property, however, turn a liability into an asset by working with nature and planting the soil-filled crevices with low-maintenance alpine or succulent plants, rather than trying to cover the area with grass. You can also grow alpine and rock plants in raised beds or containers providing the loose, gravelly, well-drained conditions such plants demand. Rock plants can also be tucked into the gaps and crevices in wood, stone, or masonry raised-bed walls.

A drystone rock wall makes an excellent vertical gardening space. Fill the crevices with rich potting soil and hold in place with sphagnum moss or coco fiber. Plant succulents and trailing plants into these soil pockets, and rock garden plants along the top and bottom.

TABLE 9-6:
Rock garden plants

Plant	Description	Zone
Campanula rotundifolia (harebell)	Sky blue flowers all summer; 6 inches to 2 feet. Full sun. Perennial.	1–5
Cryptogramma crispa (rock brake)	Crinkly leaved fern to 1 foot. Acid soil; full sun or light shade.	3–7
Dryas octopetala (alpine avens)	Small-leaved, mat-forming plant with white flowers in late summer. Full sun.	3–7
Echinocereus triglochidiatus (claret-cup cactus)	Scarlet flowers April–June on spiny, low-growing plant.	6–9
Engelmannia pinnatifida (Engelmann daisy)	Yellow daisies densely cover plant April–July. Full sun.	3–8
Epilobium latifolium (alpine fireweed)	Low mound with large pink flowers June–August. Moist soil; full sun.	3–7
Erythronium grandiflorum (glacier lily)	Bright yellow flowers on delicate plants. Naturalizes easily. Moist soil; full sun.	3–7
Gentiana calycosa (mountain gentian)	Deep blue, bell-shaped flowers on small, bushy plant July–August. Moist soil; full sun.	3–7
Geranium spp. (cranesbill)	Low-growing, spreading plant. Blue, pink, or white flowers. Very hardy.	4–8
Heuchera spp. (coralbells)	Low plant; red or pink flowers borne on 1- to 2-foot stalks. Very tolerant.	3–8
Lewisia rediviva (bitterroot)	Leafless plant with pale pink flowers in early spring.	3–7
Melampodium leucanthum (blackfoot daisy)	Low, mounding plant; white daisylike flowers. Full sun.	3–8
Phlox multiflorus (cushion phlox)	Creeping plant with white or pink flowers throughout summer. Full sun or partial shade.	3–7
Polypodium virginianum (rock polypody)	Slow-creeping fern to 8 inches. Acid soil; sun or shade.	1–5
Potentilla tridentata (wineleaf cinquefoil)	To 12 inches. Evergreen leaves; white flowers. Full sun or light shade.	1–5

continued

TABLE 9-6: (Continued)

Plant	Description	Zone
Sanguinaria canadensis (bloodroot)	Single, blue-green leaf with pure white flower. Moist, slightly acid, shady soil.	4–8
Silene acaulis (moss campion)	Tiny-leaved, mat-forming plant covered with bright pink flowers throughout summer. Full sun.	3–7
Townsendia parryi (townsendia)	Dark green with pink or lavender daisylike flowers. Full sun.	3–7
Zinnia grandiflora (wild zinnia)	Open branching plant with yellow-orange flowers. To 1 foot.	6–9

Succulents, lichens, ornamental grasses, flowers, and a number of dwarf shrubs and trees do well in the dry, well-drained, light-soil conditions of the rock garden. Keep the bed well mulched with pebbles, crushed stone, or gravel, and any weeds that take root there will be very easy to pull up.

THE HERB GARDEN

Herbs are some of the easiest plants to grow. Even if your garden consists of just a few pots on a windowsill, you can still enjoy growing, harvesting, and using a number of herbs. They need a sunny, south-facing window, good air circulation, and fairly cool temperatures (50 to 70 degrees F). Among the easiest windowsill herbs to grow are basil, bay, catnip, chervil, chives, coriander, myrtle, oregano, rosemary, sage, summer savory, and sweet marjoram.

Outdoors, herbs add color, scent, and texture to the accessible landscape. Perennial herbs such as sage, chives, thyme, mint, and germander can be spotted into the mixed flower border. In the vegetable garden, culinary herbs provide an instant garnish for the salad you're gathering. Certain other herbs can be placed strategically throughout the garden to attract or repel certain insects. Other herbs can be a sort of natural "first-aid station," offering quick relief from the scratches, aching muscles, and sunburn that often come with toiling out of doors.

The uses of herbs, both culinary and medicinal, are beyond the scope of this book. Before using any herb as food or medicine, consult with a reputable herbalist or your doctor. Many medicinal herbs, including foxglove, valerian, and even chamomile, can be dangerous if used incorrectly. If you are using prescription or over-the-counter medication, potentially dangerous drug interactions can occur with the medicinal use of some herbs.

THE MOONLIGHT GARDEN

In many areas, summer afternoons are too hot and humid to enjoy out of doors. If you have respiratory or circulatory problems, have had skin cancer, or are on medications that make your skin or eyes sensitive to sunlight, consider planting a moonlight garden. Even if you have no problem with the heat and glare of the midday sun, by the time you get home from work or school, most of your garden may have gone to sleep for the night. And summertime guests may not get a chance to enjoy your garden once the sun has gone down.

A moonlight garden takes advantage of the coolest part of the day. Fill your nighttime garden with pale-colored, fragrant plants that are visible after dark—lilies, night-scented stock, peonies, and climbing roses. Night-blooming water lilies, in a small pool or tub garden attract fireflies and frogs to the nighttime garden; flowering trees and shrubs like mock orange, dogwood, Bradford pear, and weeping cherry add privacy and seclusion.

To make your accessible garden more enjoyable after dark, select plants that are at their best at night and plant them where they are most visible from windows, patio, or deck. Under low-light conditions, reds, yellows, deep pinks, and other bright colors fade to gray or disappear altogether. White, pale yellow, and pale pink flowers glow under moonlight; variegated foliage sparkles at night; and the soft, silvery hues of senecio, lamb's ear, and sage acquire an almost metallic luster.

Many night-blooming flowers are especially fragrant, and even daytime flowers can take on a special glamour in moonlight. Good choices for an after-dark garden are fragrant white *Nicotiana alata,* or flowering tobacco; *Matthiola bicornis,* or night-scented stock; *Datura meteloides* 'Evening Fragrance'; white *Phlox paniculata* 'Mount Fuji'; and pale yellow *Oenothera missourensis,* or evening primrose. If you garden in a semitropical location (Zones 9-11), vines like star jasmine, stephanotis, frangipani, and mandevilla are a must. Also use evocative plants like white poppies, lunaria, love-in-a-mist, moonflower, and mugwort, a fragrant-leafed variety of artemisia.

CHAPTER TEN

Accessories for
Accessibility

An accessible garden need not be an entirely outdoor garden. But in the average house or apartment, it may be virtually impossible to grow plants with high light requirements—which include most flowering plants, fruits, and vegetables—without supplemental lighting. And if you're enthusiastic about starting your own garden plants from seeds or cuttings, it's easy to inundate your home with pots and flats, all vying for limited windowsill space.

Besides extending the growing season, greenhouses, cold frames, hot frames, propagators, and other accessories allow the accessible garden to be brought indoors to varying degrees, out of the vagaries of weather and the accessibility problems posed by difficult locations. And for housebound or bedridden gardeners, bringing a small portion of the outdoors inside can mean a great deal in terms of quality of life and improved emotional health.

Other garden accessories exist purely to extend our enjoyment of the outdoors. The accessible garden, large or small, is part of the living space of any home and should be both accommodating and inviting.

Add a small potted tree and a comfortable bench to a utilitarian vegetable garden to make it more welcoming. Cool and enliven a sun-baked patio or paved area with a calm reflective pool or a fountain. Put a picnic table and benches beneath a tall, shady tree. Strategically place a pergola or gazebo, covered with flowering vines, to provide shade and comfort from which to enjoy your neatly trimmed lawn and flower beds.

Keep these adjuncts to pleasurable gardening in mind when designing your accessible landscape. They will repay their cost many times over in years to come in the form of hours of additional pleasure and comfort.

From Charles A. Lewis, horticulturist, Morton Arboretum, Lisle, Illinois:

" "People respond to plants and to caring for plants. This response is often beneficial, even therapeutic and rehabilitative. How can this be? We know that many people talk to plants, but do the plants talk to us, too? They may not speak in words, but they do convey meanings that can be understood in terms of human values. Simple horticultural practices such as the growth of seedlings or the rooting of cuttings, the unfolding of a flower, all elicit subtle responses that can be beneficial and that symbolically fulfill many human needs."

GREENHOUSES

Greenhouses and add-on sunspaces (12, 15, 16, 49, 67, 114, 160) bring the garden indoors—ideal for those who find working outdoors uncomfortable or impossible—and make active gardening possible all year round. Most greenhouses and sunspaces today are almost entirely solar-heated; in fact, the addition of a sunspace to your home may lower your overall heating bills during fairly mild winters.

A greenhouse or sunspace can create a world in miniature, tailored to any specific climate or region: a cool, dry alpine zone fresh with the scent of herbs and pines; a steamy tropical rain forest dripping with orchids and banana plants; a warm, inviting southern garden filled with the perfume of gardenias and jasmine; or a temperate indoor vegetable patch with tomatoes and peas.

Propagator kits with plastic trays, small individual pots, and clear domed lids—in effect tiny greenhouses—are excellent for tabletop gardeners and for those who want to start their own flower and vegetable seeds. Propagators with high domed lids (67, 70, 78, 95, 114) can be used as terrarium gardens, and both propagators and terrariums are excellent ways to learn the special requirements of a "contained" environment; you may want to experiment with them before making the commitment to a full-size greenhouse or sunspace.

Good planning before planting applies to the greenhouse as well as the outdoor garden. Know what you want before construction begins, and make your wishes clear to your designer or contractor. If you will

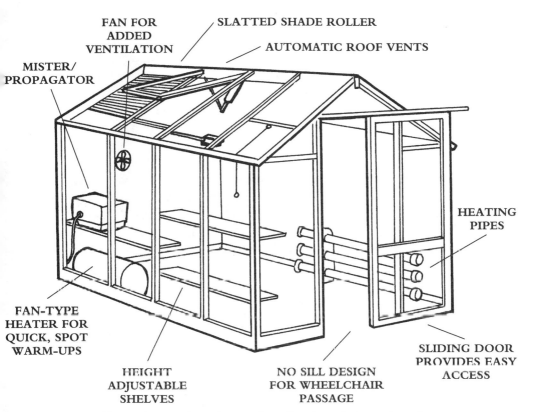

FAN FOR ADDED VENTILATION

SLATTED SHADE ROLLER

AUTOMATIC ROOF VENTS

MISTER/ PROPAGATOR

HEATING PIPES

FAN-TYPE HEATER FOR QUICK, SPOT WARM-UPS

HEIGHT ADJUSTABLE SHELVES

NO SILL DESIGN FOR WHEELCHAIR PASSAGE

SLIDING DOOR PROVIDES EASY ACCESS

An accessible greenhouse. Choose features that will make gardening easier and more enjoyable; adapt the design to your needs.

require special ventilation, heating, cooling, or misting equipment to maintain a special climate, ensure during the planning stage that these requirements will be met. Make sure that the greenhouse or sunspace will be accessible and comfortable for you as well. It should be adapted to your needs, and not the other way round. Design details require special attention, especially with prefabricated greenhouses.

Access to most greenhouses can be difficult for wheelchair gardeners because of the doorsill or threshold. When purchasing a free-standing or add-on greenhouse, look for a design that either does not use a sill or can be adapted to a sunken threshold or sill. If you're retrofitting an existing greenhouse structure for accessibility, install a shallow ramp up and over the sill, and trim or adjust the door to fit snugly over it.

Use sliding doors wherever possible, rather than traditional swinging doors. Sliding doors save space, are easier for wheelchair and scooter gardeners to open and shut, provide a tighter weatherproof seal, and can usually be adapted to use either a sunken threshold or an overhead suspension track that eliminates the need for a bottom sill or threshold.

Brick and rough-textured concrete are the safest alternatives for flooring. Although terra cotta tile is often used for sunspaces because of its beauty, durability, and ability to collect and hold solar heat, it can be treacherously slippery when wet. For standing gardeners, place heavy-duty rubber matting in front of work areas to provide better traction and to reduce the strain of standing on hard surfaces for prolonged periods of time.

Potting benches (67) should be about 26 inches above the floor to be comfortably used from a seated position. Make sure that under-bench shelving does not extend out too far; leave at least 18 inches of under-bench clearance so that you can pull your chair under the bench just as you would a desk or table. Use a comfortable work table to determine the best working height for you, whether you expect to work from a seated or standing position. All work tables, sinks, and storage shelves in the greenhouse should follow this comfortable-height rule. Demand the same comfort in the greenhouse that you would in your home or office. Cover work surfaces with smooth, water-resistant finishes like tile or laminate to eliminate the need for repainting.

Use the space beneath at least one bench as storage for compost, potting soil, and other bulky material. For seated gardeners, wide-mouthed, open barrels or trash cans mounted at an angle beneath the bench will be more easily accessible than slide-out drawers or swinging-door cabinets. Nail a 20-inch-wide piece of sturdy 1-inch plywood, notched to hold up the open end of the barrel or trash can and prevent it from rolling, between the bench legs at floor level.

For wheelchair gardeners, aisle width should be at least 40 inches. Allow for a wheelchair turnaround area at each end of the greenhouse; to give you turnaround room without sacrificing too much usable space, position swing-away shelves over this area or raise the height of nearby benches slightly so that, with a little maneuvering, you can swing your chair around partially under the benches.

Use overhead space in the greenhouse by suspending pots and baskets from pulley-operated hangers (15, 97, 165) mounted from the center ridge or on sturdy beams and poles suspended from the ceiling. Train vining plants upward on lightweight trellises of netting or string, thus making the most of vertical growing space. If you grow cucumbers or tomatoes on a trellising system, anchor the top of the trellis to a pole that is in turn suspended from a pulley. Then you can lower the vine to a comfortable height to pick vegetables growing near the top.

Jar-lid openers (13, 40, 42, 55, 61, 130), easy-reach wands, long-handled tongs (42, 52, 110), and other kitchen and bathroom aids are useful for the greenhouse as well. There are always lids to open, dropped items to pick up, and things on shelves too high to reach. Buy duplicates for your greenhouse so that you'll have the gadget where you need it, when you need it. Also have a special set of tools, scissors, buckets, and measuring spoons and cups just for the greenhouse to avoid contaminating household items with garden chemicals, minerals, and botanicals.

Equip all faucets with easy-turn handles (9, 10, 14, 40, 42, 43, 55, 61, 77, 108, 109, 149) and snap-on-and-off hose attachments (16, 26, 49, 84) to eliminate the need for carrying watering cans. Use light-weight hoses and watering wands for easy watering of overhead and back-of-the-bench plants. To save effort in watering, equip benches with capillary matting (67, 114) or drip irrigation tubing (26, 34, 49, 67, 70, 84, 114). If you need to maintain constant high humidity in the greenhouse, or if you are using it as a propagation house for cuttings, install an automatic, timer-controlled misting system (114).

Thermostats and temperature- or timer-controlled heating, cooling, shading, and ventilation systems to improve the efficiency of the greenhouse and provide a more beneficial environment for your plants. The initial cost of installing these automatic devices is far outweighed by the savings in energy costs, effort, and loss of plants.

COLD FRAMES
Cold frames (46, 95, 97, 165) lengthen the gardening season in cool-weather climates, provide shelter from sun and wind for delicate seedlings, and are used to harden off transplants before moving them to the garden. Using a cold frame in conjunction with a permanent raised bed can extend your season by as much as a month in both early spring and late autumn.

Cold frames act as low-tech solar collectors by trapping warmth beneath a lid of glass, clear plastic, or fiberglass. A simple cold frame can be nothing more than a low wall of concrete blocks or even an earthen berm built up to surround a small area of soil. Place a sheet of plastic or an old window frame over the area, and you have effectively created a heat trap that will raise soil temperatures by about 10 degrees.

By improving the heat collecting and retaining properties of a cold frame, you extend its use longer into the cold season. Build up the back wall so that the frame is tilted toward the south to catch more sunlight. Insulate the sides with bales of straw or rigid foam insulation boards to keep more of the collected heat inside. Increase the heat-retentive properties of a frame even more by adding thermal mass in the form of flat stones or bricks inside the frame or by using clay pots. These objects will absorb the sun's warmth throughout the day and slowly release it into the frame during the night.

The amount of heat that builds up within a frame during bright spring or fall days can be enormous. To prevent "cooking" your plants, raise the lid for ventilation on hot days. The routine of raising and lowering cold frame lids can be wearying, and if you forget, you may lose an entire season's worth of flowers or produce. To make this task easier, install automatic hydraulic hinges (97, 165) on the cold frame. These hinges contain fluid that gradually expands as it warms, slowly raising the lid; as the fluid cools, it contracts, lowering the lid. Solar-powered lid openers (70, 95) are also available; these open and close the frame to a preset, timer-controlled schedule. Automatic openers are usually reliable, but you should check the frame periodically, especially on very hot, very cold, or very windy days, just to make sure that everything is operating correctly.

Several good commercial frames are available. The Access Garden Frame (164) is more a miniature greenhouse than a traditional cold frame. Made of sturdy structural aluminum, it provides more than 24 square feet of ground-level growing space, plus an additional 4 square feet of space on a movable shelf. The frame is 32 inches high and has sliding side and top panels that make access easy from a standing or sitting position. For wheelchair gardeners, placing the frame on a raised bed makes it even more accessible. A hose mount and mist irrigation system come with the frame, but you must supply the glazing. Use clear polycarbonate or acrylic rather than glass; they are lighter in weight and shatterproof.

HOT FRAMES

A hot frame is a variation on the cold frame that uses both solar heat and heat from an underground source. Traditionally, this heat source has been fresh, hot manure, buried in a pit about 1 foot beneath the growing level of the bed. Horse, sheep, poultry, and goat manures are excellent hot manures; cow manure tends to be cooler. The roots and leaves of growing plants must not come in direct contact with fresh manure or they will burn.

Modern hot frames rely on heavy-duty heating cables and mats (16, 67, 70, 78, 95, 114, 147) to provide steady warmth to plants. If you want to use an electrically heated hot frame, use only cables and heating mats specifically designed for outdoor, garden use. Never use home heating pads that are intended to soothe aching muscles or sore joints. Check all cables, mats, and wiring periodically to be sure that the insulation is intact and all connections are secure. To further reduce the chance of a shock hazard, connect warming cables and mats only to a ground fault interrupter circuit (GFIC) outlet.

HYDROPONIC GARDENING

Hydroponic cultivation (82, 83) requires as little as one-quarter the space of regular growing techniques, making it an ideal medium for the accessible indoor garden. Hydroponically grown crops mature 20 to 25 percent faster than plants grown in a traditional garden or greenhouse, and because the nutrient-rich solution in which the plants grow is recycled, little water is consumed.

From Dr. Richard Mattson, HTM, Department of Horticultural Therapy, Kansas State University:

"What do we say to someone who's had a stroke and says, 'Well, I can't garden anymore'? That's just not an acceptable response! There are always new ways to do something, new ways to enjoy the garden, even if it's just starting out by feeding birds. My father had a severe stroke several years ago, and we started him out with seed catalogs. The speech therapist worked with him until he could put together a seed order, and he just progressed from there. He's back gardening today."

Hydroponic gardening kits, produced by Hydrofarm Gardening Products Company (82), are self-contained units that supply the gardener with everything needed to begin successfully growing plants without soil. Several tabletop models are available, all equipped with automatic aeration, water, and feed pump systems that practically grow the garden for you. The compact Hydrogarden, an 11-by-21-inch tub system, will comfortably fit just about anywhere. The larger Emily's Garden system is equipped with individual pots that can be moved around within the main hydroponic reserve tub. The Megagarden (24 by 24 inches) and Hydrofarm Ebb & Flow (44 by 26 inches) systems have movable containers within the main tub capable of growing large houseplants and even vegetables indoors.

GROW-LIGHT SYSTEMS

Even the sunniest window may not provide enough light to grow sun-loving plants and seedlings. Grow lights (15, 67, 114) meet plants' light needs by reproducing natural sunshine. Complete multishelf light-rack units (67, 114, 147, 164), available in a variety of sizes, are a good choice for the indoor disabled gardener.

Fluorescent fixtures duplicate sunlight more closely than any other type of artificial lighting, because they emit light in a nearly complete

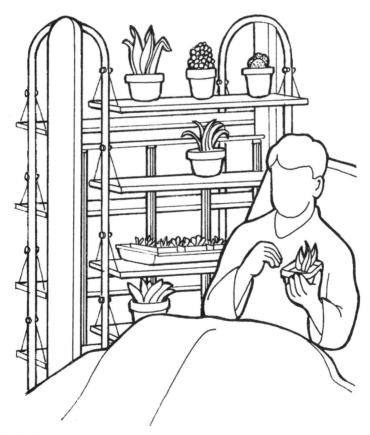

Even bedridden gardeners can enjoy tending plants with the RotoGro rotating shelf lighting unit. Powered by a quiet, efficient electrical motor, the shelves move slowly up, over, and down around the central light bars. Each shelf is front and center every two hours, so no plant is beyond the gardener's reach. Available through the Home Gardener Manufacturing Co., 30 Wright Avenue, Lititz, PA 17543.

spectrum of colors. Cool-white bulbs are also a good, economical choice for grow lighting. Avoid incandescent and halogen lights, which produce huge amounts of heat and lack much of the full spectrum of sunlight.

You'll get the most out of any kind of grow lights by keeping them lit for sixteen hours a day—especially important for starting seedlings. Most light-loving plants need at least this much light to grow compact and full. Use an inexpensive timer to cycle the lights on and off for you.

The most intense light is produced near the middle of long, tube-shaped fixtures. Rotate your plants from the ends to the middle of the bench daily to ensure that every one gets its fair share of light.

Keep the bulbs and the under-hood reflector clean; even a thin film of dust can dramatically decrease the amount of light available to plants. If possible, paint shelves, tabletops, even nearby walls bright white to reflect as much light as possible back onto the plants, and strategically place mirrors, shiny baking sheets, and foil-covered cardboard pieces to reflect additional light. Do not use mirrors to reflect natural sunlight; mirrors can concentrate bright sunshine intensely and cause a fire.

Position grow lights low over the plants, about 4 inches above the foliage. Ensure that no foliage touches the bulbs, which could damage the plants.

TABLES AND BENCHES

When adding seating to the accessible garden, comfort is paramount. A garden bench (15, 34, 67, 84, 90, 97) should be a place to relax, dream, or even doze. Avoid outdoor furniture made of flimsy aluminum tubing that is easily toppled, heavy cast-iron that reaches scorching temperatures in the sun, splintery old wood that may catch skin and clothing, and slippery, unattached cushions that may cause injuries by sliding out from under the body. Also watch out for sharp edges on seats and armrests that can cut off circulation to arms and legs, cording or webbing that might cut into the skin at pressure points, sharp or protruding corners that could injure someone who falls or bangs against them, and legs or feet that splay out at an angle from the seat, posing tripping hazards.

Look for sturdy, stable chairs, tables, and benches with smooth, non-conductive surfaces like finished wood or resin plastic. Wide seats make it easy to slide from scooter or wheelchair to bench and back. Armrests should be no wider than 3 inches, with rounded edges, to make it easy to hold on for support when raising or lowering yourself. Cushions should be tied down securely and backed with skidproof material.

Table height is important. Raising or lowing picnic or patio tables may make them more comfortable for use by wheelchair gardeners. To

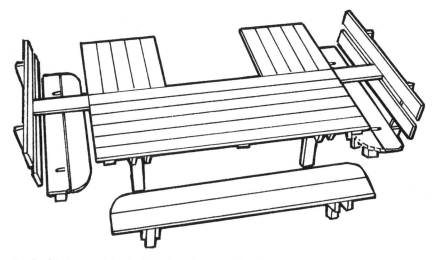

A wheelchair-accessible picnic table with a specially designed cutout that allows a wheel-chair user to sit comfortably with others. Pedestal-style legs allow easy transfer from wheelchair to bench, when desirable. Several different patented designs are available through Roger Pearson & Associates, Inc., P.O. Box 484, Hagerstown, MD 21740.

raise a table, simply place it on bricks; to lower it, you may have to saw the legs. Tables with a single central support are easier to slide under than four-legged ones, and tables with attached benches are much less accessible than those with pull-out benches. Avoid tables made from pressure-treated (CCA) wood; the arsenic and heavy metals used in weatherproofing the wood can leach out into food or onto hands.

WATER GARDENS

Just as garden beds filled with earth can be raised above ground level, so too can water gardens be raised up to make them more accessible.

A water garden need not be large to be effective. If this is your first venture, start small. An excellent choice for an accessible water garden is a cedar or plastic half barrel lined with plastic sheeting. About 22 inches in diameter and 16 inches deep, these barrels are perfect for a few plants and goldfish. Set the barrel on a wheeled plant dolly before you fill it, and you have a pool that can be moved wherever and when-ever you want.

To build your miniature water garden, you'll need a 5-by-5-foot sheet of UV-stabilized, EPDM plastic sheeting designed for use in water gardens. Don't use regular plastic sheeting, which will probably leak and may contain chemicals harmful to fish and aquatic vegetation.

To line the half barrel or other container, press the plastic down firmly into the bottom. Add 4 inches of garden soil (do not use compost or peat moss, which would cloud the water). Turn under a 3-inch collar around the top, and staple the sheeting to the inside rim of the barrel. Slowly add a few inches of water, and you're ready to plant.

After plants are in, cover the exposed surface of the soil with a layer of clean, coarse gravel or pebbles, and finish filling the tub. A pebbly bottom looks nice and will prevent fish from dislodging the plants.

Wait a week before adding fish, to allow time for the plants to become established and for waterborne chemicals to evaporate.

Fish are essential in all but the smallest containers; they eat mosquito larvae and algae, prune excess vegetation, and provide natural fertilizer. Stock the water garden with 2 inches of fish for each square foot of surface. A half-barrel water garden would accommodate one medium-size goldfish or two small ones. Consult a local aquarium store for the best easy care fish species for your area.

Once your water garden is complete, the trick is to keep it in balance. Patience is the key. Expect a week or so of murky water, wilted

A raised water garden differs from a raised bed garden only in the growing medium. A recirculating pump can be used to add a fountain or waterfall to the raised pool; fish and aquatic vegetation create a balanced underwater environment.

plants, and an occasional fish casualty. Resist the urge to "fix" things by draining and refilling the pool, adding chemical clarifiers, or installing filtration systems. Left alone, fish, plants, and microorganisms will achieve a natural balance: The water will clear, plants grow, fish thrive.

An overall greening is normal and natural; sunshine, nitrates, and carbon dioxide will cause algae growth. But if slimy, hairlike strands form, your water is polluted with excess nutrients. Scoop out the strands and reduce the amount of food you give your fish. The problem should right itself within a week.

Once you've had success with a small water garden, you may want to try a larger, permanent pool. Using an EPDM liner, you can make a pond of whatever shape and size you like. (A minimum depth of 18 inches is required to overwinter fish outdoors.) By varying the depth and creating underwater ledges, you can plant a wide variety of aquatic plants in and around the pool. A raised pool, lined with EPDM plastic sheeting, can be made of poured concrete, concrete blocks, or bricks, or by stacking landscape timbers or railroad ties to the desired height. Incorporate wide ledges all around the raised pool to accommodate the leaning elbows of anyone who wishes to spend some time gazing into the watery depths.

OUTDOOR LIGHTING

No outdoor landscape is complete without some form of nighttime illumination. Besides providing safety and security, outdoor lighting (15, 34, 67, 72, 92, 129, 140, 148, 150) allows you to spend more time in your garden. In hot climates, where high temperatures may keep you indoors most of the day, outdoor garden lighting is especially valuable.

When planning for outdoor illumination, consider safety as well as aesthetics. Safety lighting illuminates pathways and steps, driveways, and entryways. If you live in a high-crime area, consult with the local police or neighborhood-watch association for tips on security lighting.

Begin your overall lighting scheme with a sketch of the entire property. Locate obvious areas that should be lit: pathways, doors, garage entrances. These areas should get first attention in any lighting installation. For pathways, choose downward-pointing fixtures that cast a broad, even light onto the path, not into the eyes. Space fixtures evenly along both sides of the path; uneven spacing is confusing and may lead to accidents. Indicate abrupt changes in grade—steps, ramps, raised patios—with strip lighting across the path, preferably in a different color from the normal pathway lighting, or if path lighting is bright enough, with reflective strips.

Doorways, including garage doors, should be flooded with light. All doorknobs, doorbells, locks, sills and intercoms or speakerphones should be brightly illuminated. House numbers should be prominently displayed near the front door and well illuminated so that if necessary, emergency help will be able to read them easily from the street.

Take a look around your property at night and pinpoint any other areas that may pose a security or safety hazard. Are there dark areas behind the garage or toolshed that may invite loiterers or mischief makers? Is the driveway entrance hard to see after dusk? Place additional lighting in these locations.

Dramatic visual effects can be achieved with light, and you may be able to place security light fixtures so that they enhance the nighttime landscape. A wide selection of fixtures is available, but stick with one or two styles to avoid a carnival-like appearance.

You can vary the direction, color, and focus of lights to achieve different effects. Downward-pointing lights spread a wide, diffused light over a broad area. By raising or lowering their height, you can increase or decrease the intensity of the light and the area it covers. Downward lighting is excellent for illuminating pathways, patios, driveways, and entryways.

Lights that point upward, such as spotlights, floodlights, or well lights, can be used to highlight plantings as well as to illuminate house numbers and doorways. Positioning a light beneath a small tree or a clump of bamboo so that its shadow is cast against a plain wall creates a dramatic effect. Special waterproof lights can be installed underwater in ponds and reflecting pools to lend a soft glow to the entire surrounding landscape. In placing upward-pointing lights, position the reflectors so that they do not shine into the eyes or into house windows.

Lighting color and intensity can be varied to help orient persons with visual impairments to the nighttime surroundings. Be judicious in the use of colored lights in the landscape to avoid a garish effect, however, and if you use lighting color to provide visual cues, be consistent. Use soft, white lighting for general illumination. Edge steps, handrails, and the beginning and end of ramps with red or orange lights. High-intensity spotlights may be valuable at gates or for illuminating garden benches and tables. Reserve blue, green, or highly diffused lights for out-of-the-way areas that will not be ventured into after dark; these colors do not provide sufficient illumination for persons with limited visual acuity.

Installation of outdoor lighting systems is best left to the experts, except in the case of low-intensity, low-voltage lighting. Before beginning any electrical installation, you or your contractor must check with local authorities regarding codes to follow, especially for 120-volt systems that will tap into your regular house wiring. Submit a detailed plan of your proposed lighting scheme to the code board before you begin work.

Most codes will require you to install a ground-fault circuit interrupter (GFCI) receptacle for any plug-in outdoor lighting. Whether demanded by local code or not, it's a good idea to use a GFCI receptacle at any location that may become wet. These special electrical outlets are equipped with a device that senses any condition in which grounding occurs on the appliance plugged into it and then immediately shuts down the electrical circuit. If, for example, someone should accidentally stick a gardening tool into a live socket, the circuit would instantly stop the current, thus preventing a possibly fatal shock.

Low-voltage lighting systems are becoming increasingly popular, and for good reason. They are safe and easy to install, provide a wide range of lighting options, and use very little energy. If you have a small property or your lighting needs are minimal, low-voltage systems may be the best choice. Use the guidelines presented above for placement and intensity of lighting along paths and stairways. Follow the manufacturer's installation instructions carefully to avoid possible shock hazards. Although it is not necessary to shut off the electricity to the outdoor outlet that the low-voltage lights will plug into, I suggest doing so—it's good to take every precaution when working with electricity.

Solar-powered lights are another option for garden lighting, but because of their high initial cost, low intensity, and fragile glass collector plates, they are best reserved for soft spot illumination rather than for lighting up large areas. On the plus side, solar-powered lights cost nothing to run, use no energy resources, and create no pollution. Because there are no wires to run, they are easy to install virtually anywhere, even in remote locations around the garden, and because there is no large amount of current present, they are very safe. Most solar lights use an electronic eye that senses when it becomes dark or light and automatically switches the light on or off.

Although manufacturers may promise up to twelve hours of light from a solar-powered fixture, actual lighting time may be four to eight hours, depending on the time of year, whether the day is sunny or overcast, and the intensity or wattage of the light bulb in the fixture. During the winter, short, cloudy days and long, dark nights may produce only enough electricity for a brief glow of about an hour. Areas that require bright safety lighting should not depend on solar-powered lights.

ELECTRICITY

As with water faucets, it's hard to imagine having too many electrical outlets around the outside of the house, especially if you use a lot of power tools in your accessible landscape. Electrical lawn mowers, hedge trimmers, weed whackers, bulb augers, and other devices are much more convenient and safer to use if you do not have to drag a long extension cord behind you. If your home has few outdoor receptacles, you may want to have an electrician install one convenient to the garden, deck, or potting shed. Make sure that any outdoor receptacle is GFCI rated.

As an alternative to installing permanent electrical receptacles, the Outdoor Power Post (15, 34, 84) is a convenient portable electrical outlet that can be used with most power tools and gardening equipment. It has three 120-volt grounded outlets and 25 feet of cord, mounted on a sturdy 5-inch stake that you push into the ground wherever you need power. It is not recommended for wet weather or permanent installation, however.

YARD AND GARDEN ORNAMENTS

Whether your tastes run to pink flamingos on the front lawn or classical statuary in a yew allée, by all means indulge yourself with garden art. The accessible garden is, above all, a place for enjoyment, and a few ornaments, lovingly chosen and carefully placed, can add immeasurably to the joy of gardening. For gardeners with visual impairments— indeed, for anyone at all— the tactile enjoyment of smooth or textured sculptural pieces and the sounds of wind chimes or wind-powered whirligigs add new dimensions to the outside world. Arches and pergolas, covered with fruit- or flower-laden vines, beckon the wanderer onward into the garden. Birdbaths and feeders encourage wildlife of all sorts into the accessible garden, and sundials and gazing balls add a sense of timelessness and mystery.

Landscape design has long recognized the importance of focal points—objects or plantings of particular interest that draw the eye. In small gardens, a carefully sized and situated piece of statuary can give the illusion of greater size and space; in large, open gardens, statuary or art objects can be used to create a sense of intimacy or mystery.

When designing and installing large garden structures like pergolas, keep the general rules of accessibility in mind: entries and pathways wide enough for comfortable wheelchair access or for two persons to walk abreast; low-gradient ramps instead of steps; skidproof paving or floor materials; handrails or grab bars where appropriate; and comfortable, easy-access seating.

CHAPTER ELEVEN

Horticultural Therapy for Professionals

Using gardens as an adjunct to the healing process is nothing new. Physicians, philosophers, and poets through the ages have recognized the benefits of gardening to the mind, body, and spirit. Through the gentle disciplines of nature, the ill or the physically disabled may achieve a renewed sense of self-esteem, self-confidence, and self-discipline that will stand them in good stead both inside and outside the garden walls.

Horticultural therapy, as a rehabilitative discipline, uses plant material and gardening techniques as a way to improve the physical, psychological, and social adjustments necessary to help a newly disabled person cope with and reenter the work world. Horticultural therapy can also be used to benefit the elderly and infirm, the mentally ill, the developmentally disabled, substance abusers, public offenders, and the socially disadvantaged by giving them a sense of achievement, control, renewed productivity, and pride of accomplishment.

A BRIEF HISTORY OF HORTICULTURAL THERAPY

In the United States, horticultural therapy began as early as 1812, under the auspices of Dr. Benjamin Rush, a Philadelphia physician and a signer of the Declaration of Independence. While working with emotionally and mentally ill patients, he observed the calming and therapeutic effects of working outdoors. By 1817, the Friends Asylum for the Insane was opened in Philadelphia, and the course of therapy offered there included working in the hospital's vegetable gardens and fruit orchards.

Therapeutic gardening programs were tried in many other institutions over the next 130 years, but it was not until the aftermath of World War II and the establishment of a number of new veterans' hos-

> *From Kathy Brock, certified therapist, HealthSouth*
> *Rehabilitation Center, Mechanicsburg, Pennsylvania:*
>
> "I work every day with brain-injured people—accident victims, stroke patients—and I've found that working with plants in different ways is a great means of relearning and improving fine motor skills. My clients have gotten a lot of benefits from starting tomatoes and peppers indoors, growing them, then later bringing the vegetables into the kitchen to prepare salads. They get to practice lots of different skills that way, and it's very rewarding for them—and for me—to see their progress. Gardening is a great way to develop both skills and confidence, not just for gardening, but for everyday life. It's an integrated program of therapy—you can tie gardening into anything!"

pitals that therapeutic gardening received its real impetus. Garden work was seen as an excellent form of occupational therapy for recovering veterans—an opportunity to learn new skills, reenter the work force, reacquire social and communication skills, and a chance to heal people wounded in both body and mind.

For many years, however, each facility developed its own programs, and breakthroughs in new tools, techniques, and professional training sessions often went unheralded. To remedy this situation, in 1973, the American Horticultural Therapy Association (AHTA) was founded to establish a clearinghouse for information and research in the field of therapeutic gardening. The AHTA now has a membership in excess of seven hundred and has encouraged almost three-hundred hospitals to use horticultural therapy as an active part of their rehabilitation programs for physically, mentally, and emotionally challenged children and adults. More than a dozen colleges and universities offer horticultural therapy training programs, and Kansas State University offers bachelor's and master's degrees in the curriculum.

For detailed information on establishing a horticultural therapy program for your facility, for the location of training programs, for receiving accreditation for existing programs, and for ongoing developments in the field, contact the American Horticultural Therapy Association, 9200 Wightman Road, Gaithersburg, MD 20879, telephone (301) 848-3010.

AMERICANS WITH DISABILITIES ACT

The Americans with Disabilities Act (ADA), which became law in July 1994, was passed to ensure equal accessibility to all public places for people with physical or mental disabilities. The act applies to employers of fifteen or more workers and to all businesses and organizations, whether they are commercial enterprises or private clubs. The outdoor recreation areas and meditational gardens of hospitals, convalescent homes, and retirement communities fall under the jurisdiction of the ADA.

Besides clearly defining the conditions that must be met for the hiring, insuring, promotion, and termination of all employees, regardless of physical or mental abilities, the ADA mandates that all areas must be made accessible to all employees and visitors "unless doing so would impose an undue hardship"—to be judged on a case-by-case basis.

The cost of retrofitting an existing area to accommodate the disabled can easily place a heavy financial burden on a small business or organization. Recognizing this financial burden, ADA also provides for tax relief to help defray the cost of barrier removal, renovations, and accessibility-enhancing improvements.

For small businesses and organizations (fewer than thirty full-time employees), no more than $250 of the cost of accommodation work must be borne by the business itself. The employer can receive a 50 percent tax credit on costs over $250, up to $5,000 of the actual cost. Accommodation costs of more than $5,000 qualify for a tax deduction of up to $15,000. Large businesses and organizations (more than thirty full-time employees or $1 million in gross receipts) are limited to a $15,000 tax deduction.

For more information about the ADA and how it applies to your business or organization, consult *What Business Must Know about the ADA: 1992 Compliance Guide,* by Z. D. Fasman, and the *Uniform Federal Accessibility Standards (1988),* which you can get from the National Council on Disability or from your state's Department of Labor. A tax attorney or certified public account (CPA) should be able to help you determine the amount of tax credits for which your business is eligible.

PUBLIC GARDEN ACCESSIBILITY

Planning and laying out an accessible garden on a public scale can be a daunting but highly rewarding experience. Given the adoption of the ADA, however, making a public garden accessible to all is no longer a matter of choice. The material presented in chapters 1, 2, and 3 provides basic information needed to design safe and accessible pathways, ramps, entryways, and so on.

In addition to the basic design, layout, stocking, and planting of the garden itself, the designer must carefully consider the public-access areas of the garden. Driveways and entry ports should be as close to the garden as possible. Allow for plenty of handicap-only parking spaces, and make as many as possible van accessible so that wheelchairs can be maneuvered out. Pave parking areas and walkways; loose gravel is difficult for wheelchair users to maneuver through.

Keep grade changes on paths leading into and out of the garden to a minimum. If curbs and raised sidewalks are necessary, install sufficient curb cuts for wheelchair and motorized-scooter visitors. Don't entirely eliminate all raised curbs, however; blind visitors find these helpful as cues to the location of roadways, parking lots, and sidewalks.

Signs guide visitors through the garden and make the experience more pleasurable and educational by providing information about certain plants and features. Don't clutter the landscape with signs, but aim for high impact with minimum intrusion. Signs should be large and easy to read, printed boldly in black ink on white or bright yellow. Braille signs and raised-line diagrams and maps must be provided for blind and visually impaired gardeners.

Use bright-colored arrows to channel traffic through the garden. Pathways and ramps must be a minimum of 7 feet wide to allow for wheelchair users to pass without collision; if the garden is small and pathways narrow, designate a specific one-way traffic flow to avoid jams and accidents.

Gates and doorways should be at least 36 inches wide. Allow at least 4 feet of clear space on either side to permit wheelchair and scooter gardeners to back and maneuver through the gate or door. Keep latches as simple as possible; spring-hinged gates that do not need latches are ideal, but they must not slam shut so quickly or so hard that fingers get pinched.

Provide plenty of seating throughout the garden, incorporating seating surfaces onto the edges of all raised beds, if feasible. Avoid dark-colored and metal surfaces, which will absorb heat and become uncomfortably hot on sunny days. Make sure that some of the seating areas are shaded, either by overhead construction or by trees. Places that provide protection from rain are also helpful.

Wheelchair-accessible water fountains are a must in the public garden. Install watering troughs or at least provide clean bowls next to fountains for guide dogs.

Plant selection should be based on local hardiness zones. Look for tough plants with a lot of color. Avoid plants that require excessive

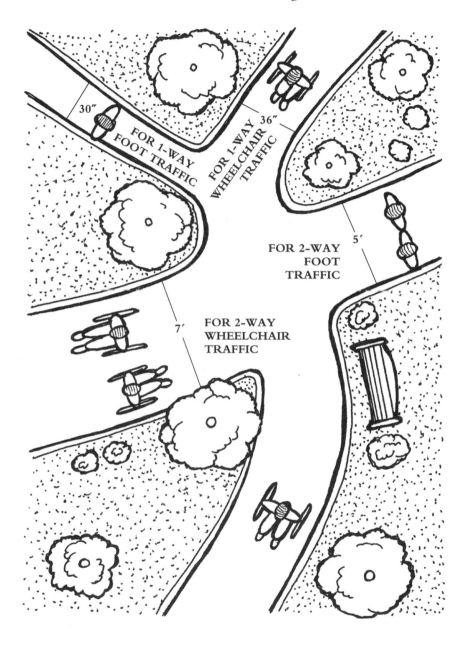

FOR 1-WAY
FOOT TRAFFIC

30″

FOR 1-WAY
WHEELCHAIR
TRAFFIC

36″

FOR 2-WAY
FOOT
TRAFFIC

5′

FOR 2-WAY
WHEELCHAIR
TRAFFIC

7′

When designing paths for public gardens, keep wheelchair widths in mind. Seven-foot-wide paths are necessary for two wheelchairs to pass easily without touching; where this is not possible, plan for one-way traffic only. Low curbs will keep feet and wheelchair or scooter tires out of planting beds.

pruning or feeding or that drop a lot of fruits, flowers, or leaves. Steer clear of poisonous plants, especially if you anticipate children as visitors to the garden. Some plants are only mildly toxic; others are toxic only if certain portions are eaten, such as daffodil or jonquil bulbs or rhubarb or tomato leaves; others, like spurge, can produce itchy skin reactions; and still others, like nightshade and foxglove, can be deadly if ingested. Common sense should be your guide.

Poisonous Plants

For the public garden, avoid these plants or place them in inaccessible locations.

Angel's trumpet	Jerusalem cherry
Azalea	Jimson weed
Bird of paradise flower	Jonquil
Black nightshade	Lantana
Buttercup	Lily of the valley
Caladium	Mayapple
Castor bean	Mistletoe
Chokecherry	Morning glory (seeds)
Christmas pepper	Mountain laurel
Climbing nightshade	Narcissus
Daffodil (bulbs)	Oleander
Daphne	Philodendron
Deadly nightshade	Pokeweed
Delphinium	Pothos
Dumbcane	Privet
Elephant ear	Rhododendron
English ivy	Rhubarb (leaves)
Foxglove	Sweet pea
Holly	Swiss cheese plant
Hyacinth	Tomato, potato, pepper (leaves)
Hydrangea	Virginia creeper
Iris	Wisteria
Jack-in-the-pulpit	Yew

Choose plants with interesting textures, shapes, and colors. Use a lot of herbs and fragrant flowers to add to the full sensory enjoyment of the garden. Keep up appearances with daily grooming, and replace dead, spent, or unhealthy plants with fresh as quickly as possible to avoid empty spots. Label all plants, in both text and Braille, if possible. If you feature edible plants in the garden, place them well out of reach unless you don't mind seeing your crops disappear as fast they develop. (Public gardeners in Britain call this phenomenon "tourist blight.")

Brochures and handouts are helpful, and guided and narrated or tape-recorded walking tours of the garden are a wonderful boon to the visually impaired or to anyone else who wants a personalized tour. Your guides should be knowledgeable about all aspects of the garden, and tape recordings and equipment should be up-to-date and in good repair.

Emergencies may arise, so plan in advance for the quick access of ambulances and medic teams. Keep a well-stocked first-aid kit, including smelling salts, bandages, bee-venom antidote, and sunscreen. During hot spells, have ice on hand. Make sure a telephone is nearby in case help must be summoned; if possible, equip garden personnel with cordless or cellular phones.

GARDENS FOR THE VISUALLY IMPAIRED

Public gardens made especially for the blind and visually impaired, which includes many elderly, present a special dilemma to the designer. On the one hand, it is only natural to want to make every accommodation possible for persons with limited eyesight, to help them enjoy the garden fully and to prevent the possibility of accidents and of legal liability. On the other hand, trying to create a "special" environment— one safe from every possible surprise or mishap—does nothing to help anyone who must function actively in the real world.

It is easy for the sighted to forget, as we try to imagine a world without sight, that blindness is more a social disability than a physical disadvantage. The typical blind person is healthy, active, alert, and independent. Blind and visually impaired people function in the day-to-day world as full participants; white cane and guide dog provide most with all the help they need in negotiating ordinary obstacles like ramps, stairs, curbs, busy intersections, and swinging doors. Most ask for no special treatment beyond the courtesy extended to any other person in a public setting and do not require special treatment in the form of handrails, rope guidelines, audible alerts, textured pavements or wall finishes, or other "detectable warning devices." In dealing with any special-needs population, it is just as important to avoid attitude barriers as it is to reduce physical ones.

Old stereotypes and misconceptions about the supposed enhanced senses of the blind persist. To be blind does not mean that one can hear better, smell better, taste better, or have a more acute sense of touch than the average sighted person; blindness does not confer "super sense" to make up for the loss of sight. Because the visually impaired

From Ramona Walhof, president, National Federation of the Blind of Idaho, Boise:

"Blindness is more an attitude problem than a physical problem—it's the attitudes of well-meaning but misguided sighted people that sometimes cause problems for the blind.

"Blind gardening is just like any other gardening. It's a matter more of knowledge and experience than of special tools and techniques. Sure, it might be hard to tell a weed from a seedling at first, but don't tell me a sighted gardener has never pulled up a vegetable plant by mistake! You just have to keep at it, keep trying, keep learning. Like anything in life, it takes a little practice."

must depend more on those senses, they may become more aware of the scents and textures around them, but to no greater degree than any sighted person would be, should he or she decide to concentrate on using them instead of sight to negotiate through the world.

Keeping these factors in mind, designing a public garden for the visually impaired should be much like designing any garden, with a few enhancements to make the garden more enjoyable to the gardener with limited or no vision.

Signs should be placed close to paths and walkways, clearly printed in raised-letter black-on-white or black-on-yellow text, with the text repeated in Braille at either the top or bottom of the sign. Keep the colors, height, location (right or left side of path), and relative position of text and Braille lettering consistent for all signs, and keep overhanging or obscuring vegetation cut back. Braille and raised-letter plant markers giving the common and Latin names are a thoughtful addition to any public garden, since gardeners are always curious about plants that have caught their interest.

Raised edging along pathways and beds can be helpful to keep accidental foot traffic off planting areas, but handrails, guide ropes, or other barrier-type devices are not necessary except in cases where it is imperative that no one—sighted or otherwise—enter an area. Keep pathways clear of tripping hazards like hoses, trailing vines, and tools—a commonsense precaution for any garden. Install handrails, also painted for high visibility, along both sides of all ramps and stairs, no matter how short they may be, and apply high-visibility white or yellow paint at the top and bottom of ramps and on the edge of each step.

Provide watering troughs beside water fountains for guide dogs that will be accompanying their handlers through the garden. Keep these animals in mind when choosing paving material, too. Black asphalt and smooth concrete can be painfully hot to paws in the summer sun; finely packed crushed gravel or shredded bark may be a kinder choice. A daily cleanup of droppings may also be necessary, and it may be advisable to keep the average guide dog's "marking height" in mind when planting urine-sensitive shrubs and other vegetation. Although working guide dogs are well trained, the call of nature cannot be ignored.

As in any garden, a variety of plants chosen for their scent and texture as well as their appearance will produce the most pleasing effect. Plants that must be touched to be appreciated—mints that release their fragrance only when rubbed or bruised, lamb's ears' silky-woolly leaves, or the crackly bark of paper birch or sycamore—should be easily accessible without excessive reaching or bending and sturdy enough to survive continual and sometimes rough handling. Bright red, orange, yellow, and white flowers are especially appreciated by gardeners with low visual acuity and are pleasing to sighted visitors as well.

Include touchable sculpture in the garden. Opt for low-cost cast concrete or resin rather than bronze or marble; over time, the acids from human sweat and oils will erode the surface of most natural stones and metals.

Fountains to provide a refreshing background sound and still pools in which to trail fingers are nice additions. For the safety of small children, keep water depth to no more than 2 or 3 feet, and make sure all children are carefully supervised near water.

If your budget allows, consider either guided or tape-recorded tours through the garden, especially if it covers a large area and presents many interesting but easily missed features. If you opt for tape-recorded tours, keep the equipment and recordings in perfect working order and up-to-date.

Consult with your local chapters of the National Federation of the Blind, the American Foundation for the Blind, and other such organizations for design guidelines and a review of planned garden facilities. Their members will be glad to lend their experience and expertise to any accessibility project.

THERAPEUTIC GARDENS

In designing a therapeutic garden for a nursing home, hospital, rehabilitation center, or community-living facility, the garden must not only be accessible to entry, it must be accessible to *working* as well. Beds must be at a comfortable working height for those who wish to garden, and special tools and accessories must be available to make gardening easier and more productive. Chapters 1 through 3 give general guidelines on the layout and design of an accessible garden, and chapter 7 surveys accessible-gardening and adaptive tools.

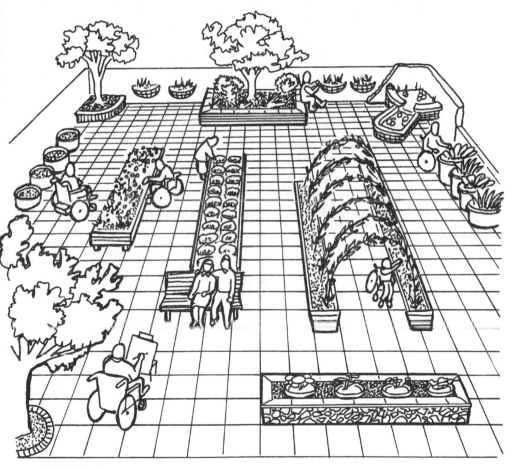

Make the therapeutic garden as multipurpose as possible. A varied schedule of programs and activities keeps the garden active throughout the year, can provide extra income in the form of admission fees for special events, and helps integrate patients with the outside world.

Once you've got the therapeutic garden in place, consider what would most benefit the group with whom you are working. Use your imagination, and ask your patients what they would most enjoy. For children and adults, an active garden where they can plant and tend their own beds of flowers, fruits, or vegetables may be best to help them regain physical strength, manual dexterity, a sense of accomplishment and hope. For elderly clients, a relaxing, less work-intensive shrub or flower garden that requires only light, periodic maintenance like pruning or clean up may be ideal for maintaining physical strength and dexterity, establishing a sense of community among gardeners, and allowing the individual to feel productive.

Above all, keep the program flexible and adaptable. Gardening cannot be done by schedule; weather, insects, blights, and seasonal changes dictate what needs to be done and when. If you live and work in an area where year-round outdoor gardening is not possible, provide light carts and as many indoor horticulture programs as possible to keep gardeners interested and involved. And, too, there are always some individuals who do not enjoy working in the earth. Respect their wishes and find some other activity that they can enjoy, perhaps flower arranging or wreath making using flowers and foliage from the therapeutic garden. For those who are physically or emotionally unable to participate in active gardening programs, just being outdoors or watching the activity of the garden through a window can be beneficial. Allow patients to come into the program at their own pace; encourage active participation, but don't push it on anyone.

Try to include interaction with the outside community in the therapeutic gardening program. Open workshops and lecture series that allow gardeners in the program to interact with gardeners from the local community are especially helpful in maintaining and reestablishing social and communication skills and for reintroducing recovering patients to general society. Trading anecdotes, tips, techniques, and plant materials and establishing new friendships and support groups are of benefit to all gardeners involved in such interactive programs. By asking for donations or charging a reasonable fee for outside gardeners to participate in certain events, additional funding for the therapeutic garden can also be obtained.

For more ideas on using the garden as a therapeutic aid, an excellent source of resource and development manuals and lesson plans for horticultural therapy can be obtained from the Chicago Botanic Garden's Horticultural Therapy Services office. Each 130-page manual describes how to establish a successful, year-round horticultural therapy program specifically designed to benefit a particular group. Lesson plans provide step-by-step instructions for weekly activity programs that make the garden a valuable adjunct to therapy throughout the year.

From Dr. Susan Erber, principal, PS233 Queens, a school for special-needs students, New York City Board of Education:

"Horticultural activities provide excellent educational and therapeutic opportunities for students with physical challenges, blindness, and other learning difficulties. The concept of students and plants 'growing together' provides an exciting vocational and recreational environment for acquiring fine-motor coordination and receptive and expressive language skills, and is a vehicle for both science and arts instruction."

Here are examples of the programs that can be part of a comprehensive program of horticultural therapy:

• Houseplant clinics. Nursery personnel and greenhouse growers or local experts can explain the basic care of houseplants, how to divide and repot them, and how to recognize and deal with pests and diseases. Good for patients relearning or perfecting large motor skills.

• Grocery store gardening. Plants are grown from common kitchen scraps like carrot tops, lemon seeds, sweet potato ends, and avocado seeds. Especially fun for children, but good for a gardener of any age who is restricted to small-scale indoor gardening.

• Terrarium garden workshop. Terrariums made from large glass bottles, fishbowls, or large brandy snifters can be planted and tended, then taken home. Ideal for helping patients develop and maintain manual dexterity and for working on small motor skills.

• Dried flowers and potpourri workshop. Local craftspersons can demonstrate the art of flower drying and the making of sachets and potpourri, using flowers grown in the therapeutic garden. Especially good for the visually impaired.

• Bonsai gardening. Traditional bonsai takes years to develop, using slow-growing trees and techniques perfected over centuries, but lovely bonsai arrangements can be developed in a fairly short time using woody-stemmed herbs, perennials, and dwarf shrubs such as rosemary,

Bonsai is one of the most relaxing and rewarding gardening activities for the physically challenged. This "slow-motion sculpture" of living plant material is an ideal way to help improve motor skills as well as self-esteem.

sweet bay, chrysanthemums, low-growing junipers, barberry, and ivy. Local experts in the art of bonsai can lecture on the history of the craft and demonstrate the traditional tools and techniques to an open audience of patients and outside gardeners. Bonsai helps develop and maintain manual dexterity and fine motor skills with little or no heavy physical labor demands and is especially well suited to those who are chairbound or bedridden.

• Art classes in the garden. Local artists and art teachers can hold classes in the therapeutic garden, both during active gardening periods and during off hours. Introducing patients to the arts is a good way to broaden interests and develop new social contacts.

Whatever programs you choose, pace the activities to the needs and abilities of your patients. Gardeners will naturally become attached to particular plants or plots of soil; respect their "ownership" of these plants and spaces. If a patient returns home after completing a course of rehabilitative therapy, let him or her take along a plant from the garden. If possible, provide follow-up visits and offer help in establishing and maintaining an accessible garden at home, possibly through a team of trained visiting nurses. The joy of gardening is a way of life, not merely a hobby or therapeutic workout, and its life-enriching effects reach into all aspects of your patient's life and well-being.

Accessible Public Gardens

The gardens listed here use a variety of methods to make the landscape more accessible to people with physical or visual restrictions. They include gardens designed with raised beds, ramps, and pathways that are easily negotiated with a walker or wheelchair, as well as sensory gardens full of textures, scents, tastes, and sounds. These gardens can be invaluable sources of ideas and information as you plan and design your own accessible garden.

Guided or audiotaped tours, rope trails, Braille plant labels, and large-print guidebooks are available at some gardens. Accessibility varies from garden to garden, so call before you visit to determine what facilities are available and to arrange for any special help you may need.

ALABAMA

Birmingham Botanical Gardens
2612 Lane Park Road
Birmingham, AL 35223
(205) 879-1227
Touch and see nature trail with Braille labels and guide ropes.

Helen Keller Fragrance Garden
Alabama School for the Blind
705 South Street
Talladega, AL 35160
(205) 761-3259
Small flower garden with Braille markers.

Mobile Botanical Gardens
P.O. Box 8382
Museum Drive, Municipal Park
Mobile, AL 36608
(205) 342-0555
Fragrance and texture garden.

ARIZONA

Tucson Botanical Gardens
2150 North Alvernon Way
Tucson, AZ 85712
(602) 326-9255
Sensory garden with fountain, raised beds, Braille signs, and audiotape tours.

ARKANSAS

Heritage Herb Garden
Ozark Folk Center
P.O. Box 500
Mountain View, AR 72560
Fragrant and textured herbs in raised beds along paths with wheelchair access.

Garden of Exploration
Arkansas School for the Blind
2600 West Markham
Little Rock, AR 72205
(501) 324-9556
Fourteen raised beds around a pool, including scented, tactually interesting plants, and bright flowers.

CALIFORNIA

Heather Farms Garden Center
1540 Marchbanks Drive
Walnut Creek, CA 94598
Sensory garden in raised beds at wheelchair level.

The Living Desert
47900 Portola Avenue
Palm Desert, CA 92260
(619) 346-5694
Bronze topographic map of valley area, large-print and Braille guidebooks.

Sherman Library and Gardens
2647 East Coast Highway
Corona Del Mar, CA 92625
(714) 673-2261
Touch and smell garden at wheelchair height, Braille guide.

Lakeside Park Trail and Show
Gardens and Garden Center
666 Bellevue Avenue
Oakland, CA 94612
(415) 273-3186
Fragrance and herb garden with Braille plaques.

Garden of Fragrance at Strybing
Arboretum
Golden Gate Park
9th Avenue and Lincoln Way
San Francisco, CA 94122
(415) 661-1316
Plants for form, color, texture, and fragrance, Braille labels, and audiotaped tours.

Overfelt Botanical Gardens
Park Drive and McKee Road
San Jose, CA
For information:
City of San Jose
Department of Parks and Recreation
151 West Mission Street
San Jose, CA 95110
(408) 259-5477
Fragrance garden located next to the San Jose Public Library.

COLORADO

Horticultural Art Society Garden
Horticultural Art Society of
Colorado Springs
1438 North Hancock Avenue
Colorado Springs, CO 80903
(719) 475-0250.
Fragrance herb garden.

Denver Botanic Garden
909 York Street
Denver, CO 80206
(303) 331-4000
*Sensory garden oriented toward
horticultural therapy.*

CONNECTICUT

Denison Pequotsepos Nature Center
Pequotsepos Road
P. O. Box 122
Mystic, CT 06355
(203) 536-1216
*Nature center with rope and Braille-
marked trails. Group programs by request
for people with disabilities and visual
impairments.*

FLORIDA

Ellis A. Gumbel Garden for the Blind
Vizcaya Museum and Gardens
3251 South Miami Avenue
Miami, FL 33129
(305) 579-2809
*Narrated tape tours of touch-and-smell
herb garden. Special tours can be arranged
in advance.*

Mounts Horticultural Learning
Center
531 North Military Trail
West Palm Beach, FL 33415
(305) 683-1777
Touch garden.

GEORGIA

Atlanta Botanical Garden
P.O. Box 77246
Atlanta, GA 30357
(404) 876-5859
Fragrance garden

Pendelton King Park
Kissing Dower Road
Augusta, GA 30904
(706)722-5891
Touch and scent garden labeled in Braille.

IDAHO

Idaho Botanical Garden
2355 Old Penitentiary Road
P.O. Box 2140
Boise, ID 83712
(208) 343-8649
Fragrance herb garden.

ILLINOIS

Vermillion County Historical
Museum and Herb Garden
116 North Gilbert Street
Danville, IL 61832
(217) 442-2922
*Fragrant raised-bed gardens with Braille
markers.*

Hadley School for the Blind
700 Elm Street
Winnetka, IL 60093
(708) 446-8111
*Discovery garden with herbs chosen for
shape, texture, fragrance.*

Chicago Botanic Garden
Lake Cook Road
P.O. Box 400
Glencoe, IL 60022
(708) 835-5440
*Sensory garden and learning garden for
people with disabilities.*

Garfield Park Conservatory
Chicago Park District
Department of Public Information
425 East McFetridge Drive
Chicago, IL 60605
(312) 533-1281
Located on North Central Park Boule-
vard. Features flowers, vegetables, and
scented plants in raised beds, Braille
labels, and fountains.

INDIANA
Conner Prairie
13400 Allisonville Road
Nobelsville, IN 46060
(317) 776-6000
Handicapped-accessible nature trail with
Braille markers.

KENTUCKY
Kentucky School for the Blind
1867 Frankfort Avenue
Louisville, KY 40206
(502) 897-1583
Fragrant herb garden with raised beds and
wide paths, signs in Braille.

LOUISIANA
R. S. Barnwell Memorial Garden
and Art Center
601 Clyde Fant Parkway
Shreveport, LA 71101-3655
(318) 673-7703
Fragrance garden with Braille labels,
wheelchair-height raised-bed plantings.

MARYLAND
Brookside Gardens
1500 Glenallan Avenue
Wheaton, MD 20902
(301) 949-8231
Fragrance garden.

Helen Avalynne Tawes Garden
580 Taylor Avenue
Annapolis, MD 21401
(410) 974-3717
Sensory garden.

MASSACHUSETTS
Berkshire Botanical Garden
5 West Stockbridge Road
Junction Routes 102 and 183
P.O. Box 826
Stockbridge, MA 01262
(413) 298-3926
Raised beds and herb gardens, Braille
labeled, to demonstrate gardening
possibilities for physically and visually
challenged gardeners.

MICHIGAN
Fernwood Garden and Nature
Center
13988 Range Line Road
Niles, MI 49120
(616) 695-6491
Special section of the garden designed for
use by people with disabilities and visual
impairments.

Dow Gardens
1018 West Main Street
Midland, MI 48640
(517) 631-2677
Sensory trail.

MISSOURI

Missouri Botanical Garden
P.O. Box 299
St. Louis, MO 63166
(314) 577-5100
*Located at 4344 Shaw Boulevard.
Scented garden in raised beds, Braille
signs, and wind-chime sculpture.*

Jacob L. Loose Park
5200 Pennsylvania Avenue
Kansas City, MO 64112
(816) 561-9710
*Located on Warnall Street. Fragrance
and texture garden.*

NEBRASKA

Louise Evans Doole Herb Garden
Chet Ager Nature Center
2740 A Street
Lincoln, NE 68502
(402) 471-7895
Five-senses trail with Braille plaques.

NEW JERSEY

Garden for the Blind and Physically
Handicapped
1081 Green Street
Iselin, NJ 08830
(908) 283-1200
Large raised bed of plants chosen for scent.

Fragrance and Sensory Garden
Colonial Park Arboretum
R.D. 1, Box 49-B Mettlers Road
Somerset, NJ 08873
(908) 873-2459
*Fragrance and sensory garden in raised
beds with Braille labels.*

Trailside Nature and Science Center
Coles Avenue and New Providence
Road
Mountainside, NJ 07092
(908) 789-3670
Herbs in raised beds.

George Griswold Frelinghuysen
Arboretum
53 East Hanover Avenue
P.O. Box 1295
Morristown, NJ 07962-1295
(201) 326-7600
Braille trail.

NEW YORK

Bailey Arboretum
Bayzille Avenue
Latingtown, NY
(516) 676-4497
Sensory garden

Brooklyn Botanic Garden
1000 Washington Avenue
Brooklyn, NY 11225-1009
(718) 622-4433
*Fragrance garden in Braille-labeled
raised beds.*

Five Rivers Environmental
Education Center
Game Farm Road
Delmar, NY 12054
(518) 475-0291
*Herb garden and wheelchair-accessible
nature trail.*

Mather Homestead Museum
343 North Main
Box 531
Wellsville, NY 14895
(716) 593-1636
*Gardens specially marked for people with
visual impairments. Limited hours.*

Queens Botanical Garden
43-50 Main Street
Flushing, NY 11335
(718) 886-3800
Fragrance garden.

NORTH CAROLINA
North Carolina Botanical Garden
3375 Totten Center
Chapel Hill, NC 27599-3375
(919) 962-0522
Patio garden with raised beds at different heights, trellis plantings, Braille labels. Garden is planted and maintained by people with disabilities.

Bicentennial Garden
Greensboro Beautiful Inc.
Drawer W-2
Greensboro, NC 27402
(919) 373-2558
Located between Hobbs and Holden Roads. Fragrance garden.

Tanglewood Park
P.O. Box 1040
Highway 158 W
Clemmons, NC 27012
(919) 766-0591
Fragrance and rose gardens with fountain.

University Botanical Garden at
Asheville
151 W. T. Weaver Boulevard
Asheville, NC 28804
(704) 252-5190
Garden for people with visual impairments.

NORTH DAKOTA
Positive Action Committee
c/o Georgene Emard
1701 University Avenue
Grand Forks, ND 58203
(701) 775-4910
Model garden with features for people with disabilities.

OHIO
Sarbach-Werner Nature Preserve
Hamilton County Park District
10245 Winton Road
Cincinnati, OH 45231
(513) 521-PARK
Located on Poole Road, off Colerain Avenue. Trail with Braille markers.

Rockefeller Park Greenhouse
750 East 88th Street
Cleveland, OH 44108-4100
(216) 664-3103
Located off Martin Luther King Boulevard. Raised-bed texture and scent gardens with "talking boxes" and Braille labels. Talking garden with narrated tours for blind and visually impaired.

Cox Arboretum
6733 Springboro Pike
Dayton, OH 45449
(513) 434-9005
Edible landscape garden in raised beds at wheelchair height.

Boardman Township Park
375 Boardman-Poland Road
Youngstown, OH 44512
Herbs displayed in raised beds. Members of the Holborn Herb Growers Guild are available Thursday evenings to talk with visitors.

Ford Nature Center at Mill Creek
Park
840 Old Furnace Road
Youngstown, OH 44511
Half barrels and display stands at wheelchair level, labeled in Braille.

OKLAHOMA
Sensational Gardens
Oklahoma State University
Horticulture Department
400 North Portland
Oklahoma City, OK 73107
(405) 945-3358
Touch and scent garden at wheelchair height.

PENNSYLVANIA
Garden of the Five Senses
Lancaster County Central Park
1050 Rockford Road
Lancaster, PA 17602
(717) 299-8218
Fragrance garden, barrier-free paved walkways with herb and flower beds, scent boxes, reflecting pools, and interpretive signs.

Tyler Arboretum
515 Painter Road
P.O. Box 216
Media, PA 19063-4424
(610) 566-5431
Fragrance garden and guided tours.

RHODE ISLAND
Garden of the Senses
Wilcox Park
71 1/2 High Street
Westerly, RI 02891
(401) 348-8362
Flowers and herbs of distinctive taste, smell, or texture, in Braille-labeled raised beds.

SOUTH CAROLINA
South Carolina Botanical Garden at
Clemson University
Department of Horticulture
Clemson University
Clemson, NC 29634-0375
(803) 656-4949
Braille trail and hortitherapy garden for the physically disabled.

Hopeland Gardens
City of Aiken
P.O. Box 1177
Aiken, SC 29802
(803) 642-7630
Located on Dupress Place, off Route 19 South. Touch and scene trail marked in Braille.

SOUTH DAKOTA
McCory Gardens
Department of Horticulture and
Forestry
South Dakota State University
Brookings, SD
57007
(605) 688-5735
Fragrance and touch garden.

TENNESSEE
Elizabeth Burr Garden
Cheekwood Tennessee Botanical
Gardens and Museum of Art
1200 Forrest Park Drive
Nashville, TN 37205
(615) 356-8000
*Raised herb beds with railings and
Braille labels.*

TEXAS
Dallas Civic Garden Center
Fair Park
P.O. Box 26194
Dallas, TX 75226
(214) 428-7476
*Herb and scent garden in Braille-labeled
raised beds. Tours and special programs
for people with visual impairments.*

Fort Worth Botanical Garden
3220 Botanic Garden Boulevard
Fort Worth, TX 76107
(817) 870-7686
*Fragrance garden at wheelchair height,
Braille labels, and pool with fountain.*

San Antonio Botanical Gardens
555 Funston Place
San Antonio, TX 78209
(512) 821-5115
Scent and texture garden.

Amarillo Garden Center
1400 Streit Drive
Amarillo, TX 79106
(806) 352-6513
Touch and smell garden in raised beds.

Austin Area Garden Center
2220 Barton Springs Road
Austin, TX 78746
(512) 477-8672
Fragrance herb garden in raised beds.

VIRGINIA
Norfolk Botanical Gardens
Airport Road
Norfolk, VA 23518
(804) 853-6972
*Fragrance garden with Braille markers
and handrails.*

WYOMING
Cheyenne Botanic Garden
710 South Lions Park Drive
Cheyenne, WY 82001
(307) 637-6458
*Tropical plants and food crops tended by
volunteers, including senior citizens,
individuals with disabilities, and others.*

Sources of Tools, Supplies, and Information

1. AARP
   P.O. Box 199
   Long Beach, CA 90801

2. Abbey Medical Catalog Sales
   American Hospital Supply
   Corp.
   13782 Crenshaw Blvd.
   Gardena, CA 90249

3. Abeldata
   Adaptive Equipment Center
   8455 Colesville Road
   Suite 935
   Silver Spring, MD 20910-3319
   (800) 227-0216
   (301) 588-9284

4. Accreditation Council on
   Services for People with
   Developmental Disabilities
   (ACDD)
   8100 Professional Place
   Suite 204
   Landover, MD 20785
   (301) 459-3191

5. Access/Abilities
   P.O. Box 458
   Mill Valley, CA 94942
   (415) 388-3250

6. Access to Recreation, Inc.
   2509 E. Thousand Oaks Blvd.
   Suite 400
   Thousand Oaks, CA 91362
   (800) 634-4351

7. Access with Ease
   P.O. Box 1150
   Chino Valley, AZ 86323
   (602) 636-9469

8. Accessible Designs.Adjustable
   Systems, Inc.
   94 North Columbus Road
   Athens, OH 45701
   (614) 593-5240

9. AdaptAbility
   P.O. Box 515
   Colchester, CT 06415

10. Aids for Arthritis, Inc
    3 Little Knoll Court
    Medford, NJ 08055
    (609) 654-6918

11. Aids Unlimited, Inc.
1101 North Calvert Street
Suite 405
Baltimore, MD 21202
(301) 659-0232

12. Alenco Greenhouse Window
P.O. Box 3309
Bryan, TX 77801

13. AliMed, Inc.
297 High Street
Dedham, MA 02076
(800) 225-2610

14. Allied Medical, Inc.
690 Mendenhall
Memphis, TN 38117
(800) 423-4966
(800) 422-2126

15. Alsto Company
P.O. Box 1267
Galesburg, IL 61401
(309) 343-6181
(800) 447-0048

16. A. M. Leonard, Inc.
6665 Spiker Road
P.O. Box 816
Piqua, OH 45356

17. American Association for the
Advancement of Science
Education and Human
Resources Programs
Project on Science,
Technology, and Disability
1333 H Street N.W.
Washington, DC 20005
(202) 326-6670

18. American Community
Gardening Association (ACGA)
325 Walnut Street
Philadelphia, PA 19106
(212) 248-4990

19. American Foundation for the
Blind
Product Center
100 Enterprise Place
P.O. Box 7044
Dover, DE 19903-7044

20. American Horticultural Society
(AHS)
7931 E. Boulevard Dr.
Alexandria, VA 22308
(703) 768-5700

21. American Horticultural Therapy
Association (AHTA)
9200 Wightman Road
Gaithersburg, MD 20879
(301) 848-3010

22. American Occupational
Therapy Association
4720 Montgomery Lane
P.O. Box 31220
Bethesda, MD 20824-1220

23. American Printing House for
the Blind
P.O. Box 6085
Dept. 0086
Louisville, KY 40206-0085
(502) 895-2405

24. Ames Lawn and Garden Tools
Box 1774
Parkersburg, WV 26102

25. Ann Morris Enterprises, Inc.
890 Fams Court
East Meadows, NY 11554
(516) 292-9232

26. Aquapore Moisture Systems, Inc.
Gardena Watering Products
610 South 80th Avenue
Phoenix, AZ 85043
(602) 936-8083

27. Arlan and Sons
11991 Arroyo Avenue
Santa Ana, CA 92705

28. Arthritis Foundation
1314 Spring Street N.W.
Atlanta, GA 30309
(404) 872-7100

29. Association for Education and
Rehabilitation of the Blind and
Visually Impaired (AER)
206 North Washington Street
Suite 320
Alexandria, VA 22314
(703) 548-1884

30. Audubon Workshop
1501 Paddock Drive
Northbrook, IL 60062
(312) 729-6660

31. Automagic Corporation
195 South Beverly Drive
Suite 406
Beverly Hills, CA 90212
(213) 552-2101

32. Bonsai Farm
13827 Highway 87 South
Adkins, TX 78101
(210) 649-2109

33. Breaking New Ground
International Conference on
Rural Rehabilitation
Technology (ICRRT)
Box 8103
University Station
Grand Forks, ND 58202
(701) 777-3120

34. Brookstone Company/
Hard to Find Tools
1655 Bassford Dr.
Mexico, MO 65265
(800) 846-3000
(800) 926-7000

35. Bruce Medical Supply
411 Waverly Oak Road
Box 9166
Warminster, PA 18974

36. W. Atlee Burpee & Co.
300 Park Avenue
Warminster, PA 18991

37. Calais Company
5 Cold Hill Road #12
P.O. Box 355
Mendham, NJ 07945
(201) 543-5665

38. Chicago Botanic Garden
Horticultural Therapy Services
P.O. Box 400
Glencoe, IL 60022-0400

39. Clapper Company
1125 Washington Street
West Newton, MA 02165

40. Cleo, Inc.
3957 Mayfield Road
Cleveland, OH 44121
(800) 321-0595

41. Colonial Garden Kitchens
    Unique Merchandise Mart
    Building 66
    Hanover, PA 17333

42. Comfort House
    189 Frelinghuysen Avenue
    Newark, NJ 07114-1595

43. Comfortably Yours
    61 West Hunter Avenue
    Maywood, NJ 07607
    (201) 368-0400

44. David Kay, Inc.
    4509 Taylor Lane
    Cleveland, OH 44128
    (800) 872-5588

45. Denman and Company
    2913 Saturn Street, Suite G
    Brea, CA 92621

46. De Van Koek
    9400 Business Dr.
    Austin, TX 78758
    (800) 992-1220

47. Dixon Industries, Inc.
    Box 404
    Coffeyville, KS 67337

48. Dixson Health Care Products
    P.O. Box 1449
    Grand Junction, CO 81502
    (800) 443-4926

49. DripWorks
    380 Maple Street
    Willits, CA 95490
    (707) 459-6323

50. Dynamics International
    Gardening Association (DIGA)
    Drawer 1165
    Asheboro, NC 27204-1165
    (919) 625-4790

51. Edible Landscaping
    P.O. Box 77
    Afton, VA 22920
    (804) 361-9134

52. Ekco Housewares, Inc.
    9234 West Belmont Avenue
    Franklin Park, IL 60131

53. Electric Mobility Corporation
    1 Mobility Plaza
    Sewell, NJ 08080
    (609) 468-0270
    (800) 662-4548

54. Enabling Technologies
    Company
    3102 Southeast Jay Street
    Stuart, FL 34997
    (407) 283-4817

55. Enrichments
    145 Tower Drive
    P.O. Box 579
    Hinsdale, IL 60521
    (800) 323-5547

56. Environmental Applied
    Products
    Boise, ID
    (800) 531-0102

57. Fairway King
    4300 North Sewall
    Oklahoma City, OK 73118
    (405) 528-8571

58. Family Farm Rehabilitation
    Management (FaRM)
    P.O. Box 37
    Ankeny, IA 50021
    (515) 964-3868

59. FashionABLE
    99 West Street
    Medfield, MA 02052-9908
    (617) 359-2910

60. Felix Co.
    Helping Hands Division
    9 Rice's Lane
    Westport, CT 06880

61. Fred Sammons, Inc.
    Bissell Healthcare Corporation
    P.O. Box 32
    Brookfield, IL 60513-0032
    (800) 323-5547

62. Fuller Brush Co.
    Sales and Service
    P.O. Box 5100
    Rural Hall, NC 27098

63. G. E. Miller Inc.
    484 South Broadway
    P.O. Box 266
    Yonkers, NY 10705

64. Garden Way Inc.
    102nd Street & 9th Avenue
    Troy, NY 12180
    (800) 828-550

65. Gardener's Eden
    P.O. Box 7307
    San Francisco, CA 94120-7307

66. Gardener's Eye
    P.O. Box 100963
    Denver, CO 80210

67. Gardener's Supply Co.
    128 Intervale Road
    Burlington, VT 05401
    (802) 863-4535

68. Gardeners of America (GOA)
    5560 Merle Hay Rd.
    P.O. Box 241
    Johnston, IA 50131-0241
    (515) 278-0295

69. Guardian Products, Inc.
    Box C-4522
    Arleta, CA 91331-4522
    (800) 255-5022

70. Gurney's Seed and Nursery Co.
    110 Capital Street
    Yankton, SD 57079

71. Hall Enterprises
    P.O. Box 800
    West Hartford, CT 06107
    (203) 521-7052

72. Hammacher Schlemmer
    145 East 57th St.
    New York, NY 10022

73. Handi-Ramp, Inc.
    Box 745
    1414 Armour Blvd.
    Mundelein, IL 60060

74. Harriet Carter
    Department 18
    North Wales, PA 19455
    (215) 361-5151

75. Health Supplies of America
    P.O. Box 288
    Farmville, NC 27828
    (800) 334-1187

76. Health Call
    Sickroom Service, Inc.
    2523 South Kinnickinnic Ave.
    Milwaukee, WI 53207

77. Healthy Home
    5844 Alessandro Ave.
    Temple City, CA 91780

78. Henry Fields Seed &
    Nursery Co.
    415 North Burnett
    Shenandoah, IA 51602

79. Hobby Greenhouse Association
    (HGA)
    8 Glen Terrace
    Bedford, MA 01730-2048
    (617) 275-0377

80. Horticultural Therapy
    Department
    Dr. Richard Mattson
    Dept. of Horticulture, Forestry
    & Recreation Resources
    Kansas State University
    Manhattan, KS 66506-4002

81. Horticultural Therapy Services
    Chicago Botanic Garden
    P.O. Box 400
    Glencoe, IL 60022
    (708) 835-8250

82. Hydrofarm Gardening Products
    3135 Kerner Blvd
    San Rafael, CA 94901

83. Hy Dro Gro Mini Farms
    P.O. Box 118
    Fortson, GA 31808
    (404) 324-4769

84. Improvements Catalog
    4944 Commerce Parkway
    Cleveland, OH 44128

85. Independent Living Aids, Inc.
    27 East Mall
    Plainview, NY 11803
    (800) 537-2118
    (516) 762-8080

86. Indoor Gardening Society of
    America (IGSA)
    944 S. Munroe Road
    Tallmadge, OH 44278
    (216) 733-8414

87. Inkadinkado, Inc.
    105 South Street
    Boston, MA 02111

88. International Conference on
    Rural Rehabilitation
    Technology (ICRRT)
    Box 8103
    University Station
    Grand Forks, ND 58202
    (701) 777-3120

89. J. A. Preston Corp.
    60 Page Road
    Clifton, NJ 07012

90. Jackson & Perkins
    50 Rose Lane
    Medford, OR 97501-0704
    (800) 292-4769
    (800) 348-3222 TDD

91. J&J Landscape Design and
    Maintenance
    P.O. Box 21683
    Tampa, FL 33622-1683
    (813) 645-8777
    (800) 546-6724

92. Joan Cook
3200 Southeast 14th Avenue
Ft. Lauderdale, FL 33316

93. John Deere
1400 Third Ave.
Moline, IL 61265
(800) 544-2122

94. Julee Quarve-Peterson, Inc.
Accessibility Book
P.O. Box 28093
Crystal, MN 55428

95. J. W. Jung Seed Co.
Randolph, WI 53956

96. PBM Group
(formerly Kemp Co.)
160 Koser Road
Lititz, PA 17543
(800) 441-5367

97. Kinsman Co., Inc.
River Road
Point Pleasant, PA 18950
(215) 297-0890
(800) 733-4146

98. Langenbach
P.O. Box 453
Blairstown, NJ 07825

99. Lee Valley Tools
1080 Morrison Drive
Ottawa, ON K2H 8K7
Canada
(613) 596-0350

100. Let's Get Growing
General Feed & Seed Co.
1900-B Commercial Way
Santa Cruz, CA 95065

101. Lighthouse for the Blind and
Visually Impaired
Resource Center
20 Tenth Street
Suite 220
San Francisco, CA 94103
(415) 431-1481

102. Link to Assistive Products
(LINK)
CAT/UB
515 Kimball Tower
Buffalo, NY 14214-3079
(800) 628-2281

103. Living Wall Garden Company
R.D. #3 Tobey Street
Naples, NY 14512
(716) 374-2340

104. LS&S Group, Inc.
P.O. Box 673
Northbrook, IL 60065
(800) 468-4789
(708) 498-9777

105. La Motte Chemical
P.O. Box 329
Chestertown, MD 21620
(800) 344-3100

106. Lillian Vernon
510 South Fulton Avenue
Mount Vernon, NY 10550

107. Liparus Associates
3001 Redhill
Building 5, Suite 108
Costa Mesa, CA 92626

108. Luba, Inc.
226 Northwest 5th Avenue
Hallandale, FL 33009
(800) 327-3768

109. Lumex, Inc./Swedish Rehab
100 Spence Street
Bay Shore, NY 11706
(800) 645-5272

110. Maddak, Inc.
Bel-Art Products Subsidiary
6 Industrial Road
Pequannock, NJ 07440-1993
(201) 694-0500

111. Mantis/HJS Enterprises, Inc.
1458 County Line Road
Huntington Valley, PA 19006
(800) 366-6268

112. Maxi-Aids
42 Executive Boulevard
P.O. Box 3209
Farmingdale, NY 11735
(800) 522-6294
(516) 752-0521

113. Medical Equipment
Distributors, Inc.
3223 South Loop 289 #150
Lubbock, TX 79423
(800) 253-4134

114. Mellinger's, Inc.
2310 W. South Range Road
North Lima, OH 44452-9731
(800) 321-7444

115. Miles Kimball
41 West Eighth Avenue
Oshkosh, WI 54901

116. NASCO
901 Janesville Avenue
Fort Atkinson, WI 53538
(800) 557-9595

117. National Association for Visually
Handicapped
22 West 21st Street
New York, NY 10010
(212) 889-3141

118. National Council of State
Garden Clubs
4401 Magnolia Avenue
St. Louis, MO 63110
(314) 776-7574

119. National Council on Disability
1331 F Street N.W.
Suite 1050
Washington, DC 20004-1107
(202) 272-2004

120. National Federation of the Blind
1800 Johnson Street
Baltimore, MD 21230
(301) 659-9314

121. National Gardening Association
(NGA)
180 Flynn Avenue
Burlington, VT 05401
(802) 863-1308

122. National Institute on Disability
and Rehabilitation Research
Office of Special Education and
Rehab Services
U.S. Department of Education
400 Maryland Avenue S.W.
Washington, DC 20202

123. National Multiple Sclerosis
     Society
     733 Third Avenue
     6th Floor
     New York, NY 10017-3288
     (800) FIGHT-MS (344-4867)

124. National Rehabilitation
     Information Center
     8455 Colesville Road
     Silver Spring, MD 20910-3319
     (800) 346-2742

125. National Therapeutic
     Recreation Society (NTRS)
     National Recreation and Park
     Association
     3101 Park Center Drive
     Suite 1200
     Alexandria, VA 22302
     (703) 820-4940

126. Nelson's Medical Line
     Warehouse
     5376 Ashton Center
     P.O. Box 20609
     Sarasota, FL 34238
     (800) 247-2256

127. Nitron Industries
     4605 Johnson Road
     P.O. Box 1447
     Fayetteville, AR 72702

128. No Bend Garden
     Rural Route 2
     Pawcatuck, CT 06370

129. Norm Thompson
     Box 3999
     Portland, OR 97208

130. North Coast Medical, Inc.
     187 Stauffer Boulevard
     San Jose, CA 95125-1042

131. Nu-Day Creations
     Suite 7029
     111 East Drake Road
     Fort Collins, CO 80525

132. Obex, Inc.
     P.O. Box 1253
     Stamford, CT 06904
     (203) 975-9094

133. One Step Closer
     P.O. Box 691
     Weston, MA 02193

134. Option Central
     1604 Carroll Avenue
     Green Bay, WI 54304
     (414) 498-9699

135. Para Medical Distributors
     2020 Grand Avenue
     P.O. Box 19777
     Kansas City, MO 64141
     (800) 245-FAST

136. Physically Challenged Farmers
     of Alberta
     #315 14925 111 Avenue
     Edmonton, AB T5M 2P6
     Canada
     (403) 486-2688

137. Plants of the Wild
     P.O. Box 866
     Tekoa, WA 99033
     (509) 284-2848

138. Plow & Hearth
301 Madison Road
Box 830
Orange, VA 22960

139. Power King
1100 Green Valley Road
P.O. Box 715
Beaver Dam, WI 53916

140. Real Goods
555 Leslie Street
Ukiah, CA 95482-5576
(800) 762-7325

141. Research and Rehabilitation for
Handicapped, Inc.
35 Lawton Avenue
Danville, IN 46122

142. Resources for Rehabilitation
33 Bedford Street
Suite 19A
Lexington, MA 02173

143. Rugg Manufacturing Co.
P.O. Box 507
Greenfield, MA 01301
(413) 773-5471

144. Ryobi America Corp.
5201 Pearman Dairy Road
Suite 1
Anderson, SC 29625-8950
(800) 525-2579

145. Science Products
P.O. Box 888
Southeastern, PA 19399
(800) 888-7400

146. Sears Home Health Care
Catalog
Sears, Roebuck and Co.
Sears Tower
Chicago, IL 60684
(800) 323-3274

147. Shepherd's Garden Seeds
30 Irene Street
Torrington, CT 06790
(203) 482-3638

148. Smith & Hawken
25 Corte Madera
Mill Valley, CA 94941-1829
(415) 383-4050

149. Smith and Nephew Rolyan, Inc.
P.O. Box 555
Menomonee Falls, WI 53051
(800) 558-8633

150. Solutions
P.O. Box 6878
Portland, OR 97228-6878
(800) 342-9988, ext. 110

151. Spanner's Company
16 Boulevard East
#108, Suite 306
Orange, CA 92668

152. Stone Container Corporation
P.O. Box 37020
Louisville, KY 40233

153. Storey's Books
Department 9315 Schoolhouse
Road
Pownal, VT 05261

154. Support Plus/FashionABLE
33 West Street
Box 500
Medfield, MA 02052-9908

155. Susquehanna Rehab Products
     R.D. 2, Box 41
     Wrightsville, PA 17368

156. Swisher Mower & Machine
     Co., Inc.
     333 East Gay Street
     P.O. Box 67
     Warrensburg, MO 64093

157. Tapestry
     340 Poplar Street
     Building 20
     Hanover, PA 17333
     (717) 633-3333

158. Technology for Independence
     529 Main Street
     Boston, MA 02129
     (617) 242-7007

159. Tetra Development Society
     Plaza of Nations
     Box 27
     770 Pacific Boulevard South
     Vancouver, BC V6B 5E7
     Canada
     (604) 688-6464

160. Texas Greenhouse Co., Inc.
     2524 White Settlement Road
     Fort Worth, TX 76107
     (817) 926-5447

161. The Cook's Garden
     P.O. Box 65
     Londonderry, VT 05148

162. Vandenberg ADL
     6811 West 167th Street
     Tinley Park, IL 60477
     (800) 872-2347

163. VisAids, Inc.
     102-08 Jamaica Avenue
     Richmond Hill, NY 11418
     (718) 847-4734

164. Walt Nicke Company
     36 McLeod Lane
     P.O. Box 433
     Topsfield, MA 01983
     (508) 887-3388
     (800) 822-4114

165. Winco, Inc.
     3062 46th Avenue North
     St. Petersburg, FL 33714-3864

USDA Hardiness Zones

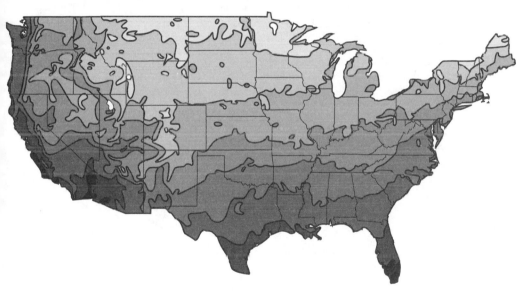

	Average annual minimum temperature			
ZONE	TEMPERATURE (°F)		ZONE	TEMPERATURE (F)
1	Below -50°	No zone 1 in U.S.	6	-10° to 0°
2	-50° to -40°		7	0° to 10°
3	-40° to -30°		8	10° to 20°
4	-30° to -20°		9	20° to 30°
5	-20° to -10°		10	30° to 40°

• BIBLIOGRAPHY •

Agency for Toxic Substances and Disease Registry. *Toxicological Profile for Arsenic.* United States Department of Health and Human Services, 1993.

Bender, Richard W. *Herbal Bonsai: Practicing the Art with Fast-Growing Herbs.* Mechanicsburg, PA: Stackpole Books, 1996.

Brooks, Howard D., and Charles J. Oppenheim. *Horticulture as a Therapeutic Aid.* New York: Institute of Rehabilitation Medicine.

Container Gardening for the Handicapped. Phoenix: Hand-D-Cap Publishing.

Field, W. E. *Agricultural Tools, Machinery, and Buildings for Farmers and Ranchers with Physical Handicaps.* Vol. 2. West Lafayette, IN: Breaking New Ground Resource Center, Purdue University, 1991.

Fleet, Kathleen. *A Manual for Blind Gardeners: Some Suggested Aids.* London: Royal National Institute for the Blind, 1978.

Fox, Sharon, and Carey Burris, Jr. *Horticulture for the Visually Impaired.* Clemson, SC: Clemson University Press, 1977.

Galarneau, D., et al. *Residues of Arsenic, Chromium, and Copper on and near Outdoor Structures Built of Wood Treated with CCA Type Preservatives.* Ottawa: Health and Welfare Canada, 1990.

210

Gardening in Containers. Brooklyn Botanic Garden Series. Brooklyn: Brooklyn Botanic Garden.

Gardening in Containers. Sunset Series. Menlo Park, CA: Lane Magazine and Book Co.

Gugerty, J. J. *Tools, Equipment, and Machinery Adapted for the Vocational Education and Employment of Handicapped People*. Madison, WI: University of Wisconsin–Madison Vocational Studies Center, 1983.

Krause, D. *Designing Barrier-Free Nature Areas*. Ithaca, NY: Cornell University Press.

Mary Marlborough Lodge, Nuffield Orthopaedic Centre. *Equipment for the Disabled*. Headington, Oxford, England.

Mattson, R. H., ed. "Health through Horticulture." Proceedings of the Seventh Horticultural Therapy Short Course. Manhattan, KS: Kansas State University, 1988.

————. "Interactive Horticulture." Proceedings of the Fifth Horticultural Therapy Short Course. Manhattan, KS: Kansas State University, 1985.

Mattson, R. H., Johanna Fliegel, and Patrick Williams, eds. "Creative Horticulture." Proceedings of the Sixth Horticultural Therapy Short Course. Manhattan, KS: Kansas State University, 1987.

Moore, Bibby. *Growing with Gardening*. Chapel Hill, NC: University of North Carolina Press, 1989.

National Council for Therapy and Rehabilitation through Horticulture. *The Easy Path to Gardening*. Mount Vernon, NY.

Ocone, Thabault. "Tools and Techniques for Easier Gardening." Monograph, Gardens for All, Burlington, VT, 1984.

Office of Environmental Health Hazard Assessment. *Arsenic in Drinking Water*. California Environmental Protection Agency, 1992.

Relf, Paula Diane. *Gardening in Raised Beds and Containers for Elderly and Physically Handicapped*. Blacksburg, VA: Virginia Cooperative Extension Service, 1987.

Rothert, Gene. *The Enabling Garden: A Guide to Lifelong Gardening*. Dallas: Taylor Publishing Company, 1994.

Rothert, Eugene, and James Daubert. *Horticultural Therapy for Nursing Homes, Senior Centers, and Retirement Living*. Chicago: Chicago Horticultural Society, 1985.

Shoemaker, J., and R. H. Mattson, eds. "Therapeutic Horticulture." Proceedings of the Second Horticultural Therapy Short Course. Manhattan, KS: Kansas State University, 1982.

———. "Therapeutic Horticulture." Proceedings of the Third Horticultural Therapy Short Course. Manhattan, KS: Kansas State University, 1982.

United States Consumer Product Safety Commission. *Project on Playground Equipment: Estimate of Risk of Skin Cancer from Dislodgeable Arsenic on Pressure-Treated Wood Playground Equipment*. Washington, DC: United States Consumer Product Safety Commission, 1990.

• INDEX •

ADA legislation, 178
American Horticultural Therapy
  Association, 177
Annuals, 149–50
Asphalt, 19

Benches, 105, 161, 164, 169–70, 179
Biennials, 145–49
Blind, 182–84
Bog garden, 152–56
Brick work, 18–19, 20–21, 35, 164
Bulbs, 150

Carts, 104
Clothing, 87, 106–7
Cold frames, 161, 165–66
Compost, 58–70
Computer software, 11
Concrete work, 16–18, 35, 164
Container planting, 36–41, 164
Contaminated soil, 56–57
Contractors, 12–14
Cover crops, 67

Designing for accessibility, 1–14
Dethatching, 121
Digging tools, 90–93
Drainage, 35–36, 37
Drip irrigation, 79–80

Earthworms, 68–69
Electricity, 172–75

Farm resources, 117
Faucets, 74–75, 165

Fences, 25–28
Fertilizers, 52–56, 118–20
Fill materials for paths, 20
Flowers, 145–50
Foundation plants, 141–44
Fragrance, 150–52, 184
Fruit trees, 140–41
Funding sources, 13–14

Garden carts, 104
Gates, 9, 25–28, 179
Gloves, 87
Grab bars, 25
Greenhouses, 161, 162–65
Grip improvements, 86–88
Ground covers, 125, 126–29

Handrails, 24–25
Hardiness zones map, 209
Harvesting, 3, 96–98
Health tips, 106–107
Hedges, 141–44
Herbs, 158–59
Horticultural therapy, 176–77
Hoses, 75–78
Hot frames, 166–67
Hydroponics, 167–68

Indicator plants, 50–51
Indoor gardens, 39–41, 161,
  162–65, 167–69
Intensive spacing, 44–45

Kneelers, 105
Kneepads, 106

Lawns, 108–30
Leverage aids, 84–86
Lighting, 168–69, 172–74
LINK Project, 84

Mapping the site, 9–11
Mesiscaping, 71–73, 131–33
Moonlight garden, 159–60
Mowing, 108–30
Mulches, 125, 130

Naturescaping, 131–33

Pathways, 6–7, 8, 15–21, 179, 180,
    183–84
Patios, 15
Perennials, 145–49
Permaculture, 131–33
pH in soil, 49, 51–52
Planning for accessibility, 1–14
Plant supports. See Trellises and
    plant supports
Planting, 102–3
Planting beds, 8–9, 11–12, 29–39,
    183–84
Poisonous plants, 181
Portable paths, 20
Potting soil mix, 40–41
Pressure–treated wood, 34–35
Pruning, 96–98, 134–36
Public gardens, 178–89, 190–97

Rain gauges, 73–74
Raised beds, 29–39
Raking leaves, 121–24
Ramps, steps, slopes, 7–8, 21–24,
    179
Reach from wheelchair, 7
Reachers, 103–4
Rock gardens, 156–58
Rocking fork, 48

Safety, 106–7
Scale drawings, 10–11
Scoots, 104–5
Seeding, 100–2
Shredders, 67–68

Shrubs, 141–44
Signs, 179, 183
Slide boards, 105
Slopes. See Ramps, steps, slopes
Snow removal, 123
Soil preparation, 46–57
Solar lawn mower, 115
Sphagnum moss, 41
Splint, 87
Spraying, 98–100
Sprinklers, 78–79
Squaring techniques, 12
Steps. See Ramps, steps, slopes
Stones, 19
Sunspaces, 161, 162–65

Tables, 169–70
Tabletop gardening, 39–41
Testing soil, 49
Therapeutic garden, 185–89
Tile, 19
Tillers, 93–94
Timers, watering, 73–74
Tools, 84–107, 198–208
Trash-bag garden, 33
Trees, 133–41
Trellises and plant supports, 41–44,
    164
Trowels, 88–90

Vermicomposting, 68–69
Vision-impaired, 182–84

Water, 71–83, 116–18, 179, 184
Water gardens, 152–56, 167–68,
    170–72
Watering wands, 76, 77
Weeding, 95–96, 120
Wetlands, 152–56
Wheelbarrows and carts, 104
Wheelchair dimensions, 8
Wildflowers, 124–25
Wood, 19, 34–35

Xeriscaping, 71–73, 131–33

Yields of vegetables, 3